Abstracts from

The Connecticut Gazette

(Formerly The New London Gazette)

*Covering
Southeastern Connecticut*

1774-1776

Richard B. Marrin

HERITAGE BOOKS
2009

HERITAGE BOOKS
AN IMPRINT OF HERITAGE BOOKS, INC.

Books, CDs, and more—Worldwide

For our listing of thousands of titles see our website
at
www.HeritageBooks.com

Published 2009 by
HERITAGE BOOKS, INC.
Publishing Division
100 Railroad Ave. #104
Westminster, Maryland 21157

Copyright © 2009 Richard B. Marrin

All rights reserved. No part of this book may be reproduced or transmitted in any form or by any means, electronic or mechanical, including photocopying, recording or by any information storage and retrieval system without written permission from the author, except for the inclusion of brief quotations in a review.

International Standard Book Numbers
Paperbound: 978-0-7884-4784-6
Clothbound: 978-0-7884-7598-6

Nature's God entitle them."
    Witness the colonists gathering together, first in protest, then in rebellion. Read first hand reports of the Battles of Lexington, Concord and Bunker Hill. It - and whole lot more - can be found in the newspaper of the day. From it, we of the Twenty First Century can better understand this concept of Liberty sought by the Colonists but still highly prized and protected today.

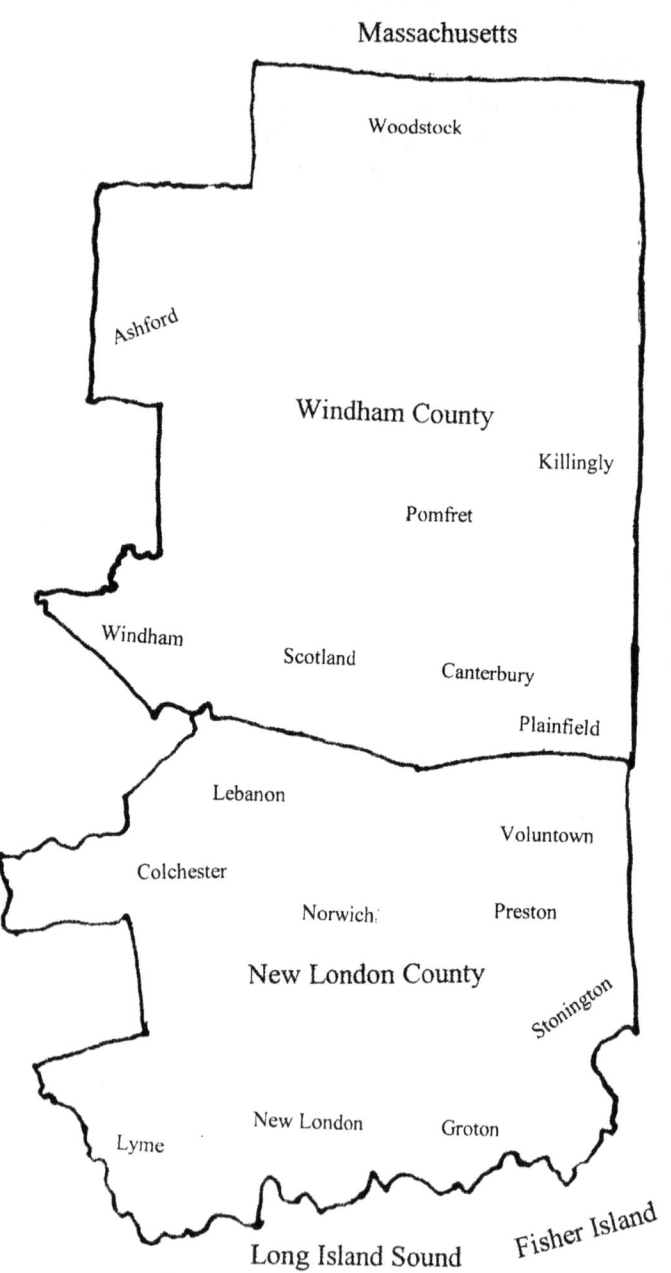

ABSTRACTS FROM 1774

From *The Gazette,* January 7, 1774

tea
The East India Company's tea has not arrived at New York as of Thursday of last.

We hear that eight chests of the East India Tea are to be sent to this town, New London, via Newport.

Monday last, arrived here at New London, William Howell in ten days from Charleston, South Carolina, who informs us that there was a dispute between the Captain of the Tea Ship that had arrived there and the consignees about the landing of the tea.

We hear that a chest of tea, which had been hoisted from out of one of the ships at Boston, was not so broken as to prevent its floating and it drove on shore near Boston Neck, where it was found by a countryman who retailed part of it at a dollar per pound. As the populace received intelligence of the affair, they carried the chest with its contents to the Commons where they made a fire which consumed it.

administration of estates
Notice by Commissioners Nathaniel Mayer, John Denison 4th and Gilbert Fanning, appointed by the Hon. Charles Phelps Judge of Probate of the District of Stonington to the creditors of the estate of Joshua Rathbun, the third, deceased and represented insolvent, that a meeting will be held at the dwelling house of John Denison, IV at Long Point in Stonington.

pay up poem

All persons indebted to him
are desired for to pay

or they will sued be
and that without delay

So will the sum amount
How can you it abide
to add to your account
trouble and cost beside?

As many debts now standing be
for seven years to crowd my books
I do protest I hate to see
such dull and heavy looks

I therefore warn debtors to come
and payment make with speed
or they will shortly hear their doom
in letters plain to read.

by Seth -Wymund Holmes, New London North Parish.
****
From *The Gazette,* January 14, 1774

Justices of the Peace appointed
The General Assembly has appointed the following gentlemen in New London to be Justices of the Peace *viz.* John Tyler of Preston; Joseph Palmer of Stonington, Thomas Mumford and William Morgan of Groton, Nehimiah Huntington and Nathaniel Backus of Norwich.

man found dead

Last Monday an elderly Negro man belonging to Mr. Ezechiel Fox of this town, New London, was found dead in a field near Mr. Fox's house. He had been left for a short time by the people with whom he had been at work, who on their return to the field, found him dead, lying on the ground.

administration of estates
Any person that has demands upon the estate of James

Mumford, late of New London, deceased, are desired to bring them in for adjustment. Notice given by Sarah Mumford and Robinson Mumford, Administrators.

All persons indebted to the estate of Jonathan Huntington, late of Windham, deceased, are requested to make speedy payment to Ebenezer Devotion, Executor.

found
in the pasture of Josephus Lovett, near Rope Ferry in New London, five sheep.

fire
About one o'clock on Wednesday night last, the dwelling house in the improvement of Mr. John Champlin took fire under a chamber hearth, but one of the family, waking just at the time it began to blaze, the fire was happily extinguished without much damage.

agricultural news
Last Christmas day, Mr. Samuel Hill of Lyme killed a swine of his own raising and fattening just 20 months old, one half of the large English breed, that weighted 21 score and 4 pounds after being properly dressed and drained.

died
On Wednesday night died here in New London, Mary Whitaker in an advanced age.

Go West
Yesterday sailed for the Mississippi to touch at Stonington the schooner *Mississippi*, Nathaniel Porter, Master, and 45 passengers who are to settle that country.

weaver
The weaver's and the clothier's business are carried on in the best manner by Dyer Willes in the West Part of the First Society in Windham on the Lebanon line.

****

From *The Gazette,* January 21, 1774

married
Last Thursday in New London was married Timothy Tiffany to the amiable Mrs. Parthenia Coit, a lady possessed of every qualification necessary for a married life.

list of letters at New London Post office

John Blackley, Norwich Landing
Benjamin Crowe, Killingly
Robert Douglass Jr., North Parish, New London
John Dolbeare, North Parish, New London
Elisha Gallup, Stonington
Mr. Holt, Shoemaker, New London
John Hillard, Stonington
Isaac Hubbard, Southampton, Long Island
Joseph Leach, New London
Thomas Monro, Stonington
James B. Nickolson, Norwich Landing
John Richards, New London
David Yeamans, New London

for sale
Just come to hand and to be sold by Moses Morss of Preston at the lowest rate for cash or short credit, a new and fresh assortment of English and West Indian goods. He still continues in the saddler's business and wants a journeyman that well understands that trade.

Fenning's Much Approved Spelling Book to be sold by the printer hereof.

John Hallam at his shop near *The Sign Post* in New London, makes and sells all kinds of goldsmith, silversmith and jeweler's work. He will take country products in payment, *viz.* beef, pork, cheese, butter, bees wax and Bayberry tallow.

found
Came in to the pasture of Abel Rathbun of Colchester, a yearling steer.

From *The Gazette,* January 28, 1774

shipwreck on Block Island
A schooner in the command of Captain Robinson from South Carolina, bound for Cape Ann, laden with pitch, rice, etc. came to anchor on the 25th *ult*. near Block Island by reason of easterly weather. The day following, a violent gale from the westward drove her from her anchorage and she's stranded on the southwest part of said island. The vessel is lost, but part of the cargo, sail and rigging saved.

agricultural news
On Wednesday of last week, a heifer belonging to Timothy Lester of this town, just 21 months old to the day, had a bull calf which the next day weighted 57 ½ pounds. It had not sucked for about nine hours when weighted.

married
Dr. Simon Wolcott to Miss Lucy Rogers.

died
Monday night last, died at Norwich of a consumption, Mrs. Lydia Lathrop, wife of Captain Elisha Lathrop.

Last Tuesday night, between the hours of 10 and 11, departed this life in Norwich, Samuel Lathrop of that Town in the 86th year of his age.

On the same day, died at East Haddam, Ruth Spencer, widow of John Spencer, in the 86th year of her age.

Last Saturday died in Groton, Miss Sarah Woodbridge, daughter of Captain Paul Woodbridge of that place.

chimney sweeping
Chimney sweeping performed by Samuel Weaver and William Line, who will, on suitable encouragement, give attendance once a quarter in the principal towns of the colony.

From *The Gazette,* February 4, 1774

died
Col. Simon Lathrop, 86 years of age; he was an honor to the respectable family from which he descended and to which he stood related. He was naturally active and industrious and enjoyed a long series of prosperity by the blessing of God; he continued in the marriage relation about 60 years; he was a parent of peculiar tenderness.

pay up
James Chapman Jr. of New London desires all persons that are indebted to him to settle up immediately or he will be put to the necessity of putting them to suit.

All persons indebted to Joseph Smith of New London are requested to settle the same without delay.

strayed or stolen
from Elisha Gleeson of Pomfret, a black mare.

farm for sale
To be sold on reasonable terms by Obidiah Kingsbury living in Norwich West Farms, five and a half acres of land with a dwelling house, barn with a good well and sundry fruit trees on the land. The land is on the road between Windham and Norwich, about halfway between the court houses in said towns. Also to be sold, four acres of woodland, about a half a mile from the premises.

Almanac
Ames Almanac for the year 1774 will be published by the Printer hereof on Monday next.

bankruptcy notice
Notice by Jonathan Nash, Theodore Sedgwick and Truman Wheeler to the creditors of the estate of Elias Ransom, late of Great Burlington in the County of Berkshire, that a meeting is

to be held at the dwelling house of Josiah Smith, inn holder in said Great Barrington.

found
in the pasture of Daniel Robertson, of Coventry, two stray mares.

land for sale in Norwich town
For sale, at the house Aariah Lathrop, inn holder in the town of Norwich, by the order of the General Assembly, lands belonging to Ebenezer Backus, deceased, including the dwelling house and shop where Backus dwelt with land of about 60 rods, lying between the two streets; eight acres and nine rods of land on the opposite side of said street, with a barn, corn house and other buildings thereon; bounded on the southeast by the land of Mr. John Post;
about two acres and three quarters of land with a dwelling house thereon on the northeast side of the Town street, near Samuel Wheat's land;
36 acres of land on the south side of the Quarter, near the town plot, by John Edgerton's land;
10 acres of land in the West Shepard Walk by the southwest corner of the land of the late William Lathrop;
17 acres of pasture land near Daniel Douglass' dwelling house;
17 acres of pasture land, near Jabez Lathrop's dwelling house;
600 feet of land at the landing place with a store house standing thereon being 20 feet on the Shetucket River near the landing place;
8 acres of land at a place called Yentick, adjoining to Uriah Roger's land;
26 acres and 133 rods of land lot down the southeast of Mr. Simon Calkin;
a handsome dwelling house, shop, a barn, out houses and land now in the occupation of Ebenezer Lord, near the Meeting House in Norwich;
two tracts of land, the first containing about 20 acres which formerly belonged to John Edgerton, the second about seven acres which formerly belonging to Dr. Elisha Lord.

inoculation
Notice by John and Elisha Ely that they have carried on inoculation for the smallpox[1] for several years past on Duck Island, which is situated near the West parish in Saybrook, during which time, about four hundred people have passed through the operation without the loss of one patient. There has also been landed on the island thirty people who were sick with small pox in the normal way, who had taken the distemper in New York, other places or in the West Indies, all of whom have happily recovered. This, we think, is an instance that rarely, if ever, has happened in America. And from the situation of our hospital, great advantage it is hoped will accrue to the public. Being near the Connecticut River, it serves as a repository for those infected with the contagious distemper and has thereby prevented the distemper from being carried into the center of this colony and propagating among its inhabitants. We therefore hope and expect that all proper encouragement will be given us, especially as we have laid out our profits of the proceeding years in another building whereby we hope and expect to have much larger and better accommodations.

Susquehanna Purchase
Notice given by Samuel Gray, Nathaniel Wales Jr., Jedidiah Elderkin, Ebenezer Baldwin and Gershom Breed, Proprietors of the Susquehanna Purchase[2], to meet at the courthouse in Windham to take into consideration the present situation of the Purchase and come to such determination there, as shall be judged best and necessary for securing the same.

****

From *The Gazette,* February 11, 1774

Susquehanna Purchase
There is now between 2000 and 3000 people at Susquehanna under Connecticut claim, people perhaps as regular and orderly as any under heaven. But in the resolutions of Pennsylvania they are represented as riotous, lawless, tumultuous and disturbers all of the peace.

accidental death.
One day last week, a child of James Haughton of the North Parish in this town, about five years old, fell into a dish kettle of hot water, which scalded it in such a manner that it died in 48 hours.

fat cow
We hear that a cow fattened by Experience Robinson in Windham was last week sold in Boston for $60.

sudden death of couple
We hear from Sharon that last Monday night a man and his wife of that place went to bed in good health and were heard by the family to talk together about the break of day, but, at about eight o'clock in the morning, they were both found dead in the their bed. They were aged persons.

fire
On the 28th seventh *ultima* about 2:00 p.m. the following melancholy accident happened in Coventry North Parish, namely as Mr. Jacob Brewster was dressing flax, he laid several bundles by his fireside in order for drying which suddenly took fire and the wind being very high, in less than two minutes, it was not practical to enter that part of the house but by the dexterity of the people present, they entered other parts of the house and threw out of the windows some few articles and, as a number of people had by this time collected, they, by dragging away the timber as it fell and quenching the fire upon the floor with snow, saved in great part of the provisions of the cellar. The loss must be very considerable as the house was 30 by 35 feet and nearly finished. About 15 bushels of corn and part of his English grain is consumed.

a record
Yesterday, Mr. James Burnam of Norwich brought to market a sled load the of wood which completes the number 2,500 loads he has drove himself to town since the year 1754. The whole of which he has drove in himself about four miles, a great part of which he cut himself and all, except about 50 loads, on his own

land. All which he has done without upsetting a cart or breaking a wheel, lost a sled or even bruising a finger or by any means damaging an ox or horse by any wound.

N.B. He imagines he has about five times as much more wood for market which he intends leaving to some other person to cut and draw as the thinks he has done his share in that way the 2500 loads he has sold for about 820 pounds lawful money.

to be sold
a sloop of about 84 tons burthen that had been mostly used in the whale fishery. It is a very strong, good vessel and a prime sailor. Horses, cattle or West India goods will be taken in payment. Inquire of W. Stewart.

Choice Muscovado sugar to be sold by Dudley Saltonstall by the hogshead and barrel.

****

From *The Gazette,* February 18, 1774

to be sold
at public vendue by the order of the General Assembly at the house of Amariah Storrs in Mansfield, all the land belonging to the late Oxenbridge Thatcher of Milton, deceased; one parcel of the lands lies on the Atchauge River and contains 183 acres, all of it unimproved lands; part of it is well timbered and is suitable for plowing, mowing and pasture. Also two other tracts of land, the one contains about 50 acres, the other 12 acres. Also about 20 acres situated about a mile east from the town street, adjoining a large pond. Inquire of Shubael Conant of Mansfield. Notice given by James Boies, Administrator.

notice of bankruptcy
Notice by Hezekiah Sears and David Smith, Commissioners to the creditors of the estate of Waitstill Smith, late of Chatham, that a meeting will be held at the house of David Smith in said Chatham.

hats for sale
Advertisement by David Nevins that he has for sale at his shop,

opposite the store of Christopher Leffingwell in Norwich, hats he has manufactured in both beaver and castor. Those who are inclined to purchase by the dozen shall have a handsome abatement made, so as to make it well worth their while to purchase in that way.

lighthouse legislation
The following Public Act was passed at the last session of the General Assembly: an Act for the erecting and maintaining of a lighthouse near the port of New London and for laying a tax on shipping in support thereof.

sudden deaths
About a fortnight ago, Mr. David Burnham of East Hartford, who for some months has been disordered in his senses and lived with two of his sons, was found frozen to death in their house.

Last Monday, a child in New Britain in Farmington about 14 months old, being left at home with some older children by the parents who were abroad on a sleight, fell into the fire and was so much burned that it died a few hours after.

hog
A hog was killed by Captain Eliphalet Bulkey in Colchester, about 15 months old, which weighted and dressed, 17 score and 5 pounds.

died
Last Saturday night, in this town, aged about 90 years, Mary Uncas, relict of the late Benjamin Uncas II, Sachem of the Mohegan tribe of Indians. Her remains were interred in Norwich on Wednesday last.

Last Wednesday. died here (New London) in an advanced age, Edward Robbins for many years a noted shopkeeper in the town.

Delaware Companies
Notice by Jabez Fitch, Isaac Tracy, Joseph Griswold and Elisha Tracy, the Proprietors of the First and Second Companies of the Delaware Purchasers, that there will be a meeting at the Courthouse in Norwich to consider the present situation of said purchases. A general attendance is desired, as matters of great importance will be transacted at said meetings.

bankruptcy notice
Notice by Justus Buck and Edward Shipman, Commissioners to the creditors of the estate of Samuel Parmele of Saybrook, deceased, and represented insolvent, that a meeting will be held at the dwelling house of Captain Edward Shipman in said Saybrook.

to be sold cheap
a very good wagon; inquire of the Printer.
****
From *The Gazette,* February 25, 1774

land for sale
Notice by Edmund Freeman and Elijah Fenton, Trustees to estate of the Reverend Ebenezer Martin of Ashford, of the sale of Reverend Martin's dwelling house and a small a lot of land. The sale will be at the dwelling house of Simon Smith, tavern keeper in the parish of Westford of such town.

clocks and watches
Thomas Harland, watch and clock maker from London, wishes to acquaint the public that he has opened a shop near the store of Christopher Leffingwell in Norwich. Clocks and watches, if left with John Champlin in New London, will be forwarded to Harland and returned with all expedition.

sleigh sinks in river
The following melancholy accident happened on Wednesday the last. As a sleigh with two horses and five people were returning from a wedding in Haddam and crossing the Connecticut River, a few rods above East Haddam Landing, the

ice broke through, when one young woman named Liddy Gates, daughter of Joshua Gates of East Haddam, was drowned with both of the horses who were carried under the ice by the current.

snake
Last Saturday, as Captain Levi Riley was going on board his vessel at Lyme, he found in his path in the snow an adder, four feet in length and very venomous which he killed.

died
in New London, last Friday, Mrs. Sarah Chappel, consort of Captain Stephen Chappel. This is the third wife he has buried in the space of around six years.

court adjourned
We are desired to inform the public that the New Haven County court is adjourned to Tuesday, March 15 next.

shipwrecks
Arrived here, February 21 via New York, Capt. Daniel Starr of the sloop *Fanny*, bound to this port [New London] from Moule who, on the 21st of January, was cast away on Barnegat Beach in a violent gale of wind. The vessel was lost, but the cargo and appurtenances saved.

The sloop *Polly*, Captain Giles Sage, on the 19th instant in a gale of wind, coming into this harbor [New London], ran aground on Goshen reef. His vessel was bilged and lost part of the cargo of sugars. The vessel has since got off and now is coming to the harbor.

anecdote of the celebrated Columbus
When Columbus, after having discovered the Western Hemisphere, was by order of the King of Spain, brought home from America in chains, the captain of the ship, who was intimately acquainted with his character, his knowledge and abilities, offered to free him from his fetters and make his passage as agreeable as possible. But Columbus rejected his friend, saying "Sir, I thank you, but these chains are the rewards

for my services to my Sovereign I have served as equally as my God and as such I would carry them to my grave."

****

From *The Gazette,* March 4, 1774

land in New London Town for sale
Notice by Marvin Wait, Administrator for the estate of Enoch Bolles Jr, deceased, to be sold at the Court House in New London by order of the Court of Probate for the district of New London, a lot of land situated on Beach street, lying south of, and adjoining, to, Nathan Baley's and containing a quarter of an acre; also to be sold household furniture, wearing apparel, saddler tools and two chaises with harness.

weaver hired
Abijah Jones of Colchester informs the public that he has engaged a workmen at the weaver and clothier's trade. Said workman learned his trade at Eleazar Jewet's of Norwich.

administration of estates
Notice by the Jonathan Prentis, Executor of the estate of Capt. Joseph Prentis, late of New London, deceased, to all those who are indebted to the estate are desired to make payment, and those who have accounts against of the estate are desired to exhibit them for settlement.

teacher available
A school master who teaches reading, writing, arithmetic, navigation and surveying would take employment at a school. N.B. He teaches arithmetic very concisely.

lent but forgotten to whom
Lent about eight years ago, a French Regular gun and then, about two years ago, an English double breech gun. As it is forgotten to whom they were lent, those who have been in their possession are requested to return same to Nathan Douglass in New London.

Norwich lottery
The managers of the Norwich Wharf Bridge lottery[3], having disposed of a great part of the tickets, will proceed to the drawing of said lottery as soon as to remainder of the tickets are sold.

horse thieves sent to prison
Last Friday, three persons were convicted in the court at Windham for horse stealing and were sentenced to four years confinement in Newgate prison and the same day they were sent off to said prison. Their names are William Crawford (of New Hampshire), John Roberts and -- Ramsdel.

died
Last Sunday, aged 58 Mrs. Doratha Huntington, relict of the Hon. Hez. Huntington;

Mrs. Mary Boscawen the, wife of Richard Boscawen died in Jamaica. She was the daughter of Avery Denison of Stonington and widow of Capt. Jesse Denison, late of St. Eustatia;

On the sixteenth, departed this life, Samuel Raynolds of Somers in the 46th year of his age, after about ten days of illness with a violent nervous disorder. He was the oldest son of the Reverend Peter Raynolds, late pastor of the Church in Enfield.

suicide
Monday night last, a man named William Noulton of Ashford, who had for some time been disordered in his senses, cut his own throat.

****

From *The Gazette,* March 11, 1774

Saybrook Bar Lottery
will be drawn on March 21. Tickets may be had of Mr. William Hart Jr. in Saybrook, David Manwaring in New London, Joseph Knight, post rider, and all managers.

standards for doctors
Any number of physicians in the County of New London in taking into consideration the great importance that those who enter into the practice of Physick should be able to prosecute it in the most useful manner, request their brother of the faculty in said County to meet at the house of Azariah Lathrop in Norwich to consider the matter and, if it is thought to be expedient, for a memorial to the General Assembly at their next session that the practice of medicine may be put under some better regulation.

administration of estates
Notice by Marvin Wait, Administrator, that by order of the Court of Probate for the District of New London that Adam Shapely and Edward Hallam have been appointed Commissioners to examine the claims of the several creditors to the estate of Edward Robinson, late of New London, deceased and represented insolvent, and that a meeting will be held at the house of Capt. Nathaniel Coit, inn holder in New London.

Notice to all creditors and debtors to the estate of Nathaniel Williams, late of Stonington, that they should bring their claims and payments to Abigail Williams, *Administratrix* of said estate.

To be sold at the dwelling house of Elisha Fitch of Norwich, part of the estate of Joseph Pride, deceased.

reward for escaped prisoner
Notice by Samuel Plumb, Constable in Stonington, that a reward is offered for the return of Samuel Dyer Hull of said Stonington who made his escape with the assistance of some evil minded persons. He was taken by virtue of a writ of attachment. Said Hall is about 27 years of age; about five feet ten inches high and round face; dark complexion; black curled hair and dark eyes.

a healthy place
A correspondent at Oyster Ponds in Southold, Long Island says that from November 10, 1771 to February 5, 1774 there has died but four persons in the East Society in Southold. The

Society consists of about 70 families. Not one of the above four persons were in a married state. Between the above said dates, there have been more than 10 births to one death. "Yet, let the living man know that they must die

died
at Preston, Mrs. Mehetabel Coit, amiable consort of Wheeler Coit, merchant, after a short confinement by sickness in the 28th year of her age. She has left behind to lament her early death, a sorrowful husband, four brethren and two sisters, beside a large circle of weeping friends and neighbors, and a number of the poor and needy who ever found her heart and hand open to feed the distressed and relieve their wants.

tea ship
A ship with the East India Company's tea on board, bound for New York, was blown off the coast and arrived at Antigua.

stolen
Notice by Matthew Talcott of Middletown that there was stolen out of his shop various items including currency.

wanted
a sprightly active boy to be an apprentice at the cordwainer's business, 14 or 15 years old, who can be well recommended. Inquire of Thomas Trapp at Norwich Landing.

lost
One day last week, on the road from Lyme East Society to Colchester, a woman's black taffeta cloak; notice given by Benjamin Lee.

****

From *The Gazette,* March 18, 1774

day of fast
His Honor, the Governor, has issued a proclamation appointing Wednesday, the 13th day of April next, for a public fast in this colony.

hog
One day last week, a hog was killed by Jabez Chapman of East Haddam which weighted 27 score and 4 pounds.

detested tea
From Lyme yesterday, one William Lamson of Martha Vineyard came to this town with a bag of tea, about a hundred weight, on horseback which he was peddling about the Country. He was about a business, it was supposed, that would render him obnoxious to the people, which gave reason to suspect that he had some of the detestable tea, lately landed in Cape Cod. Upon examination, it appeared to the satisfaction of all present to be part of that very tea, although he declared that he had purchased it of two gentlemen in Newport, one of them is said to be a customs House officer and the other the Captain of the Fort. Whereupon, a number of the Sons of Liberty[4] assembled in the evening, kindled a fire and committed the bag with its contents to the flames where it was all consumed and the ashes buried on the spot in the testimony of their utter abhorrence of all tea subject to a duty for the purpose of raising any revenue in America. A laudable example for our brethren in Connecticut.

died
at New Haven, Capt. Christopher Killey, Deputy postmaster;

at Norwalk John Belding, Deputy Postmaster at that place.

Mohegan leases
Notice by Richard Law, on behalf of the Committee, appointed by the General Assembly to assist the Mohegan Indians in leasing out their lands, are to meet on said business at Haughton's, inn keeper, halfway between New London and Norwich where all those that are now tenants on said the lands are desired to meet and settle their leases.

administration of estates
Notice by James Stedman, Administrator of the estate of Deacon Thomas Stedman, late of Windham, deceased, that such

part of the estate sufficient to raise the sum of 264 pounds will be sold at the house of Jacob Simons, Inn holder in Windham;

Notice by Edward Hancox, Elnath Rosseter, Nathan Palmer, Jr. Commissioners appointed by the Court of Probate, District of Stonington, of the estate of Joseph Chesebrough, late of Stonington, deceased and represented insolvent, that a meeting will be held at the dwelling house of Captain Andrew Palmer in Stonington.

Susquehanna Purchase
Notice by Jonathan Gardiner, Clerk of the Proprietors of a township now called Newport in the Susquehanna Purchase, lately surveyed, that a committee consisting of Prince Alden, John Comstock and Captain Cyprian Lothrop of New London, chosen for that purpose, will meet at the dwelling house of Simon Gager, inn holder in Norwich, to hear the report and see the survey of said committee, choose officers for the said town and do any business proper at said meeting.

****

From *The Gazette,* March 25, 1774

to be sold on reasonable terms
by the Thaddeus Cooke, living in Preston, North Society, about 310 acres of land with a large dwelling house, barn and sundry other buildings, a good well of water, and a large orchard on the premises. Said land is well watered with constant streams and springs. About 200 acres of land is in a good improvement and remaining well wooded; said land lies within a mile off two of some iron works and several other mills. Also to be sold, two acres of land with a good saw mill, about half a mile from the above premises.

runaways
from Elijah Phelpes, an apprentice boy named Guy Chapel; about 18 years old; by trade a shoe maker.

from Samuel Chapman of Tolland, a well built fellow, named Israel.

From *The Gazette,* April 1, 1774

heart attack
Last Friday, Ebenezer Hamblin of Colchester was seized with a pain in his breast as he was walking to a neighbor's and, being carried home, died in a few hours. He was aged 76 years.

to be sold
a farm in Mansfield containing 220 acres, 40 of which is under improvement with a new and convenient dwelling house, barn and corn house. For further particulars, inquire of Isaac Perkins living on the premises.

flax for sale
Choice flax to be sold by John Geer on board the schooner *King of Pussia*, lying at Capt. Jabez Perkins' wharf at Norwich Landing.

not responsible
Notice by Joshua Wheeler that gives notice to all persons from not trusting Abeleny, wife or concubine, on his account upon their peril for he will not pay a penny of her accounts.

for sale
a convenient mansion house two stories high and on a small lot of choice land adjoining, situated a few rods southerly of the Reverend Mr. White's Meeting House [5] in Windham with a well of water on the premises. For further particulars, inquire of John Baker Brimmer at Chelsea in Norwich.

Colchester Lottery
Messrs. Gershom Bulkey, Henry Champion and Jacob Isbain Jr. are appointed managers of said lottery by the town of Colchester, pursuant to the grant of the Assembly and the inhabitants of the same town have given bond to the Governor and to the Colony of Connecticut that said lottery shall be faithfully managed and completed in 12 months from the grant and that each fortunate adventurer shall be surely paid.

strayed
from Noah Day in Colchester, a sorrel colt.

****

From *The Gazette,* April 8, 1774

just published
and to be sold by Timothy E. Green, a choice collection of hymns and spiritual songs intended for the edification of sincere Christians of all denominations by Samson Occom, minister of the Gospel.

please pay
Notice by Nathan Arnold, who, for a number of years, has been in the practice of physick in Mansfield, that he is now about to remove a considerable distance and desires every person indebted to him to settle accounts without the delay or further notice.

conviction
At Superior Court held at Norwich last week, Daniel Humphrey of Windsor was convicted of burglary in breaking into the cabin of the sloop *Dove* in this harbor, New London, and stealing 100 pounds of coffee and was sentenced to six years confinement in Newgate Prison, Simsbury Mine.[6] Also, one James Williams and a transient person were convicted of robbery on the highway and sentenced to two years confinement at the same place. And, on Monday last, they took that departure for said prison properly guarded.

wanted to buy
Cash given for a small furs, bees wax, old pewter and copper by John Baker Brimmer.

notice
The inhabitants of the Town of New London are hereby notified to bring their weights and measures to Nathan Bailey, Sealer, to be sealed as the law directs.

passage boat
Springer's New London and Norwich Passage Boat continues to ply every day in the week, except Sunday, wind and weather permitting.

died
at Milford, of the smallpox, Mrs. Mary Fowler, consort to John Fowler.

In this town, New London, Wyllys Hubbard, son of Colonel Leveret Hubbard, aged 19.

****

From *The Gazette,* April 15, 1774

please pay up
Notice by Elisha Paine of Plainfield that there are a considerable number of debts owed him for business done in the law department and, as he is going out of the Colony and soon expects to be removed, his family desires all persons to settle the same with Nathan Wales.

to be sold
at the dwelling house of Samuel Branch, late of Preston deceased, good land lying west of the road near William Witter, a black Smith's shop, near the dwelling house of Edward Mott and sundry other articles. For further particulars, inquire of Hannah Branch.

administration of estates
Notice by the Richard Law, Nathaniel Shaw, Jr. and Russell Hubbard, , Commissioners appointed by the Court of Probate for the District of New London to the creditors of the estate of James Mumford, formerly of New London, deceased and represented insolvent, that a hearing will be held at the mansion house of the said Mumford in New London.

newly elected
The following gentlemen are chosen representatives of the General Assembly

New London: Richard Law and William Hillhouse;
Norwich: Isaac Tracy and Benjamin Huntington;
Groton: Thomas Mumford and Captain William Morgan;
Stonington: John Deane and Nathaniel Miner;
Lyme: Major Samuel Holden Parsons and William Noyes;
Windham: Nathaniel Wales, Jr. and Maj. Jedidiah Elderkin;
Lebanon: Col. Arnot and William Williams;
Glastonbury: Jonathan Welles and Ebenezer Plummer;
Colchester: Maj. Henry Champion and Daniel Foot;
Haddam: Capt. Jabez Brainerd and Capt. Joseph Brok;
East Haddam: Daniel Brainerd and Jabez Chapman;
Saybrook: Hezekiah Whittlesey and William Worthington.

shipwreck
Last Sunday, a sloop, about 35 tons, Davis, Master, belonging to Norwich in its passage from Boston to this place (New London) was lost on a shoal called "the snowdrift" near Nantucket. Her cargo consisted chiefly of European goods which has received considerable damage.

died
On the 20th of last month, died at Plainfield, the widow Ann Underwood in the 88th year of her age. It is remarkable that she never had a fit of sickness but she died with the infirmities of old age. She was greatly resigned to the will of God. Her death is sincerely lamented by her children and friends;

in New Haven, departed this life in new beauty and innocence, Mrs. Mary Perit, consort of Mr. Anthony Perit and the elder daughter of Benjamin Sanford at the 18th year of her age.

to be sold
at the dwelling house of Capt. Dudley Wright in Colchester in Hartford County, about 27 acres of land, well wooded and watered. It lays by the New London Road about 1 mile and a quarter from the Meeting House in said Colchester; notice given by Humphrey Lyon and Jabez Chapman Jr.

ran away
from David Bolles of Ashford, an apprentice boy named Benjamin Pitt; about 19 years old; five feet ten inches high; light complexion; brown hair tied in the neck, his foretop combed back.

to be sold or let
by Ely Warner of Hartford, a convenient dwelling house situated at East Haddam Landing, near the River, three quarters of an acre of land adjoining the said House with a small barn standing thereon and a good well; also seven acres of pasture land within a quarter of a mile of the above and six acres of lands; very convenient for a merchant, coaster or tradesman.

escaped
A few night's since, the noted Steel made his escape from goal.

****

From *The Gazette,* April 22, 1774

storm at sea
Capt. Job Easton, who is arrived at Newport from Hispaniola, spoke with the Brig *Minerva,* Eliphalet Roberts, from this port, New London, who met with a heavy gale of wind in which he was overset and lost his main mast and two horses. Captain Easton threw over a top mast for them, but the sea was so high they could not get it on board.

died
at Groton, Mrs. Mary Chester. aged 78, relict of Capt. John Chester;

Elijah Walworth;

Mrs. Mary Burrows, wife of Samuel Burrows Jr.

administration of estates
Notice by Lathrop Niles and Edward Eells, Administrators of the estate of Joshua Rathbun, late of Stonington, deceased and represented insolvent, that a meeting of creditors will be held at

the house of Capt. John Denison on Long Point (so called) in Stonington.

ran away
from Abraham Page of Branford, an indentured servant named Joshua Chappel; he was born in New London; is about 22 years old; somewhat thick set; of dark complexion and has short, dark hair and a flat nose.

to sail
The schooner *Indian King,* Robert Avery, Master, will sail for Nova Scotia.

formation of medical society
At a meeting of physicians, lately held in Windham, who desired to establish in this Colony a learned collection of physicians, which must in the end be beneficial to the public utility of mankind and the safety of every individual.
Parker Morse, Joshua Elderkin, David Abrams, Nathan Arnold, John Clarke, Benj. Palmer, Eleazer Fitch, Elijajh Lyman, Elisha Perkins and John Brewster were in attendance.

****

From *The Gazette,* April 29, 1774

to stand stud
The *Leopard* of the one eyed *Ansley* horse, his sire, was brought from England by lawyer Ingersoll. It is a horse of size and of beauty and fine carriage and is a very swift runner. Inquire of Ebenezer Welch Jr., near Wales Bridge, 8th Society of Norwich.

medical society
At a meeting of the physicians of New London County at the house of Thomas Allen in New London, the following physicians were selected a committee to represent the other physicians of the county at a meeting with other counties to be held in Hartford: Doctors Joseph Perkins, Elisha Tracy, Benjamin Gales and Eleazer Matther.

administration of estate
Thankful Smith is appointed *Administratrix* of the estate of Joseph Smith, late of Norwich, deceased.

ran away
from Robinson Mumford, a mulatto wench, Kate, 23 years of age; born in this country; she is tall and likely to look at; has bushy hair and dresses neat.

****

From *The Gazette*, May 6, 1774

prison break

Last Saturday night, the prisoners at NewGate prison in Simsbury opened a place that had been stopped that lead from their place of confinement into a long deep shaft that was partially filled with rocks and stones. William Johnson Crawford and Daniel Humphrey (sometimes called Daniel Collyer Humphrey) being more bold than the rest sought to pull away the stones from over their heads and so went upwards in the old shaft and, as these two in the shaft pulled the stones, three other prisoners below moved them out of the way to keep a communication between them and all promised themselves a speedy escape, when, at about three o'clock in the morning, the rocks stones etc. in the shaft gave way and sank in the shaft where Crawford and Humphrey were at work to the great consternation of the three prisoners below who say they really believed that Humphrey and Crawford are buried under the floors. But whether they are really buried or by some means escaped remains uncertain by those who have observed the place and conjecture the latter. Therefore, this is to give notice that any person or persons who will take Humphrey or Crawford or both and shall convey them to NewGate shall receive a 10 dollar reward for each to be paid by John Viets, Keeper of said Prison.

Norwich Bridge lottery
Notice by Commissioners Joshua Lathrop, Samuel Tracy and Rufus Lathrop.

for sale house and real estate
One hundred acres of divided land; also a right to the commons in a place called Riverhead in the township of Southampton, Long Island, together with a fulling mill. The house is admirably situated for a merchant or tradesman, being 40 rods from the County Hall. The mill is built upon, and has the command of, a stream, which is equal to any on the Island; inquire of John Albertson.

coasting
Sloop *Victory*, Job Rathburn Master, proposes to follow the business of coasting between Norwich Landing and Windsor.

rape of child
Yesterday the trial of Lemon came on in the Superior Court. He was indicted for a rape on an Indian girl of 4 years old, upon which indictment he plead guilty. Whereupon, the court sentenced him to sit upon the gallows with a rope around his neck for one hour and to be whipped 39 times at a Cart's tail which sentence was immediately carried out.

remarkable
Alvin Avered of Wallingford had a black ewe that lambed four white lambs, which are all living and likely to do well. Last year she lambed three lambs at one time.

for sale
Job and Samuel Tabor at the head of the Niantic River have for sale an assortment of English goods.

runaway
from Elisha Miller of Lyme, a Negro man named Tim; 28 years old; small of stature.
****
From *The Gazette*, May 13, 1774

Susquehanna Purchase
Notice by Samuel Gray to the Proprietors of the Susquehanna purchase that there will be a meeting in Hartford.

wine and spirits for sale
Notice by Thomas Coit that he has for sale at his store in Norwich Landing wines by the bottle, gallon or cask, Madeira, Lisbon, Malalga, claret and Jamaica spirits, coffee, tea, sugar, brown sugar, etc.

administration of estates
Notice by Luke Perkins, Executor of the estate of James Perkins, deceased, of Groton to creditors to settle accounts.

$10 reward
for thief and items stolen out of the fulling mill of Daniel Allen Jr.

fire
On Monday night last, the dwelling house of Daniel Austin Jr. of Suffield took fire and was entirely consumed.

****

From *The Gazette*, May 20, 1774

American Post Office
Wednesday night in this town (New London) William Goddard arrived here from the eastern colonies on his way to Hartford and the southern colonies. His proposal is for establishing an American post office on constitutional principles (which have been warmly patronized by our brothers in the neighboring governments) and meets with the entire approbation of the inhabitants of New London and Norwich who are now subscribing with great liberality for the purpose of carrying the important design into complete execution. It is not doubted but the whole colony will cheerfully cooperate in giving success to this most noble independent undertaking so indispensably necessary in the present alarming crisis of American affairs.

administration of estates
Charles Miner and Stephen Niles have been appointed Commissioners of the estate of Seth Jones of Stonington, deceased and represented insolvent, give notice to creditors that a meeting of creditors will be held at house of Mrs. Joanna

Frink.

for stud
The half English horse *Jolly* in Lyme; notice by Stephen Johnson Jr.

The horse *Paoli*; notice by John Watson of East Windsor.

strayed or stolen
a horse from Joseph Johnson of Colchester.
****

From *The Gazette*, May 27, 1774

died
in Norwich, Thomas Lathrop; aged 94 years.

bound for Nova Scotia
the sloop *Cumberland,* Thomas Ratchford, Master, lying at Norwich Landing.

administration of estates
Notice by Samuel Latimer Jr. to the creditors of the estate of Samuel Latimer of New London to file any claims.

runaway
from Elijah Philips of Pomfret, an apprentice girl named Abigail Ide; about 14 years old with brown hair.
****

From *The Gazette,* June 3, 1774

protest
Yesterday, being the first of June, the day the cruel edict of the British Parliament respecting the people and port of Boston, it was observed here in Lebanon with marks of distinction. The bells of the town early began to toll a solemn peel and continued the whole day. The town house door hung with black with the Act affixed thereto. The shops in the town were all shut and silent. Their windows covered with black and other ensigns of distress. Towards evening, a respectable number of

freeholders of the town and others appeared at the town house where the Act was read.

died
Mrs. Sarah Smith, wife of Jonathan Smith.

Capt. John Daley of this town (New London) died in New York.

At Newent in Norwich, Mr. Joseph Read, aged 94. He had an uncommon healthy and strong constitution and was seldom known to be sick, but ,through the decay of ages and exercise of strong pain, his constitution began to wear out. He was a professor of religion for a number of years and had the character of a very religious man. His funeral was preached by the Rev. Mr. Benedict. He left a widow of 70 years, his fourth wife, five children, a great number of grand children and great grandchildren and one of the fifth generation.

lottery winner
Number 75 was the winning ticket in the Norwich Lottery. It drew 300 dollars and was in the possession of Mr. Fuller.

bankruptcy notice
Notice to the creditors of John and Eliphalet Bulkley of Colchester that there will be a meeting at the house of Azariah Lathrop where they should bring claims.

Notice that the General Association is to meet at the house of Rev. Daniel Welch of Mansfield.

taken up
by Benjamin Atwell, Jr in New London, North parish, a reddish roan mare.

notice to Susquehanna land purchasers
The Proprietors of Winchester on Fishing Creek of the Susquehanna Purchase are to meet at the house of Captain Edward Palmes of New London; notice given by John Owen, Proprietors' Clerk.

From *The Gazette,* June 10, 1774

in the House of Representatives of the Colony of Connecticut
This House taking into serious consideration sundry acts of the British Parliament in which their power and right to impose taxes and duties upon His Majesty's subjects in the towns and plantations in America for the purpose of raising a revenue are declared, attempted to be exercised and, in various manners, enforced and carried into execution and especially a very late act of penalties and pains are inflicted on the capital of a neighboring province, a precedent justifiably alarming to every colony in America, and which put their Lives, Liberties and Properties at the mercy of a tribunal where innocence may be punished upon the accusation and evidence of wicked men without defense and without ever knowing their accusers, a precedent intended to terrify them into submission and silence, while they are stripped of their Liberties and Rights, do think it expedient and their duty at this time to renew their claims to the Rights, Privileges and Immunities of freeborn Englishmen to which they are justifiably entitled by the laws of Nature, by the Charter of his late Majesty King Charles the second and by long and uninterrupted possession.

Norwich Town Meeting
At a very full meeting of the inhabitants of the town of Norwich, the Hon. Jabez Huntington, Moderator, it was voted that we will, to the utmost of our abilities, assert and defend the liberties and immunities of British America and that we will cooperate with our brothers in this colony and others in such reasonable measures as in this Assembly and otherwise, be judged most proper to relieve us on the burdens we now feel and secure us from greater evils we fear will follow from the principles adopted by the British Parliament respecting the town of Boston:
VOTED that Captain Jedidiah Huntington, Christopher Leffingwell, Dr. Theophilus Rogers, Capt. William Hubbard and Capt. Joseph Trumbull to be a standing committee to keep up correspondence with the towns of this and neighboring ones; notice by Benjamin Huntington Jr., Town clerk.

estate sale
Notice by Ebenezer Devotion, Executor of the estate of Hon. Jonathan Huntington of Windam, deceased, that a sale of the personal property of the estate will be held at Jonathan Devotion's house.

passage boat
Notice for Braddick's Passage Boat between Norwich and New London. She is an exceptionally fine sailor and is new and large and has excellent accommodations for travelers. For passage or freight, agree with Braddick at this house in Chelsea or in New London at the London Coffee House.

taken up
in Pomfret, by Israel Putnam, a brown mare.

****

From *The Gazette,* June 17, 1774

to be sold
by Jeremiah Clement at his store in Norwich, sundry cloths and other items;

by Simon Woolcot, at his shop near the Court House in New London, the best double refined English loaf sugar; also best drugs and medicines;

by John Bolles at his farm, flax, wool, oats and two good yoke of oxen.

administration of estates
Notice by Samuel Jones, James Green and the Elijah Metcalf, Commissioners appointed by the Court of Probate for the District of East Haddam on the estate of Simon Ely, late of East Haddam, deceased and represented insolvent, that a meeting will be held at the dwelling house of the widow Abigail White in said East Haddam.

please settle up
Notice to all those indebted to the partnership of Green and

Spooner, lately expired, to settle accounts. Note well that the printing business is still performed by said Spooner in the most expeditious and correct manner at his office in the store of Christopher Leffingwell in Norwich.

****

From *The Gazette,* June 24, 1774

Preston Town Meeting
A town meeting, legally warned, was held on Monday, the 13th day of June 1774, in the town of Preston with Col. Samuel Coit as the Moderator. This meeting took into consideration the dangerous situation of the British colonies in North America from the principles lately adopted by the Parliament of Great Britain by inflicting pains and penalties on the town of Boston without any legal trial, or even notice of fault, and likewise another Act is pending, and far advanced, for vacating an important part of the Massachusetts charter and by sundry Acts of Parliament, all of which, being carried into execution, would render the lives, liberties and estates of all the inhabitants of said colonies precarious and entirely dependent on the arbitrary will and pleasure of a British minister of state: therefore, it is:
voted that the Royal charters to the colonies ought to be maintained as the only sacred and indissolvable bond of union between the Crown of Great Britain and the colony.
voted that we will join in with the towns in this and in neighboring colonies in all reasonable measures as shall be thought best by a General Congress or other general agreements to assert and maintain our rights and privileges and transmit them inviolate to posterity.
voted: that, if it is thought by said Congress to break off all trade with Great Britain as the best means to attain such and end, although we are not a seaport town, yet we cheerfully will deny ourselves all those advantages that a rise to us from said trade.
voted: that Col. Samuel Coit, William Witter, John Avery, Jr. John Tyler, Captain William Belcher, Samuel Mott and Benjamin Coit be a committee for keeping up a correspondence with the towns of this and neighboring colonies.

new laws passed in Colony
The following public acts as at the last session of the General Assembly:
An amendment regulating and governing the public goals or workhouse in the copper mines[7] in Simsbury and for the punishment of certain atrocious acts and penalties;
an act to regulate the fishery at the mouth of the Niantic River;
an amendment to the act forming and regulating the militia and for the encouragement of military skill for the better defense of this colony.

administration of estates
to be sold by John Leffingwell, Administrator of the estate of Captain John Leffingwell, late of Norwich and deceased, sundry lots of land lying on the West side of the cove at Chelsea in Norwich.

All those that have any demands against the estate of Nathaniel Williams, late of Stonington, deceased, are desired to bring in their accounts to Abigail Williams, A*dministratrix* for settlement.

for sale
Good white fine boards and shingles to be sold by Nathan Douglass at his wharf in New London.

****

From *The Gazette*, July 1, 1774

pamphlet for sale
Just published and to be sold by Solomon Southwick in New port, T. Green in New London, Aaron Bushnel and Nathan Bushnel of Norwich, Jacob Fellows of Tolland, Ebenezer Hovey of Canada, David Belding of East Haddam, Joseph Knight and Moses Allen of Enfield (Constitutional Post Riders) "*The Judgments of Whole Kingdoms and Nations concerning the Rights, Powers and Prerogatives of Kings and the Rights, Privileges and Properties of the People* by Lord Sommers.

for sale
superfine and fine Philadelphia flour, just imported on the Sloop *Elizabeth,* Luther Elderkin, Master; also hemp, rye and white beans, all to be sold at the Distillery in New London.

New London Town Meeting
At a Town Meeting held in New London on June 27th, Richard Law chosen Moderator. "This town taking into consideration the alarming situation in the American North America colonies with regard to the divers acts of the British Parliament for raising a revenue on the subjects of said colonies without their consent and also a late act of Parliament for blocking the port of Boston province which had afforded the utmost aid to Britain and her dominions and being advised that divers other acts have probably been passed since whereby their charter privileges will be utterly destroyed and the residents of said colony, unless relief can be had, reduced be to a state of abject vassalage, we, consider that the Province of Massachusetts Bay to be the first victim of Ministerial tyranny and after her the other colonies will share the same fate. It is manifest to us that the design of the British ministry is to subject North America to slavery with as much rapidity as possible. Therefore, we hold it an indispensable duty both to ourselves and posterity to exert the powers Heaven has endowed us with to contribute everything within our power in a constitutional manner to avert the calamity hanging over the colony.
We declare and resolve:
First, we do most expressly declare recognize and acknowledge his Majesty King George III to be the lawful and right full King of Great Britain and all his dominions and countries and that it is our indispensable duty, as being part of his Majesty's dominions, always to bear pay full and true allegiance to his Majesty and to defend to the utmost of our power against all attempts upon his person crown and dignity;
Second, the cause of Boston is a common cause of all of the North American colonies;
Third, that the preservation of the Lives, Liberties and Properties of the subjects in North America depends (under GOD) on a strict union of all the colony throughout the

continent;

Four, that we earnestly wish for and will promote all in our power a General Congress of Commissioners from all the colonies on this continent to be convened with all possible speed;

Five, that it is our hearty desire that said General Congress should among others of their determined issues, resolve to stop all imports and exports to and from Great Britain and otherwise discontinue trade as they shall think fit; that a General Congress should be held annually on this continent and plan out a method for best affecting a design on which the future happiness of the colonies greatly depends;

Six, that we will religiously abide by the resolves of the General Congress of the United North American colonies;

Seven, that the resolves of the General Assembly of this colony in their session in May the last, be recorded at large in the Town Book;

Eight, that Richard Law, Col. Gurdon Saltonstall, Nathaniel Shaw Jr., Major Samuel Holden Parsons and Capt. Guy Richards be appointed a committee to correspond with the Committees of Correspondence in this or any of the colonies in North America and are hereby directed to transmit a copy of the resolves to the Committee of Correspondents in Boston.

Town Meeting in Windham

At a meeting of the inhabitants of the town of Windham, legally warned and held in Windham, Nathaniel Wales Jr., Moderator: "This meeting being impressed with a deep sense of the present alarming aspects of Divine Providence over the British colonies in North America arising from the present depressed situation and condition of the capital of the neighboring province and having their harbor and port locked up by ships of war in hostile array, to the terror of the people in actually obstructing all commerce and trade into or from said port, thereby forcibly preventing the performance of all private maritime contracts and rendering useless the whole navigation stores and wharves built and erected at a vast expense of the inhabitants, a principle which threatens ruin and destruction both to Liberties and Properties of every subject throughout the whole British

Empire. A bill late pending before the Parliament written for regulating government of Massachusetts Bay, too long to be here recited, is replete with arbitrary threatened destruction of all corporations in Great Britain and of all chartered rights in America. In the view of these, as well as many other impending changes, calamities and from our firm belief and persuasion that there is a Supreme Almighty infinitely good and merciful being, who sits at the helm of universal nature, by whom King's reign and princes decree justice and who is the hearts of all princes and potentates of the earth which is in his hands and under his Almighty control, we therefore sincerely wish and hope a day will soon be set apart for solemn fasting and prayer as recommended by our last General Assembly.
Samuel Gray, Town clerk

food for Boston
The town of Windham collected between two and three hundred fat sheep which were to set off to Boston for the benefit of the poor of that place. A most laudable example for other towns.

died
at Middletown, Mrs. Elizabeth Southmayd, wife of William Southmayd.

strayed
from Gershom Bulkley of Colchester, a mare.

from Samuel Latimer of New London, a mare.

Susquehanna Purchase
Notice by John Owen on behalf of the proprietors of the Town of Winchester of the Susquehanna Purchase that at a meeting a tax of one dollar and a half was assessed against all Proprietors to defray the cost of surveying lots.

runaway
from Daniel Tyler of Canterbury, a mulatto slave named Samson; five feet, eight inches tall; 30 years of age; of slender build; has thick lips and curly mulatto hair uncut and goes

stooping forward.

****

From *The Gazette*, July 8, 1774

town meeting at Woodstock
At a meeting of the citizens of Woodstock, Nathaniel Child, Moderator, the resolves of the General Assembly of this Town were read and unanimously approved; that the thanks of the Town are given to Elisha Child and Jedidiah Morse, the representatives of this Town for voting for the resolves at the General Assembly as such resolves do honor to the worthy representatives of a free loyal and virtuous people, are very expressive of the sentiments of the inhabitants of this Town and by them judged necessary in times such as these when we have the most convincing proofs of a fixed determination of the British Administration to overthrow the Liberties and to subject the people to a bondage, which our father did not, and would not, but fled into the wilderness so that they might not, and God grant that we the posterity may not bear.
A Committee of Correspondence consisting of Capt. Elisha Child, Charles C. Chandler, Jedidiah Morse, Samuel McClennan and Nathaniel Childbert was appointed.

for stud
Flying Dragon, owned by Ebenezer Backus of Windham; stands 16 hands high.

administration of estates
Nathan Douglas and Roger Gibson are appointed Commissioners of the estate of William Potter, notice by Abigail Potter, *administratrix.*

died
at Wethersfield, Col. Elizur Goodrich, who completed his 81st year;

at Sharon , Col. John Williams, Judge of the Lichfield County Court;

at Westerly, William Champlin, a gentleman of an ancient and venerable family.

married
The Rev. David Jewett to Mrs. Mary Prince, widow of William Prince;

Jedidiah Strong of Lichfield to Miss Ruth Patterson of the same place.

bound for Albany
the schooner *Dolphin*, lying in the Niantic River, will sail for Albany; for freight or passage, inquire of Constant Crocker or Hezekiah Russel, both of New London.

rape
Last Wednesday, a Negro slave named Lemon, belonging to John Ives of Wallingford, was brought to goal in this Town (New Haven) charged with committing a rape on an Indian girl of 4 years old and using her in such a brutal and barbarous manner that it is thought impossible that she can recover.

****

From *The Gazette,* July 15, 1774

East Haddam Town Meeting
At a meeting of the citizens of East Haddam, Joseph Spencer, Moderator, the following is what was thought necessary and unanimously voted: that the Declaration of American Rights, Liberties and Immunities, the unconstitutional and oppressive acts of the British Parliament to raise revenues in the American colonies; the blockading of the Town and Port of Boston; the ways and means for removing those acts; the methods of supporting that town now suffering the greatest hardships and cruelties for the common cause of America, have so frequently been made public by notable towns and cities in this and neighboring colonies, more especially by the House of Representatives of the colony of Connecticut, that a repetition of this is unnecessary, this town being fully satisfied with their resolutions and determinations, for the present we recommend a

general subscription for the necessaries this Town can supply the Town of Boston under distressed circumstances and that Nathaniel Brainerd, Humphrey Lyon, Silvanus Tinker, Gibbons Jewett, Ichabod Olmsted and Christopher Holmes to be a Committee to keep correspondence with the towns of this and neighboring colonies and to transmit the sentiments of this town with the Committee in Boston and also to receive and transmit all such donations as shall be made by the inhabitants of this town to the Overseers of the Poor in Boston.

died
Mrs. Meriam Bolles, wife of John Bolles;

very suddenly at Canterbury, John Curtis, formerly of New London.

Susquehanna purchase
Notice by Jacob Simons, James Stedman, John Brewster Committee for the Proprietors of the Townships of Hancock and Bedford into the Susquehanna Purchase and Thurlow in the Lackawana Purchase to meet at the dwelling house of Jacob Simons, inn keep in Windham to hear the report of the committee who have been to survey the lands.

administration of estates
Notice by Marshfield Parsons and Samuel Mather Jr. Commissioners appointed by the Court of Probate for the District of New London, calling creditors of the estate of Jedidiah Brockway, late of Lyme and deceased, to a meeting at the dwelling house of Marshfield Parsons in Lyme.

South Hampton town meeting
At a town meeting in South Hampton, a Committee of Correspondence was chosen, comprised by John Foster, Chairman, Elisha Howell, Obidiah Jones, Uriah Rogers, Silas Halsey, David Hedges, Henry Herrick, Elias Cook, Capt. Elias Pelletreau, David Topping and John Hu.

town meetings in Pomfret and Middletown
A town meeting was held at Pomfret, where Ebenezer Williams was chosen Moderator and George Sumner, Town Clerk and at another meeting at Middletown with Jabez Hamlin chosen Moderator and Titus Hosmer, Clerk.

Glastonbury town meeting
At a town meeting at Glastonbury, Elizur Talcott, Chairman, a Committee of Correspondence was chosen, comprising William Welles, Ebenezer Plummer, Isaac Mosely, Thomas Kimberley, Josiah Hale and Elisha Hollister.

a thank you from Boston
Upon a motion made and seconded, it was unanimously voted [by the Freemen of the Town of Boston at a Town Meeting at Faneuil Hall]that the thanks of this Town be and hereby are given to our worthy friends, the inhabitants of the Town of Windham, in the colony of Connecticut, for the kind and generous assistance they have granted this Town under its present distress and calamity, in voluntarily sending 250 sheep, a present for the relief and support of the poor industrious citizens of this place, who by a late cruel and oppressive acts of Parliament for blocking up the Harbor of Boston are prevented from getting subsistence for themselves and their families.
attest: William Cooper, Town Clerk

Plainfield Town Meeting
At a Town Meeting legally warned and held in Plainfield, Isaac Coit , Moderator
This Town, taking into serious consideration the alarming steps lately taken and taking by the Parliament of Great Britain, respecting the English colonies in America, and especially the late and very extraordinary edict for blocking up the port and harbor of Boston, are humbly of an opinion:
that this very extraordinary act is not only the creature of revenge, but the exercise of power without regard to right or wrong and, while enforced, perhaps one of the most flagrant instances of tyranny that the annals of English history can furnish.

That the Town of Boston and the Province of Massachusetts Bay ought to be considered as only the first objects of Parliamentary chastisement and that the same iron rod is now lifted over every port town and colony, with all their inland towns, under which, in their turn, they will inevitably fall victims unless HE, by whom kings reigns, should immediately either turn the hearts of those in power or displace them or cause that British America, by an indissoluble union of her sons and a most vigorous stand by them made to preserve their Liberties and Privileges inviolate to posterity, should avert the final blow

Therefore, unanimously voted, that the Resolve passed by the Honorable Assembly of the Colony of Connecticut in May last, respecting the Liberties and Privileges of the English colonies, are most salutary and very heartedly adopted by this meeting and that it is the earnest desire of this meeting that deputies from the respective colonies meet as soon as may be in general congress, for the purposes aforesaid, in whose wisdom they can heartily confide and with whose result they have no doubt they shall most cheerfully acquiesce in and that they heartedly rejoice at the prospect of its speedily taking place.

VOTED that we are willing to contribute our mite, with our neighboring towns, to those of the poor of Boston who may be distressed by the late cruel and inhuman act and that Capt. Joseph Eaton, James Bradford, Robert Kinsman, Andrew Backus, Abraham Sheperd, Dr. Ebenezer Robinson, Joshua Dunlap, Perry Clark and Curtis Spalding be a committee to receive subscriptions for that purpose.

Voted that James Bradford and Isaac Coit, Maj. John Douglas, Dr. Elisha Perkins and William Robinson be a committee to correspond with the towns in this and neighboring provinces
        attest: William Robinson, Town Clerk

protest
So obnoxious to the people of this colony were the signers of the address to Governor Hutchinson that they met with a very unwelcome reception in the towns through which they passed. We hear that one of the signers was coming to Windham a few days since, he was threatened with a visit from the populace, to

avoid which he immediately rode out of town and, the next day, coming to Norwich, he was dealt with in a like manner when he thought proper immediately to leave that place and directly set out on his return to Boston.

Mississippi

Those persons inclined to settle the lands on the Mississippi, said to be the first in America, the company of military adventure being in formation, they may hear of an opportunity of going in a good vessel to sail from Middletown about the first of September next. For particulars, inquire of John Elsworth

administration of estates

Notice by Anne Jennings to those obligated to the estate of Daniel Jennings, late of New London deceased, to make payment to Samuel Champln at the Harbor's Mouth in said New London.

to be sold

at the stores of Charles Jeffrey and Jonathan Douglas in New London a quantity of "damnified flour" fit for making stock, pate, eating hogs;

linseed oil to be sold at be Printing Office.

Committee of Correspondence meetings

The Honorable Committee of Correspondence for the Colony of Connecticut met at this Town, New London, on Wednesday last and nominated the Hon. Eliphalet Dyer, William Samuel Johnson, Erastus Wolcott, Silas Deane and Richard Law – that is to say any three of them – on behalf of this Colony to attend the General Congress of Commissioners of the English American colonies to be held in Philadelphia on the first of September next, with them to consult and advise on proper measures to promote the general good and welfare of the whole and for obtaining redress of the grievances under which we labor. Being a matter of great expectancy, a number of gentlemen from the neighboring towns attended. About four o'clock, the gentlemen committee declared to the expecting people the choice, upon which a royal salute was fired from our battery and also a salute from the shipping in the harbor. Peace, decency, good order and loyalty were conspicuous in all ranks and degrees of the people.

murder
We hear that, about a fortnight ago, a Negro girl at Mattituck on Long Island killed her own child and is committed to goal for trial.

****

From *The Gazette,* July 22, 1774

East Hampton Town Meeting
At a meeting of the inhabitants of the town of East Hampton in the county of Suffolk, Eleazer Miller, Moderator
Voted: that we will assert to the utmost of our abilities, and in lawful manner defend, the Liberties and Immunities of British America and that we will cooperate with our brethren in this Colony in such matters as from time to time appear to us the most proper and best adapted to preserve us from the burdens we fear, and in a measure already feel, from Principles adopted by the British Parliament, respecting the Town of Boston in particular and the British colonies in North America
Voted, that a non importation agreement throughout the colonies is the most likely means to save us form the present and future troubles.
Voted, that John Chatfield. Col. Abraham Gardiner, Burnet Miller, Stephen Hodges, Thomas Wickham, John Gardiner and Capt. David Mulford be a standing committee to keep up correspondence with the City of New York, with the others towns of this colony, and if there is an occasion with the other colonies.
Voted unanimously, not one contrary vote.

ordination
Wednesday se'nnight[8], the Reverend Mr. Sage was ordained to the pastoral office over the Church and Society of Suffrage in Simsbury.

died
Last Monday, departed this life at Norwalk, the Honorable Thomas Fitch, late Governor of the Colony of Connecticut;

Deacon Thomas Fosdick;

At Norwich, Mrs. Abigail Knight, widow of Jonathan Knight.

administration of estates
Notice by Elijah Wiatt, Administrator, that the real and personal estate of Seth Jones, late of Stonington, will be sold at the dwelling house of said deceased.

pay up
All persons indebted to T. Green for newspapers, advertisements or otherwise are requested to make immediate payment.

leather for sale
Choice sole leather by the side. Also a few sides of upper leather to be sold by Jesse Edgecomb in New London.
****
From *The Gazette,* July 29, 1774

administration of estates
Notice by Joseph Starr, John Avery and Amos Chesebrough, Commissioners appointed by the Probate Court in Stonington on the estate of Mrs. Margaret Ashcraft, late of Groton, deceased and represented insolvent, that a meeting will be held at the house of Capt. Jonas Belton, Inn holder in said Groton.

Whereas a seaman named Neal Scarman lately died on board the Brig *Pitt,* Andrew Perkins, Master, from the West Indies who has left a small interest in the hands of the said master. These are to inform the heirs of said Scarman that they may receive the said interest on application to Andrew Perkins in Norwich.

Delaware Purchase
Notice by Ebenezer Baldwin, Neh. Waterman Jr., John Post, Committee for the Proprietor's of a township or district in in Delaware First Purchase, lately laid out and surveyed by Messrs. Uriah Chapman and Thomas Huntington, to meet at the Courthouse in Norwich to hear the report and see the survey.

Free Masonry
Just published and to be sold by J.P. Spooner at his printing office near the store of Christopher Leffingwell in Norwich: "*Jachin and Boaz*", an authentic key to the door of Free Masonry, calculated not only for the instruction of every new made Mason, but also for the information of all who intend to become brethren.

day of fasting and prayer
His Honor, our Governor, on the advice of the Council, has appointed Wednesday, the 31st of August next, to be observed as a day of fasting and prayer throughout this colony on account of the gloomy aspect of public affairs.

the poor in Boston
We hear the inhabitants of Groton are making a collection for the poor and distressed in inhabitants of the Town of Boston.

died
at Milford, of the smallpox, David Ingersol;

at New Haven of apoplexy, Capt. Stephen Mansfield.

****

From *The Gazette,* August 5, 1774

good harvest
Accounts from all parts of the country agree that the harvest this season is very plentiful.

died
in Middletown, Robert Lee, Block Maker;

Mrs. Elizabeth Mills, relict of the late Reverend Gideon Mills of Suffrage in Simsbury.

bell foundry
Isaac Doolittle of New Haven, having erected a suitable building and prepared an apparatus convenient for bell founding and having had good success in his first attempts, intends to carry on that business and will supply any that are pleased to employ him with any size bell, as commonly used in this or neighboring provinces. Said Doolittle pays cash for old copper.

church opens membership
Mr. Green, you are desired to insert in your paper that the church in Hadlyme, under the pastoral care of the Rev. Mr. Rawson, have lately come to an agreement to allow persons of sober life and conversation and competent knowledge to *own the covenant*, and receive Baptism. The above Church, from its first founding, had practiced the admission of none to baptism, but such as were in full communion.[9]

****

From *The Gazette,* August 12, 1774

town meeting at Colchester
At a town meeting of citizens in Colchester, Henry Champion, Moderator, Henry Champion, Elias Worthington, Capt. Dudley Wright, John Watrous and Joseph Isham Jr. were appointed to the Committee of Correspondence.

replacements to Connecticut Colony's Committee of Correspondence
Three of the gentlemen lately nominated by the Committee of Correspondents for this colony to meet the Committees of the other colonies in the proposed Congress at Philadelphia have been obliged by previous engagements and the state of their health to decline attending. In consequence of which, the Committee met at Hartford and appointed the Hon. Roger Sherman and Joseph Trumbull, one of which gentlemen with the Honorable Eliphalet Dyer and Silas Deane, previously appointed, will attend to that important business.

died
at Fairfield, Mrs. Martha Silliman, consort of Selleck Silliman.
****
From *The Gazette,* August 19, 1774

administration of estates
Notice by Oliver Coit and Nathan Lord, Commissioners, to the creditors of the estate of William Green, late of Preston, that a meeting will be held at the house of Moses Tyler in Preston;

Notice by Nathan Douglas and Roger Gibson, Commissioners, to the creditors of the estate of William Potter of New London, deceased and represented to be insolvent, that a meeting will be held at the house of deceased.

ran away
from James Sherman of New London, an apprentice boy named Abner Brown, 14 years of age and rather small for his age.

lots for sale in Norwich
to be sold by Jonathan Hall of Chelsea lots for building, fit for gentlemen and merchants on the main road, near the Great Bridge.

strayed
from Charles Eldridge of Groton, a horse.

Liberty Pole in Coventry
A number of the inhabitants of Coventry and neighboring towns met and erected a liberty pole[10] to the exalted height of the Babylonith Ministry Gallows with a scarlet flag on top and an inscription, half way up the height of the pole, that read
"BURKE[11] AND LIBERTY"
After the business was completed, loyal toasts were drunk to our King and to the Friends of Liberty.

accident
A few days ago, a child of Mr. McColl of Lyme fell from a

bridge in the town and is so hurt, his life is despaired of.

Wednesday night, we had a delightful shower of rain after several weeks of drought.

died
Jonathan Lester of Groton at an advanced age
****

From *The Gazette,* August 26, 1774

administration of estates
Notice by Marvin Wait, Administrator, that all the estate of Edward Robinson, late of New London, deceased, consisting of a few rights of land in common in New London and household furniture, will be sold at public vendue.

clocks and watches
mended and repaired by Robert Douglas Jr.

Godspeed
On Monday last, Silas Deane, one of the delegates from this colony to the Congress in Philadelphia, set off from his house in Wethersfield, accompanied by a large number of gentlemen who rode out 11 miles with him. On Tuesday, at Fairfield, he joined the Hon. Eliphalet Dyer and the Hon. Roger Sherman, the other delegates from this colony. On Wednesday, they departed for Philadelphia.

break in
On Wednesday night, the shop of Ephraim Terry, Jr. of Lebanon was broken into and sundry articles taken.

strayed
a red cow with a bell around her neck; reward, if returned to London Coffee House.
****

From *The Gazette*, September 2, 1774

reward offered
Notice of reward by Ephraim Terry, Jr. of reward for return of goods stolen from his shop.

administration of estates
Notice by John Stocker and Elihu Starr, Administrators to the estate of Isaac Solomon, deceased, late of Middletown, that a meeting will be held at the dwelling house of Ephraim Fenne, Innholder in Middletown.

Susquehanna Purchase
Notice by Elijah Backus and David Hough, to the Proprietors of a Township called Warwick in the Susquehanna Purchase that was laid out by last fall by Zachariah Lathrop, that they are desired to meet at the house of Zachariah Lathrop to consider what they will do respecting the laying out of said township into lots and granting money to defray expenses.

poison gas
On the 17th last, the following remarkable disaster befell a number of persons. John Wildman, a young lad about 16 years old, apprentice to Benjamin Knapp, had occasion to go down into his mother's well being about 12 feet deep to bring up something he had dropped into it. The water was not more than two feet in depth. The lad was seen to fall into the water before he had regularly descended to it. Mr. Knapp immediately went down after the lad and having seized him, the master was heard to say. "The boy is dead" and brought him up about 3 feet when they both fell back into the water together. After this, two more men went down successively in a well, fainted and fell upon one another upon the lad and Mr. Knapp. By this time, the neighborhood was alarmed and a fifth person was let down by a rope but he was not able to bring up any of the men by reason of a faintness. There was no way now but to take up the persons by a hook attached to the end of a pole which was accordingly done. The first two who were thus drawn up, revived in a few minutes after they were exposed to the open air, although they

were extremely weak and feeble. But Mr. Knapp and the lad had been 15 or 20 minutes in the well of appeared to be dead. As they would brought up they were rolled for some minutes on Barrel. Mr. Knapp in a short time seemed to have a life in him and vomited and, after great distressing convulsions, he was able to speak and was for some time and the delirious. But the lad was beyond recovery after and the methods were used for in the revival such as rolling rubbing laying him on a bed of warm ashes etc[12]. Knapp continued the week in a distorted state, although his life is not despaired of. He remembers nothing about his going too well at all. The other two men have not recovered their strength. This account is published to show the fatal effects of damps and to warn others to try by candle or otherwise whether the well or pit into which they are about to descend is not filled with these noxious exhalations.

died
at East Hampton, David Gardiner of the Isle off Wright, after a lingering illness of some months, he was carried to the Isle and interred; there. He left a widow, the daughter of Rev. Bull to mourn his exit and two sons too young to have any deep sensibility of the great loss they have just suffered.

General Assembly
The following were chosen members of the honorable House of Representatives
for New London: Richard Law and William Hillhouse;
for Norwich: Isaac Tracy and Benjamin Huntington;
for Groton: Thomas Mumford and Stephen Billings;
for Stonington: Major Charles Phelps and Samuel Prentice;
for Lyme: John Lay II and Ezra Selden.

stolen or strayed
from the pasture of Samuel Bull of Middletown, a red mare. Reward offered if delivered to Nathaniel Shayler of Middletown or to Thomas Allen of the London Coffeehouse in New London.
****

From *The Gazette,* September 9, 1774

pay up
Richard Deshon takes this method to inform all persons who have open accounts with him to come and adjust same before the next Court, otherwise they may depend upon being called in a way very disagreeable to them and ,perhaps more so, to those who have no inclination to come to an adjustment.

runaway
from Nathaniel West, an apprentice boy, named Joseph Robbins, 17 years of age; light complexion; short brown hair; has a scar under his chin occasioned by the Kings Evil[13]; easy to get acquainted; quarrelsome among children;

from Amos Bolles of New London, an apprentice Comfort Chappel, in the 21st year of her age; short and thick set; dark complexion.

just printed and to be sold
by T. Green *A New Gamut or Rules of Music*; compiled by Mr. Bull.

administration of estates
Notice by Joshua Barker and Elijah Hyde, Jr, Executors of the estate of Capt. Ignatius Barker, late of Lebanon, to creditors and those indebted to the estate, to file claims and make speedy payment;

Notice by Silas Burrows, Administrator of the estate of Joseph Packer in Groton, of one acre of salt marsh for sale.

strayed
from Henry Ladd in Coventry, a mare.

to be sold
a small boat nearly 20 feet keel, a prime sailor and the best of her length of any kind in the harbor of New London; she is about three years old and will be sold for one third her original

cost; also ten acres of land with a dwelling house thereon in Groton and also a small shop on Pine Island about 12 feet square; inquire of James Smith living on said island.

found
by Morris Fowler of New London Great Neck, a Moses boat on the shore between Goshen and Lester's Rock.

Susquehanna Purchase
Notice by John Owen to the Proprietors of the District of Winchester in the Susquehanna Purchase to meet at Capt. Edward Palmes in New London to hear the report of Harris Colt and Moses Warren who were appointed a committee to set out such district.

attack on Boston
Last week the alarming account that the regular troops and ships of war were cannonading the town of Boston and massacring the inhabitants without distinction of age or sex, was spread throughout the country and flew like lightning. In less than 36 hours, the country side was rallied more than 170 miles in extent. It must give great satisfaction to every well wisher to the Liberties of this country to see the spirit and readiness of the people to fly to the relief of the distressed brethren. The unshaken fortitude and determined resolution to conquer or to die, which appeared in all ranks on the arrival of the news, would do honor to veteran troops. Expresses were sent from town to town with the greatest expedition. And the readiness with which all ranks and ages armed and equipped themselves is astonishing. In many towns almost every man able to bear arms marched for their relief. In others, it was equally difficult to repress the ardor of the people. The numbers actually armed in this colony has not yet been attained with sufficient precision to publish but, from the most authentic intelligence we heretofore have been able to procure, it is highly probable that not less than 10,000 men actually marched and as many were ready to march from this colony only when the news was contradicted. By accounts on Saturday morning, we learn that the number of men who had arrived in the neighborhood of that

town were computed to be at least 40,000.

The alarming news of the destruction of the Town of Boston by the regular forces and ships of war reached Saybrook last Sunday morning, when a large body of men voluntarily appeared to enroll themselves to march for the relief of badly distressed brethren and were properly equipped for battle and on their march before noon. When the soldiers were enlisted, one Hezekiah Whittlesey of that town used every method in his power to prevent any aid for the relief of the country and uttered many disagreeable expression concerning the people of Boston, the country and the General Assembly, of which he has been very frequently and now is a member, which gave great offense and, on Monday evening, a large body of from Saybrook and Lyme assembled and, under the conduct of many aged, substantial persons for both towns, went to the Justice for satisfaction. After proper application to him, he came forth, mounted a high horse block, and read and published a confession and recantation.

After had published his confession, he joined in three huzzas with the people and thanked them for the kindness with which they used with him, upon which they all dispersed and returned to their several places of abode. The whole was conducted with the greatest decorum and good order.

****

From *The Gazette,* September 16, 1774

Haddam town meeting

At a meeting of the inhabitants of the town of Haddam, Phineas Brainerd, Moderator, the following votes were passed, namely:

That the American colonies had just reason to be alarmed at the present stretch of Parliamentary power now attempting to be exercised over them, as it has a threatening aspect upon the precious Liberties which our fathers purchased at the expense of much treasure and the effusion of blood;

That we cordially sympathize with our sister colony of Massachusetts Bay and, in particular, with the Town of Boston, now struggling in the front of opposition;

That we are freely and willing to join in with the neighboring towns and colonies in any righteous way or method that shall be thought convenient to affect the universal good of the American system.

The resolves of the Honorable House of Representatives of this colony, being read, was unanimously approved of.

As a strict union among neighboring towns and colonies in this day of danger is of the greatest importance, we do hereby appoint:. Jeremiah Hubbard, Cornelius Higgins, Hezekiah Brainerd Jr., James Hazelton, Charles Smith, Joseph Brooks and Jabez Brainerd, a Committee to Correspond with neighboring towns and colonies as occasion shall require.

Looking upon a non-consumption agreement as a fatal weapon to subdue importation, Joseph Brooks and Jabez Brainerd are appointed a Committee to attend the County meetings to be held at Hartford.

Being willing to extend charity to the sufferers of the common cause, we do appoint Phineas Brainerd, Charles Hazelton, Joseph Selden, Nehemiah Dickerson, Joseph Smith, Abner Smith, Elijah Brainerd and Nathan Brianerd, a Committee to receive those donations and to forward then to the to the relief of the poor in Boston.

                Neh. Brainerd, Clerk

joint meeting of delegates of the towns of New London and Windham counties

At a meeting of delegates of the towns in the counties of New London and Windham, convened at Norwich, to consult for their common safety, Hon. Gurdon Saltonstall, Chairman and William Williams, Clerk

This convention, taking it to consideration the serious state of this country and that we are threatened with the loss of our Liberties and Constitutional Rights; and when we view its state as to arms, military knowledge, proper stores, and the attention of this people in their just defense then, whenever it shall so happen that any common enemy shall rise against us and attempt our subjection by force of arms, we cannot but be animated to address ourselves to all business that attend on military affairs.

In the first place, we do seriously recommend to the selectmen of every town within the counties of New London and

Windham that they as speedily as possible supply their town stock with full complement of ammunition, as by law required Secondly, we recommend to every particular troop and military company in the two aforesaid counties. both officers and soldiers and all others living within their several and respective limits who by law are required to provide and keep arms and ammunition, to as speedily as possible arm and equip themselves agreeable to the directions of the laws of this colony of New London and Windham;

Thirdly, we seriously recommend to all, as a matter of very great importance, that they expeditiously as may be, improve and learn to use and design their arms by artillery exercises or otherwise that so they may answer the important purpose of their institution when such occasion shall require and become fitted to attend their colonel and other field offices when by are called to regimental reviews.

mobilization
The alarm which went through the country last Saturday and Sunday reached New York on Monday evening and in Philadelphia on Tuesday afternoon and, had not the account soon been contradicted, it is very certain that there would have been between 80,000 and 100,000 men in arms near Boston, not as some Tories would insinuate "for the purpose of rebellion" but in defense of all that valuable, dear, holy and sacred.
    ****
From *The Gazette,* September 23, 1754

Liberty Pole in East Haddam
On the 14th instant, at East Haddam Landing was lifted a large union flag, finely decorated with the embolism of Liberty with an image of America fighting tyranny, upon a pole 147 feet high. Three cheers were given by a large body of the Sons of Liberty and several guns fired upon the location and various laudable resolves entered into to promote good order and unity.

cash given
for small furs, bees wax, old pewter and copper by John Baker Brimmer at his store at Norwich Landing.

stolen
out of the enclosure at of Danielle Glad in New London, a Dutch horse.

river farm for sale
to be sold a farm containing about 140 acres of choice land, very pleasantly situated on Mystic River with a large and good dwelling house thereon, well finished and a good barn and outhouses. The land is under good improvement and well fenced with stone walls. It is well watered and has a large orchard upon it. The River is an advantage to said farm and affords a great plenty of fish. Inquire of William Gallup, living on the premises.

****

From *The Gazette,* September 30, 1754

Whereas a number of loyal persons of the towns of Ashford and Mansfield have convened together on suspicion that John Stevens was an enemy to the Constitutional Rights of American Liberty and a committee was formed to which he gave the following satisfactory account. "That I never wrote any letters against the rights of American Liberty to any person and never received any such letters. However, I have talked to sundry persons at sundry times against the charter Rights of American colonists and humbly ask for forgiveness and I further declare that I will never talk or act against these Sons of Liberty but to solemnly declare that I am at the Sons of Liberty's call and will remain so for my natural life. The committee consisted of Steven Johnson, Richard Fletcher, John Keyes, Aaron Whitmore and Nehemiah. Howe

****

From *The Gazette,* October 7, 1774

horse thief
At the Superior Court held here this week, John Scott, a transient person was sentenced to 18 months confinement in Newgate prison in Simsbury for the crime of horse stealing.

accident
We hear from Kensington that a few days since a person was instantly killed as he was assisting in erecting a pole to be dedicated to the goddess Liberty. We did not learn the particulars.

deserted
from the onboard the sloop *Betsy and Polly*, Hezekiah Perkins, Master, belonging to Norwich, a seaman named Zepheniah Hatch; middling stature; short black hair and black eyes; slender built. Whoever will take up said Hatch and bring him to Messrs. Breed and Howland, merchants at Norwich or Thomas Allen at New London, shall receive five dollars reward.

****

From *The Gazette,* October 14, 1774

shipwreck
Last week David Squire in a sloop and Captain Peleg Swain in a schooner, 13 hands on each, set out in company from Nantucket on a whaling voyage and, at about eight o'clock in the evening, both vessels ran on the shoal called the Great Rip where, having several of their boats stove, two white men and three Indians, belonging to Captain Squires, took a boat and left the vessel and got back to Nantucket. Both vessels and the people left on board are supposed to be lost, there being a heavy sea. A number of the people belonged to Long Island.

brass foundry
Ebenezer Dennis hereby informs the public that he has set up the brazier and brass foundry business at his shop opposite the church in New London, where gentlemen may be served in the shortest notice.

please pay
Notice by Samuel H. Parsons of New London to those obligated to him to settle up;

Notice by Daniel and Joshua Lathrop of Norwich to their debtors to settle up;

Notice by Ebenezer Hovey to those who owe him for a delivery of last year's papers to settle up.

administration of estates
Notice by the Administrators, William Coit and Samuel Belden, of the estate of Daniel Coit to debtors to settle accounts;

Notice is hereby given that, agreeable to the order of the Court of Probate for the District of Windham, all the personal estate of William Cummings, late of Mansfield deceased and declared insolvent (saving what the court has set off and allow to the widow of the deceased) will be sold at public vendue at the dwelling of Miriam Cummings, *Administratrix;*

Notice by Samuel Chesebrough that by order of the Court of Probate for the District of Stonington, the personal estate of Colonel Amos Chesebrough, late of Stonington deceased and represented insolvent, with the encumbrances of one third part of the real estate belonging set aside to the widow of said deceased, will be sold at the house of Captain Giles Russell, innholder in Stonington;

Notice by Elijah Marshall Jr. and Cornelius Starr, Commissioners appointed by the Court of Probate of Windham of the estate of John Hunter, late of Mansfield, deceased and represented insolvent, that a meeting will be held at the dwelling house of Amariah Starr, innholder in said Mansfield;

Notice by Samuel Leffingwell, Executor of the estate of Captain John Williams, late of Norwich, deceased, that those obligated to the estate are desired to make speedy payment.

cash given
for flax seed, old brass, beeswax and small furs by Ebenezer Douglas at his shop in New London.

reward offered
by Samuel and Daniel Leffingwell of Norwich for the capture of the person who calls himself Joseph Greenhill; about 25 years

old; about five feet six or seven inches tall; well set; has bushy hair and a down look; he broke in and stole certain items from the house.

Susquehanna purchase
The proprietors of the district of Winchester in the Susquehanna Purchase are hereby notified to meet at Captain Edward Palmes in New London to consult and determine on some proposed plans for speedily settling the district.

buckskin breaches
This is to inform the public that I have for sale at my dwelling house at East Haddam Landing, a quantity of good deer and buckskin breaches, made by an excellent workmen. Inquire of Elijah Attwood at said East Haddam Landing.
****
From *The Gazette,* October 21, 1774

shipwreck
In our last we gave an account of the loss of two whaling vessels on Nantucket shoals, but we learn that, there being a light breeze, they happily drifted on Nantucket Island, the people missing. Thirteen of them reached Nantucket Island after being 24 hours on a raft in the most perilous situation as the raft was barely able to support them above water. The other eight of the crew got on the quarter deck of the vessel which was beat to pieces and so drove on Nantucket Island. For three days, they had no provision than three cod fish to subsist on. Note well in our last account, five of the people had been taken up in a boat which, with the other 21, made the whole crew so that no lives were lost.

vessel capsizes
Last Monday afternoon as Captain Ebenezer Webb and his son were returning from Long Island in Captain Webb's passage boat, the wind blowing hot from the North West, the boat overset and sunk. Happily, a boat in sight made for their relief and took up the people. The boat with a quantity of grain is entirely lost.

Delaware Purchase
At a meeting of the proprietors of the Township lately laid out by Messrs. Uriah Chapman and Theophilus Huntington in the Delaware First Purchase voted that all those who do not pay their taxes by the first of November next, will forfeit their rights. Notice given by Ebenezer Baldwin, Nehemiah Waterman and John Post, Commissioners.

small pox inoculation
The public is hereby informed that inoculation for the smallpox is suspended for the season at the hospital on Duck Island. Notice by John and Elisha Ely.
****
From *The Gazette,* October 28, 1774

flax seed wanted
Choice rock salt or cash given for flax seed by Ebenezer Way, Jr.

drugs and medicines
Thomas Coit at his store at Norwich Landing has for sale an assortment of drugs and medicines.

farms for sale
Thirty four acres of land for sale lying on the Post Road, near Mystic Meeting House, in Stonington, having a dwelling house, barn and orchard thereon; the land well fenced and under good improvement; for particulars inquire of Daniel Douglas living on said premises or Giles Russel, innholder in Stonington;

A good farm lying in Lebanon, First Society, about a mile from the Meeting House, containing about 133 acres, 8 of which under good improvement; well wooded, watered and fenced with good stone wall; a good house and barn thereon. Inquire of David Fanning, living on the premises.

saddles for sale
Advertisement by Asa Burnham that he carries on the saddler's business in all its branches at the house of Capt. William

Belcher in the upper part of Preston.

Susquehanna Purchase
Notice given to the Proprietors of the Salem District in the Susquehanna purchase to meet at the house of Paul Hebbard, Inn holder in Windham to consider on what shall be expedient ways of settling such town. Notice given by Jacob Simons and Aaron Cleveland, Committee for said Town.

runaway
from Ashbell Burnham, a Negro boy named Danstable; about 15 years of age; pretty large and somewhat pitted with the smallpox on the nose. It is supposed that he run off with a Negro boy, belonging to Captain Wylyss.
****
From *The Gazette,* November 4, 1774

day of thanksgiving
The 24th of November is appointed to be observed as a day of public Thanksgiving throughout this colony.

delegates return
Last Thursday at twelve o'clock in the afternoon, Eliphalet Dyer, Roger Sherman and Silas Deane, members of the late Continental Congress, are arrived at New Haven by land from Philadelphia. They were met at Milford by a number of the members of the General Assembly now sitting in New Haven and of the gentlemen from that place. On alighting from the carriages, they received the compliments of numbers of gentlemen of the government who were collected and several cannons were discharged on the occasion.

burglar sentenced
At the last session of Superior Court held at New Haven on Friday of last, Richard Steel, a noted and notorious offender in the thieving way, was tried for burglary in breaking open the house of the Reverend Silvanus Waterman of Wallingford and stealing from thence sundry articles of plate. He was sentenced to 10 years confinement in the Simsbury mines. After he had

received his sentencing, he asked the Chief Judge whether he was to be sent to that place in the capacity of a tutor or a scholar.

administration of estates
All persons having any accounts against of the estate of Joseph Hurlbut Jr. late of New London, deceased, are desired to bring them to the subscriber, Mary Hurlbut. *Administrarix* of said estate, for settlement and those indebted are desired to make speedy payment.

found
on the shore of Goshen Reef on the first of November, a vessel's long boat, half worn, 12 or 13 feet keel and a large cable, 3 or 4 fathoms long; stern is broken and numbered 16. The owner may have her again on applying to Nathan Rogers in New London, Great Neck and paying charges.

broke into the enclosure
of James Hebard of Windham, a light sorrel mare.

lost property
Joseph Coit of New London has in his custody, a small chest, probably from Nova Scotia; also a timber chain which were left on his wharf sometimes since.
****
From *The Gazette,* November 11, 1774

non exportation of sheep
The Committee of Correspondence for the town of New London hereby notifies all concerned that they think it is their duty to enforce the observance of the seventh article of the Association against the exportation of sheep, as recommended by the General Congress. All vessels sailing from this port will be strictly inspected and observations are being paid to every article of said Association, in such manner and as by the Congress directed.

town meeting in Mansfield
At a meeting of the inhabitants of the town of Mansfield resolved:

That his Majesty King George III and his rightful successors are entitled to our allegiance and that we and our posterity, so far as our influence can extend to them, will be faithful subjects of that illustrious King;

That we will defend with our lives and fortunes our natural and constitutional rights and, in obedience to the second great commandment of the moral law of the law of Nature, we shall assist our neighbors as occasion rises. Law and Nature are the same;

That in all our efforts, we will injure no one's property nor restrain, terrify or afflict any man's person by any means whatsoever, or be accessories in any coercive proceedings, unless the same becomes necessary in the common cause and indicated as undoubted reason;

That, as union and uniformity of conduct are necessary, we rely on the wisdom of the Continental Congress in Philadelphia to recommend such measures as may be recently adopted by our brethren on the continent and by us;

That, in this time of danger and difficulty, it is necessary that a correspondence should be maintained between the several towns in this and neighboring governments and, as this town might be supplied with a Committee to Correspond as above, we have chosen John Salter, Constant Southworth, Major Joseph Storrs, Edmund Freeman and Capt. Experience Storrs as a Committee of Correspondents in said town and we made choice of a respectable number of the inhabitants of said town to take in the subscriptions for the relief of our brethren suffering in the cause of Liberty in Boston and take proper measures that the same should be seasonably transmitted to the Overseers of the Poor in Boston.

                Con. Southward, Town Clerk

runaway
Notice by Andrew Campbell of Middletown that an apprentice boy, named Abner Bevins, about 18 years old; light complexion; sandy hair with a speech impediment, has run

away from him.

****

From *The Gazette,* November 18, 1774

representatives to General Congress appointed
The General Assembly of this Colony has appointed, Eliphalet Dyer, Roger Sherman, Silas Deane, Titus Hosmer and Jonathan Sturgis, to be members of the General Congress to be held at Philadelphia on the 10th of May, unless our grievances should be redressed before that time, any three of whom to attend.

ship sinking
Last Wednesday se'nnight, a small sloop sailed from Pechanga in Saybrook, loaded with flax seed and wood for New York, and the next night, she overset in a squall of wind about the middle of the Sound. There were three people on board, one of whom named Kelsey was drowned on Thursday afternoon. The other two stayed on the vessel, until about sunset of the same day when she drifted along Long Island, where, with great difficulty, they got on shore.

drowning
Last Monday morning, Elizabeth Rogers of this Town (New London) went from her house (supposed not too have been a free exercise of reason) and was found in the afternoon in the River. A jury of inquest was summoned who determined she that she had accidentally fallen into the River, which was the occasion of her death.

sheep impounded
Wednesday, Captain Starr arrived here from Middletown, bound to the West Indies, having on board a few sheep belonging to the sailors. The Committee of Correspondents immediately waited upon him and advised that to export any sheep would be contrary to the Association recommended by the Congress. Captain Starrs expressed the utmost willingness to comply with their desire. The sheep were accordingly landed and sold.

wool
John Deshon has employed at his house a worsted-comber from England. He is an excellent workmen and whoever will employ him may depend upon his dispatch and wool being done in the best and cheapest manner.

came into the enclosure
of Joshua Raymond of New London, a sorrel, about 4 years old.

weaving
Abijah Jones of Colchester advises the public that he carries on a weaver and clothier's business in all its branches in Colchester.

indentured servant available
Whereas Mary Crocker, an able bodied young woman, now in goal in the Town of New London, is in debt to the Selectmen of that Town in the sum of 20 pounds, the said selectmen hereby give notice that said Mary will, at her own free consent, be bound out to service for the payment of said debt to any proper person who will purchase Mary's service for such reasonable time and shall pay such debt.

bound for the Massachusetts Bay colony
The schooner *Two Sisters*, Benjamin Hill, Master, will be at Norwich Landing the first of next week; freight or passage to Massachusetts Bay is for sale; inquire of William Coit or Thomas Allen of New London.

wanted
an apprentice to the printing business, a boy 13 or 14 years old, who can read well; inquire of the Printer.

****

From *The Gazette,* November 25, 1774

sentenced to the copper mines
At a Special Superior Court, held at Norwich, the 21st of this month, the notorious villain John Brown, alias Joseph Greenhill, and Joseph Atwood, well known in the province of

Massachusetts Bay, were both sentenced to Simsbury Mines for the crime of burglary. They set off from Norwich last Wednesday morning, well secured, where, it is hoped, they have both safely arrived.

died
At Chatham last Monday, died in the 25th year of his age, Halfuld Freeman, second son to Nathaniel Freeman, after a short, but very distressing, illness of about 10 days which he endured with great patience and gave good evidence of an unshaken faith in Christ and a well grounded hope of future glory.

prison break
We hear that a few days since all the prisoners made their escape from Simsbury Mines.

strayed or stolen
from the enclosure in Branford, a very dark brown mare, about 6 years old; give notice to Moses Butler of Hartford or to Josiah Blakslee of Enfield.

wharf repaired
David Manwaring has repaired the wharf etc., formerly occupied by David Griner in New London, making it convenient for vessels.

stolen property
Notice by Samuel H. Parsons that he has in his possession a number of the articles of property, stolen by the notorious burglar John Brown.

pay up
Notice by James Flint to those indebted to him to pay their accounts in Windham.

watch repair
Advertisement by Thomas Harland, clock and watch maker in Norwich, that he has a complete assortment of warranted

watches and clocks for sale as well as different types of jewelry.

broke into enclosure
of Jason Fergo of the North Parish, New London, a red heifer.
****
From *The Gazette*, December 2, 1774

tax for relief of poor in Boston
The citizens of the Town of East Hampton on Long Island have laid a tax upon themselves sufficient to raise 100 pounds, New York currency, for the support of the industrious poor in Boston. A subscription is also set in every parish of the County of Suffolk on Long Island to raise donations for the same laudable purpose. A committee has been appointed in each parish to receive the same and instructions given to John Foster of South Hampton to collect such grain, flax etc, as should be subscribed and transport the same to Boston in the month of March next.

recantation
The Committees of Correspondence for the Towns of New London and Groton, being informed that Mr. Philip Dumar, a merchant of Boston, who was one of the addressors to Governor Hutchinson, just arrived at New London last evening and put up at Mr. Thomas Allen's, innholder. "Thereupon, we waited on said this day at 9:00 a.m. and informed him that it would be disagreeable to the inhabitants of the above town for him to continue longer in New London and entered into a free conversation with him relative to said address. He assured us that he was sorry he had ever signed it and gave us the unwritten declaration which was well approved by said committee: 'I signed an address to the Governor Hutchinson in which I had no other view than the welfare of Great Britain and the colonies and a reconciliation between which I imagine would be forwarded thereof, but being now sensible that it was an error I am very sorry that I signed it and hope his sincere declaration will reinstate me in the favor of true friends of the Constitution in both countries.' "

Preston Town meeting
At a meeting of the Freemen of the Town of Preston in consideration of the great advantages that will accrue from a steady and resolute adherence of all the towns and parts of America to the resolves of an Association of the late General Congress, held in Philadelphia, the Freemen of this town chose a large and respectable Committee of Inspection for the purposes directed in the 11th article of the Association of said Congress and the Freemen and Inhabitants of said town are freely and heartily disposed to comply with all the doings of the Congress.
    Roger Sherry, Clerk of the Committee of Inspection

accident
The following is a report on an accident that happened at Groton last Monday. After public training, Mr. Ebenezer Davis of that town in discharging a musket, it split and a small sliver from the barrel entered his breast and killed him instantly. He was about 30 years old and has left a widow and one or two children.

died
at East Hampton Long Island Mrs. Hannah Osborne, wife of Deacon Osborne of that town

administration of estates
All persons indebted to the estate of William White, late of Boston, are desired to pay the same to Phillip White of South Hampton in the Province of New Hampshire, Executor of the last will and testament of said William White. Inquire of said White in the shop of Mrs. Margarette Phillips on Cornhill

pay up
Notice for the third and last time to request all those who are in any way indebted to the estate of Elisha Hurlbut, late of Windham, deceased, to make immediate settlements with the estate. Notice given by Thomas Fanning, Administrator.

came into my enclosure
Notice by Christopher Raymond in New London, North Parish that two calves came into his enclosure.

runaway
from Samuel Brownon Jr. in Stockbridge a Negro man servant, about 27 years old speaks fast and broken English; well set; about 5 1/2 feet high. He has a fillon on one thumb and the nail grows quite over the end of the thumb. He was formerly owned by Colonel Brown of Salem and lived with Mr. John Mumford of Colchester where he was called by the name of Sambo, but since by the name of Pomp.

stolen
or taken by mistake out of a trunk in Windham, a light red string sack and petticoat. Return the same to the house of Mrs. Elecer Cary in Windham.

Notice by John Wright Jr., innholder in Chatham, that there was stolen out of his house sundry articles including a new beaver hat and deerskin breeches.

strayed or stolen
from Abijah Ranney of Middletown, a dark brown mare;

from Elisha Scovel in Colchester, a Bay colored horse. Horse maybe returned to the subscriber or to Mr. Joseph Webb of Wethersfield or Mr.. Joseph Knight, post rider

Stolen or has been lost, a man's saddle, almost new, belonging to Ebenezer Avery, Jr. in Groton at the house of Captain Jonas Belton.

****

From *The Gazette*, December 9, 1774

drownings at sea
At half after eight o'clock in the evening Captain Benjamin Meegs was drowned out of the sloop *Fancy* laying in Fishers Island Harbor. Whoever finds him and buries him decently may

be satisfied by applying to Falmouth in the County of Barnstable in New England.

N. B. The names of the men with him were John Swift and Joseph Rowley belonging to said sloop. Benjamin Walsh and Latham Macey, belonging to Nantucket, were passengers

child drowns
We are desired to inform the public that Captain Jeremiah Harris of Norwich Landing has a son missing since last Tuesday, about a three year old, and the greatest probability is of its being drowned in the river. If the body should be found, notice may be given to its afflicted parents.

break in
Notice by David Yeamans that his house in Westchester Parish in Colchester was broken open and various items stolen.

****

From *The Gazette,* December 16, 1774

wanted to purchase
Cash given for small furs, old brass, beeswax, copper and pewter by David Gardiner Jr. at his shop near the Court House in New London; he has for sale ship chandlery as usual.

to be let
A dwelling house near the Court House in New London by Joseph Hurlbut, convenient for a tavern and has been one for some years, having been improved in that business by Joseph Waterman.

bankruptcy notice
Notice that Edward Freeman and Elijah Fenton have been appointed Administrators to the insolvent estate of Rev. Ebenezer Martin of Ashford; meeting of creditors to be held at Josiah Consant, inn holder in Mansfield.

administration of estates
Notice by Joshua Barker and Elijah Hyde, Jr, Executors of the

estate of Captain Ignatius Barker of Lebanon deceased; meeting of creditors to be held at the house of Hannah Barker, innholder in Lebanon.

rooms for rent
Boarders taken in by Sarah Hallam, near courthouse in New London, she has genteel accommodations for that purpose; ten shillings a week.

threat of attack
On last Friday, all the cannon at Fort George at Newport, except for four, were carried with shot to Providence, to be easily conveyed to any part of the country to meet the Indians and Canadians[14] with which the colonies are threatened. And on last Friday, the battery of this Town (New London) was removed into the country for the same purpose.
****
From *The Gazette,* December 23, 1774

town meeting in Windham
At a town meeting in Windham, Nathaniel Wales Jr. Moderator and Samuel Gray, Town clerk, a resolution was entered that this town does accept, approve and adopt the resolutions of the Continental Congress in Philadelphia, last September, and do oblige themselves religiously to follow the same and do the utmost to insure that the same are observed and kept.
The following persons are appointed a Committee of observation: Nathaniel Wales Jr., Hezekiah Bissel, Samuel Gray; Dr. Joshua Elderkin, Samuel Webb, Capt. Hezekiah Huntington, Nathaniel Warner, Ebenezer Wolsey, Capt. John Howard, Joseph Burnham, Joseph Durkers, Dr. John Brewster, Ebenezer Devotion, Sanford Kingsbury, Capt. Zebulon Hebard, James Luce and Dr. John Cary.

town meeting in Groton
William Williams was Moderator and the " town being of a strong belief that a strict adherence to and observation of the resolutions of the Continental Congress in Philadelphia, last

September, are of the utmost importance for the preservation of American Rights and Liberties.

The following persons are appointed a Committee of Observation: Ebenezer Ledyard, Thomas Mumford, William Williams, Reddham Gallup, William Avery, Capt. Solomon Perkins, David Avery, William Morgan, John Elderkin, Joseph Packer, John Hurlbut, Ebenezer Avery 2d and Amos Geer.

died
in Fairfield on November 28, 1774 suddenly in the 69th year of her life, Mrs. Elizabeth Reynold, relict of the Rev Peter Reynold, late of that place; granddaughter of Edward Taylor, minister in Wesfield and only daughter of Samuel Taylor with his wife, the daughter of James Fitch, late minister in Norwich.

vessel wanted
Any person who has a strong, well built schooner or sloop, of about 50 to 60 tons burthern, to sell, may hear of a purchaser by contacting Roswell Saltonstall of New London, who also has to sell choice superfine and common burr flour, corn, rye, white beans and a few potatoes.

administration of estates
Notice by Daniel Fish, Administrator, that the remaining real estate of estate of Joseph Chesebrough, deceased, late of Stonington, will be sold, subject to the encumbrances belonging to the wife of Captain Fanning of South Hampton, late widow of Joseph Chesebrough; sale to be held at the house of Andrew Palmer, Stonington, innholder.

runaway wife
Notice by Dufty Jacobs that his wife Katurah, having left his house and family for unknown reasons and has not returned, that he will not be responsible for her debts.

strayed sheep
Notice by Abijah Hall of Chatham of seven strayed sheep.
****

From *The Gazette,* December 30, 1774

town meeting in Lebanon
At a full meeting of the inhabitants of Lebanon , the following was passed on and voted as a declaration, resolve and covenant: "Whereas the present ministry and Managers of the Court of Great Britain have departed from the paths of truth and justice in adopting a system of colonial administration, illegal, cruel, unjust and highly oppressive and such as their predecessors never attempted which has a direct tendency to alienate the affections of this Country totally from His Majesty's Person and Government and forever dissolve all friendly relations with the British Nation which we have heretofore delighted to call our Parent State and our Mother County; and
Whereas they have already in part executed and are vigorously pushing the completion of their design to reduce these colonies to miserable bondage and, with that view, have invaded our country with men of war and troops in warlike posture and hostile apparatus; and
Whereas on a thorough consideration of our convictions of the justice of our cause resulting from the Laws of God, the nature and reason of civil government, of the British Constitution under which principles the inhabitants of this colony first settled, it is our fixed opinion and apparently the united view of all the country that it is right to defend this important cause of civil liberty at the expense of property and lives; and
Whereas a General Congress of the united colonies was lately held in Philadelphia for the sole purpose of consulting and securing their common just rights, putting their trust in God Almighty, have plainly expressed their resolution never to part with or yield those rights to any power in the world and yet ardently desire to preserve their duty and loyalty to the King in which this country has been singularly united and to preserve for as long as possible that brotherly affection and sincere good well and friendship so deeply rooted in our breasts towards our fellow subjects of Great Britain (very few of whom are concerned with the bloody tragedy happening here).
Therefore we have come with one voice into many wise and

salutary doings and resolves including, among others, an Association relative to a non importation and non consumption of English or Irish goods and, relating to slaves, a non exportation agreement and for promoting and sale of our own manufactures and many other matters needless to list,
We the inhabitants of this town lawfully assembled do heartedly approve of the doings of said Congress in general and the Association mentioned in particular and we do hereby agree, engage and covenant with and to each other, strictly to adhere and be bound by them;
We do further agree to the recommendations of said Congress and nominate and appoint William Williams, Joshua West, John Clark, Benejah Bill, Jonathan Trumbull, Peletiah Marsh, James Pinnco, Capt. Veach, Williams, Capt Elijah Hide, Nathan Carver, Samuel Hide Jr., and, Noah Colman, all of said Town, a Committee of Inspection or Safety whose business should be to attentively observe the conduct of all persons in town in matters touching on said Association and, by all proper ways and agreeable to said recommendations, endeavor that the same be inviolably kept and observed, until our common grievances as stated by the Congress shall be addressed.
Wm. Williams, Town Clerk

Norwich Town Meeting
At a meeting of the committees of Observation and Inspection of Norwich, it was resolved that all goods prohibited by the Continental Association agreement, which shall be brought into this Town after December 1, shall be considered to have been imported in violation of this agreement, unless the importer of them can produce a certificate of the Committee of Observation and Inspection of those places from whence said articles were brought, declaring that they were imported before th first day of December.
published by order of the Committee
Dudley Woodbridge, Clerk

New London Town Meeting
This day, at a very full town meeting in New London, the

inhabitants made choice of thirty respectable people to be a Committee of Inspection and directed them to take the most effectual care that the Association of the Continental Congress, held in Philadelphia on September, 1774, be absolutely and bona fide adhered to. Any seven of said Committee can be a Quorum and upon any emergency to call such Committee together to meet at the Court House in New London, at such times as they think proper.

Saybrook Town Meeting
In a full meeting of the inhabitants of the town of Saybrook, legally warned, in which there was present a number of the freemen of the colony, upon taking into consideration the Resolves of the Continental Congress, they unanimously voted their approbation of them and they will endeavor to the extent possible to strictly adhere to every article of the Association accordingly. According to the 11th article, they chose Dr. Samuel Field, Capt. Richard Dickinson, Capt. John Cockran, Benjamin Williams, Capt. Uriah Hayden, Dr John Ely, Jonathan Lay, Capt Edward Shipman and Abraham Waterhouse Jr. as a Committee of Correspondence for that town and attentively to observe the conduct of all person touching the Association and the Town taking into consideration the unhappy circumstance of their distressed brethren in Boston who are still pressed under the iron yoke of despotic powers and did direct such committee to forward a subscription for a voluntary contribution for the relief of the suffering poor of that devoted Town.

to be sold
by Jonathan Trott at his shop near the Court House in New London cheaply, an assortment of winter goods.

Benjamin Dyer has just imported in the ship *Tristam*, Captain Shand, a fresh assortment of drugs and genuine patent medicines.

administration of estates
Notice to creditors by Abraham Gardiner and David Mulford,

Executors to the estate of David Gardiner, late of the Isle of Wright, in the county of Suffolk.

Notice to the creditors of the estate of William Potter are to meet at the house of Abigail Potter in New London.

wanted
cash given for mink and weasel skins by David Main in Stonington.

strayed
from Benjamin Collins in Mansfield, ten sheep, including one ram and some lambs.

ABSTRACTS FROM 1775

From *The Gazette*, January 6, 1775

sheep
Whereas the grand Continental Congress has recommenced an increase in sheep, it is earnestly desired that our brethren in the country will kill only their very fat sheep and will likewise use all means in their possession to preserve and increase their flocks. And it hoped that the inhabitants of this Town, New London, will not encourage a mutton market of a different kind.

town meeting in Lyme
At a meeting of the inhabitants of the Town of Lyme, Richard Wait, Jr. Marshfield Parsons, Joseph Mather, Ezra Selden, James Goold, Elias Bingham, Abner Comstock, George Griswold and Moses Warner were chosen a Committee of Inspection, agreeable to the 11th Article of the Association of the late Continental Congress.
    John Lay, 2d, Clerk

shipwreck
About three weeks ago, a sloop belonging to Casco Bay, Luce, Master, bound from thence to the West Indies with a cargo of spars, was drove ashore at East Hampton beach; the vessel lost, but the people and part of the cargo saved.

agriculture – hogs and cattle
On the 24th of last month was killed by Henry Champion of Colchester a hog, when neatly dressed, weighted 715 pounds. The lard, when taken out, weighted 176 pounds.

On the first of last month, Nathaniel Cone of East Haddam slaughtered a cow which weighted as follows: forequarters 761 pounds; hide 78 1/2 pounds, tallow 123 1/2 pounds.

died
in a fit of apoplexy, Mrs. Deborah Williams, the amiable consort of Ebenezer Williams of Stonington;

William Beebe of New London, deacon of the Sabbatarian Church; in the 78th year of his life having borne up for some years under the suffering of a long and insidious consumption;

also Ebenezer Beebe.

administration of estates
Notice by Charles Eldridge Jr, Ezekiel Baly, Ebenezer Avery 3rd, Commissioners for the estate of John Barnes, late of Groton; appointed by Charles Phelps, Probate Judge in Stonington to creditors to meet at the house of Edward Jeffrey of Groton, Inn holder.

Notice by Benjamin Bill, Silas Phelps, James Thomas, Commissioners appointed by order of Probate Judge Shubael Conant to the creditors of the estate of Capt. Josiah Fitch, late of Lebanon, to meet at the house of Simon Gray, inn holder in Lebanon.

****

From *The Gazette,* January 13, 1775

day of fasting and prayer
declared by Gov. Joseph Trumbull "considering the present unhappiness and increasing differences between Great Britain and the colonies in America" will be the subject of wise deliberation and counsel of the British Parliament in the next session.

married
Last Sunday was married in this Town [New London] Mr. Edward Hallam, merchant of New London, to Miss Polly Sage of Middletown, daughter of Capt. Comfort Sage of that place

died
Mrs. Ruth Deshon, aged 70 years, wife of Daniel Deshon of New London;

Mrs. Jennaham Holt, wife of Ebenezer Holt of New London.

administration of estates
Notice of Marvin Wait to the creditors of the estate of Capt. Benjamin Green, late of New London, deceased, to settle accounts.

pay up
Notice by Jedidiah Huntington to those who owe him to pay up.

taken up
in the Sound at Execution Rocks by Conklin of Southold, Long Island, a cable and anchor.

strayed
from James Rogers of New London Great Neck, two cattle.

****

From *The Gazette*, January 20, 1775

died
in New Haven, Deacon Jonathan Mansfield; aged 89 years.

list of letter at New London Post Office

William Avery - Groton
Abner Benedict - Middlefield
John Clarke - Colchester
Jonathan Curtis - Waterbury
Thomas Seth Cote - New London
James Eldridge - Stonington
Dr. Pelatiah Fitch - Groton
William French - Durham
Samuel Grave - Stonington
Sarah Hallam - New London
Stephen Herrod - New London
Mr. Halrant - New London
John Hillard - Stonington
Nathaniel Hewit - Stonington
Rebecca Johnson - Shelter

Island
Dennis Kenedy - New London
Samuel Mason - New London

Daniel Mecoy - New London
John Vilby - New London
Amos Whiting - Stonington

farm for sale in Colchester
four hundred acres, lately the property of Samuel Tozer and improved by Elisha Scovel; lies well situated on the road running from New London to Hartford and another road running from East Haddam to Norwich; inquire of Joseph Webb of Wethersfield or Elisha Scovil in Colchester.

settle up
Notice by David Adams of Windham to his creditors to settle accounts with Mr. Experience Robinson of Scotland.

runaway
Notice by David Fanning that his son Elisha Fanning has run him into debt and absconded; 18 years old, five feet, six inches tall, slender built and of a light complexion.

found
in the pasture of Joshua Randal of Stonington, a red steer;

a bag of peppers in the road about a mile out of New London on the Norwich road; apply to Nathaniel Rogers in New London.

Notice by Thomas Jones that he found in his enclosure in New London a bull.

****

From *The Gazette,* January 27, 1775

town meeting at Colchester
At a meeting of the inhabitants of the Town of Colchester, Capt. Dudley Wright, Moderator:
Voted that ths Town does approve of the doings of the

Continental Congress, as published, and do adopt the plan of Association and correspondence therein recommended. At the same meeting the following persons were chosen a Committee of Inspection, agreeable to the 11th Article of said Association *viz.* Capt. Elijah Smith, John Watrous, Peter Bulkey, Capt. Dudley Wright, Levi Welles, Elias Worthington, Moses Yeamans, Asa Foot, Charles Foot, David Day, James Ransom, Silvanus Blish, Perpont Bacon, and Noah Pomeroy.

At the same meeting was voted that there be a second collection for the relief of our oppressed brethren in Boston and a committee set up to collect and send such donation, consisting of Maj. Henry Champion, John Watrous, Elias Worthington, Capt. Dudley Wright, Ebenezer Strong, Asa Foot, James Ransom and Israel Foot.

died
on the coast of Barbary Amos Leech, son of Joseph Leech of this Town, New London.

pay up
Notice by Ebenezer Devotion of Windham to his creditors to settle accounts.

administration of estates
Notice by Commissioners Nathan Chesebrough, Nathaniel Peleg Chesebrough and Robert Chesebrough to settle accounts with the estate of Nathan Chesebrough of Stonington.

Susquehanna Purchase
notice by Samuel Gray, Jacob Simons, Nathaniel Warner, to the Proprietors of the Township of Salem on the Susquehanna River to come to meet at Paul Hibbard, Inn holder in Windham to draw lots for their 100 acres of allotted lands.

taken up
by Pygan Adams of New London, an old black mare.

****

From *The Gazette* February 3, 1775

Connecticut River farm for sale
To be sold, a farm containing about 140 acres with a large dwelling house with a well of excellent water near the house; lying in Lyme, adjoining to the Connecticut River at Saybrook ferry. Said farm is fenced on two sides with water and has an orchard of excellent fruit and well sized, with land of the best quality for feeding, mowing and plowing; produces annually nearly 50 loads of good hay; has a considerable grove of young timber on it. For further particulars, inquire of Joseph Maher, living on the premises.

ran away
from Nathaniel Sillick of Westerly in the colony of Rhode Island, a Negro man servant about 30 years old; six feet three inches high; well set; has a large feet; was born in Ridgefield in the colony of Connecticut. He was on a whaling voyage last season from Newport. He is in the employ of Gideon Worden's; dressed in sailor's garb. He is a good fiddler and has a squaw about 20 years old with him who calls herself Hannah Pygan and is well dressed in the English habit.

New London town meeting
Upon a thorough and candid conference and discussion of the matter [Congress suggested measures for carrying out intent of Association] we happily find ourselves unanimously united in a similarity of sentiments, both upon the construction and upon the mood of executing the several articles of agreement in said Association. We are fully of the opinion that the true intent, spirit and meaning of those articles are all well comprised in and comport with their literal one. We are fully resolved that we will all do diligence in a candid and deliberate matter to enforce, to the utmost of our abilities, a strict and universal adherence and conformity thereto.
     G. Saltonstal,l Chairman

New London supports poor of Boston
At a town meeting held in New London, a Committee was chosen to take a subscription for the support of the poor inhabitants of Boston under their present distress and transmit the same as soon as may be possible to the Committee appointed at Boston to receive donations for the poor of the said town. Voted that the following be a committee for the above purpose will:

Richard Law	Nathaniel Shaw, Jr.
Captain Guy Richards	Capt Nicholas Bishop
Ezekiel Fox	Capt Jeremiah Taber
James Haughton	William Douglas
Thom Harris	Tomas Durfee
William Hillhouse	

seizure and sale
In Norwich, to be sold at public auction to the highest bidder, three chests and six casks of medicinal drugs, imported in the ship *Lady Gage* from London, via New Yor, agreeable to the 10th article of the Continental Association.

wildcat
Last Friday, Shepherd Wheeler, Jr. of Stonington, discovering in a field near the center of the town an animal which he took to be a large dog, and he having with him two dogs, he set them upon it, but it beat them off, on which he went toward it and again set the dogs on, but they being badly wounded, retreated toward him. He then discovered it to be a very large wildcat, which immediately made at him. But he, having a good club in his hand, fortunately wounded it at first blow and afterwards killed it.

counterfeiting
We hear from Windham that one Elisha Barber of Pomfret was convicted before the Superior Court sitting in Norwich last week of counterfeiting and passing Spanish milled dollars and sentenced to two years imprisonment in the mines at Simsbury.

died
last week in New York, Miss Fanny Waley.

****

From *The Gazette,* February 10, 1775

twins daughters married
We hear from Preston on the 12th of last month were married in that town Messrs. Jonas and Allen Geer to Misses Marsha and Mary Burton, twin mates, daughters of Israel Burton of that town.

town meeting in Killingworth
The inhabitants of the Town of Killingworth at a town meeting, taking into consideration the abridgment of the natural and constitutional Rights of the American colonies by the operation of the several late acts of the British Parliament, the Association and Resolves of the Continental Congress being read, it was thereupon voted that this Town approve this Association and the several Resolves and do hereby recommend this same to be duly observed in his Town and, accordingly, it was voted that Doctor Samuel Gale, Messrs. Benomi Hillard, George Eliot, Martin Lord, Caleb Baldwin, Elisha Crane and Aaron Stevens be a Committee of Correspondents and Inspection and are hereby requested to use all proper measures that all proper Resolves of said Congress be made to be fully observed and they publish the names of any who shall presume to violate this;
Aaron Eliot, Town Register

charge
A respectable in number of the inhabitants of East Haddam preferred a complaint to the town's Committee, setting forth facts that Doctor Abner Beebe of said Town had been guilty of being inimical to the Liberties of the people in America in sundry instances, both in words and actions, which complaint was well supported and he refusing to make reasonable satisfaction, the Committee made their report to the Town and the Town voted to one man that they will have no commercial

intercourse with said Beebe, until he shall have made reasonable satisfaction to the Town for his offense; published by the Order of the Committee.
   Jabez Chapman, Clerk

Susquehanna Purchase
The proprietors of the Township of Warwick in the Susquehanna Purchase are advised to meet at the courthouse in Norwich in order to receive the report of the Committee appointed to lot out said Township and to do anything else proper to be acted upon incident to said meeting; notice by Elijah Backus, David Hough and Ebenezer Baldwin. It is expected that no one will be allowed to draw their lots until their taxes are paid up.
     ****

From *The Gazette* February 17, 1775

for sale in Groton
a farm containing about 100 acres of land pleasantly situated in Groton with a convenient dwelling house, barn and other accommodations, lately occupied and improved by William Walworth of Groton, deceased. Inquire of the heirs, John Kneeland of Boston or Elisha Williams and living in Groton.

Delaware Purchases
The Proprietors of the First and Second Delaware Purchases are hereby advised to meet at the townhouse in Norwich to transact any matters of importance may be fairly offered, relative to their purchases; notice by Jabez Fitch, Isaac Tracy, Joseph Griswold, Elisha Tracy, Committee.

to be sold at public vendue
as much of the real estate of John Robins, late of Windham, deceased, as will raise the sum of 49 pounds. Said sale to be at the house of Jacob Simon, Inn holder; per order of Thomas Fuller, Executor

take up the rogue
notice by Ebenezer Cesey that, on the 25th of November last, his shop in Abington in Pomfret was broken open and sundry articles stolen.

choice rum
to be sold by Lucy Gaylord in New London.

administration of estates
Notice by Hezekiah Sears, David Smith, Commissioners appointed by the Judges of Probate for the District of Middletown to receive and examine claims against the estate of Simeon Young, late of the Chatham, deceased and represented insolvent, that there will be a hearing at the house of Robert Young in said Chatham.

wanted
by Nathan Byley in New London, a journeyman gunsmith who is a good workman; also an apprentice to the blacksmith's business, a likely boy about 14 years old.

weaving
Stephen Miner of Stonington Point hereby informs his customers and others that he weaves cover lids of all sorts; makes them and knots the fringes, all in the neatest manner for one dollar each. Note well it takes 72 knots of common fineness, 72 for chane, 72 knots of under filling and 72 knots of double knotting. For half a dollar more, he will embroider on them the owner's name with diamonds etc.

drifted or stolen
from Daniel Byrnes of New London, a canoe.
****

From *The Gazette,* February 24, 1775

silk dyer
Nathaniel Wollys, silk dyer and clothier carries on the clothing business in its several branches: fulling, coloring, shearing,

pressing and dressing; he also dyes linen and cotton; direct inquiries to Elder Nathan Avery in Stonington.

to be sold at public vendue
at the dwelling house of Jonathan Goodwin in a part of Lebanon called the Village, the real estate of Samuel Clark of Lebanon, put in the hands of his trustees for the benefit of creditors: J. Robinson, Ashel Clark and Jonathan Goodwin.

Southampton Town Meeting
At a Town Meeting, held in Southampton, January 6, 1775, Voted unanimously that this Town look upon it that they are bound by the ties of Virtue and Honor, to adopt and strictly adhere to the Rules prescribed by the venerable Continental Congress and that we will cheerfully comply with them; Voted unanimously that a Committee of twenty one Gentlemen be chosen to act as a Committee of Correspondence and Inspection and receive the donations for the Poor of Boston, which Committee was accordingly chosen;
Thereafter, at a meeting of that Committee, on February 7, 1775, it was voted that all our merchants who shall after this time import any goods, should procure a Certificate from the Committee of the place whence such goods are shipped, of their having been brought in agreeable to the dictates of the Continental Congress. Also that this Vote be published in the New London and New York papers, so that all persons who travel may be duly notified of this, our Proceedings, and that they may govern themselves accordingly, as we are determined to purchase no goods of any person or persons, but what are brought in agreeable to the Dictates of the Congress.
By Order of the Committee, John Foster, Chairman

horses wanted
Notice by Ebenezer Backus that he wants a number of shipping horses and swine within next few days; he also has at this store in Windam, a number of English goods for sale.

Notice by Christopher Leffingwell of Norwich for shipping

horses.

horse stolen
Notice by Hez Leffingwell that his horse is thought to be taken by Russel Beebe; 19 years of age; thick set; one arm and one leg shorter than the other.

****

From *The Gazette*, March 3, 1775

homes, farms and lands for sale
in Norwich a large and convenient dwelling house and lot, with a barn, chaise house and wood house thereon; pleasantly situated on the Great Road leading from the Town of Norwich to the landing. The lot on which the house is built contains six acres of excellent land. It has two gardens thereon and two good wells with a good spring or run of water running through the same. The house and out houses all well finished and the land under good improvement and well fenced. The whole is most agreeably situated for a private gentleman, merchant etc; also to be sold, about 14 acres of a good choice land either for mowing, pasturing or plowing; said lot is mostly enclosed with a stone wall and lies about 100 rods distant from the above said house on the road leading to be said landing. The above premises will be sold very cheap for cash or on one year's credit with good security on interest. For further particulars, inquire of Captain William Hubbard living on the premises, Mr. Nathaniel Shaw Jr. of New London or Hugh Ledlie of Hartford; also to be sold by Hugh Ledlie of Hartford, four dwelling houses in Windham and two barns, one large shop convenient for a merchant and about 40 acres of excellent land, fit for lot building spots, mowing, pasturing or plowing; said land and buildings all situated near the Courthouse in Windham;

to be sold or let a large and commodious dwelling house with four rooms on the floor pleasantly situated at the mouth of New London harbor; about 30 acres of land contiguous and good well water, barn, orchard and a number of fruit trees. For further particulars, inquire of Joseph Hurlburt;

to be sold on reasonable terms, a farm containing upwards of 80 acres of good land, dwelling house and good accommodations around the same, lying in Chesterfield Society, about three quarters a quarters of a mile from the meeting house in the Society. For further particulars, inquire of Euseebius Bushnell, living on the premises.

please settle accounts
Notice from John McKee of East Haddam to his creditors that, since he intends to move to a considerable distance, he would desire they settle accounts. Otherwise, their accounts will be left with an attorney to be sued, which will be disagreeable to him and perhaps more so to those indebted to him.

administration of estates
All persons having any demands on the estate of Stephen Hempsted, late of New London, deceased, are desired to bring their accounts in for settlement. Notice given by Thomas Hempsted and William Hempsted, Executors.

whale bone for sale
A quantity of choice long split whale bone to be sold cheap by Thomas Mumford at his store in Groton. [15]

horse stolen
Notice by Hezekial Leffingwell that his horse was taken by Russell Beebee, who was lately advertised in the *Norwich Packet* as a runaway; he is about 19 years old; one leg and one arm shorter than the others.

shunning
We hear that at a town meeting held in New Haven on Tuesday last, it was unanimously voted that no person in the town streets is to entertain the deputies expected from the Towns of Ridgefield and Newton to attend the General Assembly, which is now sitting in New Haven, which Towns had defected from the Association of the Continental Congress.

new pastor
The Church and Congregation in the parish of Chesterfield in this town (New London) have made a choice of Mr. Joseph Avery for their pastor and Wednesday is the 22nd is fixed on for his ordination.

accident
Wednesday se'nnight, a child of Solomon Tarbox, 11 months old, swallowed a brass pin more than 2 inches alone. It lay for four days in the child and then came away without doing any damage to the child.

how to keep sheep in the pen
It may be of great advantage to those who keep sheep to be informed of a method to prevent their jumping over stone walls. The method is as follows. Drill a hole through each part of the hoof of the forefeet where the hoof divides and secure the parts together by a wire. This it is said to effectually answers the purpose.

died
Captain Peter Harris, aged 74 years.
****
From *The Gazette*, March 10, 1775

subscription for the poor of Boston
Whereas, the citizens of New London at their late meeting appointed to the following of persons -*viz*. Richard Law, William Hillhouse, Nathaniel Shaw Jr., Guy Richards, William Douglass, Ezekiel Fox, James Haughton, Nicholas Bishop, Jeremiah Tabor, Thomas Harris and Thomas Durly as a Committee to receive in and transmit donations for the relief of the sufferers at Boston.
These are to acquaints the public that we had severally opened subscription for that purpose and it is to be hoped that people will not be backward in contributing according to their ability to the relief of the distresses of their brothers in Boston who are thus suffering in the common cause, who would before now,

and must eventually sink under the weight of the arbitrary burdens laid on them, unless assisted, supported and spirited up by the justice and humanity of the neighbouring colonies.

died
in New London, Mrs. Sarah Starr, wife of Jonathan Starr, Jr.

small pox
The hospital on Duck Island is now open for the reception of patients who choose to have the smallpox by inoculation.

Notice by Silas Hallsey Jr. to the public that he has erected a convenient hospital at Sag Harbor where gentlemen and ladies may be inoculated for the smallpox, having good nurses and other necessaries found at $10 each.

to be sold
a good dwelling house with six rooms on the lower floor of the house and a shop under the house. The premises is very pleasantly situated on the west side of New London harbor at a place known by the name of Green's Harbor. There is 40 acres of good land adjoining the house. It has on it a good barn and an orchard of 400 apple tree; there is in a good well of water contiguous to the house. For further particulars, inquire of John Rogers, living on the premises.

Susquehanna Purchase
The Proprietors of the district of Chester in the Susquehanna Purchase are hereby notified to meet at the house of Captain Nathan Douglas, Inn holder in New London on Thursday, the 16th, at two o'clock, to pursue some business of importance relative to said district. Notice given by Joseph Hurlburt, Guy Richards, Silas Church, David Manwaring and Elipalet Lester, the Proprietors' Committee.

administration of estates
Notice by J. Robinson, Dijah Fowler and Jeremiah Mason, Commissioners appointed by the Probate Court in the District

of Windham, to receive the claims of the several creditors to the estate of the late Captain John Wattles of Lebanon, deceased and represented insolvent. A meeting will be held at the dwelling house of Charles Hinckley, Inn holder in Lebanon on the 20th day of March. All persons indebted to the above estate are desired to make immediate payment of their balances to Messrs. Jabez West and Sluman Wattles Administrators of said estate to prevent cost and trouble.

****

From *The Gazette*, March 17, 1775   254

Stonington farm for sale
To be sold a good farm, lying in Stonington, about a mile above the head of the Mystic river; containing 300 acres, good dwelling house, barn, corn house and a good orchard thereon. For further particulars, inquire of Joshua Hempsted, Jr. of New London or Robert Hempsted of Stonington, living near said farm.

Lyme farm for sale
To be sold, a farm with 150 acres of land, three young orchards and the whole well watered; a large dwelling house of five rooms on the lower floor and five in the chambers; a good cellar under two third of the house and a good well of water; pleasantly situated on two roads; very commodious for a tavern, tradesman or trader; with a barn, chaise houses and other out buildings; it lies about a mile and a quarter from the Meeting House in the northern quarter of Lyme; lies about 40 rods from a school; for further particulars, inquire of Joshua Powers living on the premises.

farm in *Windham*
for sale in the Second Society of Windham; about 100 acres, good dwelling house, farm and orchard; about 60 acres under improvement and is well watered and has a road by the house; for further particulars, inquire of Nathaniel Ford, living on the premises.

administration of estates
Notice to creditors by Mary Brainerd and Hezekial Brainerd, Executors of the estate of Hezekial Brainerd of Haddam, deceased, to bring their accounts for settlement;

Notice by Marvin Wait to all those who have claims against the estate of Capt. Bejamin Greene of New London, deceased, to come forward and file claims;

Notice to creditors or debtors by Philip Mortimer, of Middletown, Executor of the estate of John Keith, deceased, late of Hartford, to file claims or make payment.

new tavern opened
Nathan Douglass hereby informs the public that he has opened a tavern at the sign of the Golden Ball, near the Post Office in New London where all gentlemen and ladies, travellers and otherwise may depend upon entertainment and attendance N. B. Oysters, fried and otherwise dressed, may be had upon the shortest notice.

apprentice wanted
Notice by Simeon Smith of Groton that he wants an apprentice to the tanner's and saddler's business; a smart, likely boy of good education, 15 or 16 years of age.

notice of elopement
by James Green that his wife, Elizabeth, has eloped from his bed and board without reason and that he will no longer be responsible for any debt of her contracting.

grains and cider for sale
Wheat, rye, Indian corn, oats and cider to be sold cheap by John Bolles in New London.

runaway
from Joseph Billings in Preston, an apprentice, named John Ayers; age 19 years.

****

From *The Gazette*, March 24, 1775 729

died
Miss Elizabeth Devotion, the fourth daughter of the late Rev. Ebenezer Devotion of Windham, in the 23rd year of her life. At her funeral the Rev. M. T. Hart of Preston made a very pertinent prayer and the Rev. Mr. Huntington of Coventry delivered to a very numerous and affected audience an excellent discourse from *Deut* 32. 29.

school funds
Notice by Richard Law to the several school districts in New London to bring in the amount of their several lists in order to receive their respective portions of the County school money.

bound for Nova Scotia
the good sloop *Victory*, John Avery, Master; for passage or freight, inquire of Capt. Nathan Douglass of New London, John Breed of Norwich and said Avery in Lebanon.

****

From *The Gazette*, March 31, 1775

fire
Last Lords Day se'nnight, a malt house belonging to Noadiah Gates of East Haddam took fire and was burnt to the lower floor, by which means, one hundred barrels of grain and upwards of seven hundred weight of Gammons were destroyed.

shipwreck
Wednesday se'nnight, a brig from New Haven, belonging to Mr. Adam Babcock, bound out on a whaling voyage, ran onto the rocks near Oyster Pond, Long Island and is bilged.

died
at Cohees, Mr. Charles Hill, formerly of this Town (New London) and late of Norwich, aged 64 years;

Mrs. Abigail Gardiner, wife of Mr. Samuel Gardiner, of New London, aged 51 years;

at Stonington of the 14th instant, died Mrs. Rebecca Hewit, the amiable consort of Nathaniel Hewit of that place.

administration of estates
John Hale, Administrator of the estate of Elijah Ripley of Coventry, notifies creditors that a meeting will be held at house of Ephraim Root of Coventry.

Stonington lottey
The Manager of the Stonington Point Meeting House Lottery gives notice that the drawing will be held on April 10th and a few remaining tickets may be had of T. Green in New London and of the several post riders.

for sale
Notice by John Wells that will be sold at he house of Noah Tryon in Glastonbury, the frame of a vessel, 58 feet keel, 23 feet beam, single deck, 10 foot hold.

lot of land for sale
in New London, a little north of the Court House and adjoining the land of Jonathan Brooks.

bound for Nova Scotia
The sloop *Cumberland,* Thomas Ratchford, Master; apply to the Master at Norwich Landing for freight or passage.
****

From *The Gazette,* April 7, 1775

Yale closures
We hear that at the requests of the students of Yale College, all pubic exhibitions in that seminary will be discontinued until national affairs assume a more favorable aspect and that the senior class has appointed a committee to wait upon the

Authority of the College with a petition for private commencement.

please pay up
Notice by John M'Curdy of Lyme that he has quitted the shop keeping business and would desire his former customers to settle accounts.

horse stolen
Notice by John Stuart of Wethersfield that his horse, a bay gelding, was stolen out of a barn belonging to John Hanmore.

Fennings much approved Spelling book
to be sold by Nathaniel Patten, book binder and stationer, at the foot of the Green, Norwich; cheaper by the gross or dozen than any imported.

land for sale
to be sold by Ann Hancock of New London, 22 acres of choice wood land, lying in New London about a mile and half from the head of the Niantic River.

****

From *The Gazette,* April 14, 1775

convicted of attempted poisoning
We hear from Norwich that Josiah Wright Jr. and Ezekiel Wright of Saybrook and David Thompson, Jr. of Guilford were last week convicted before the Superior Court of a conspiracy to poison the cattle of their neighbors and procuring and preparing poison for that purpose. They were adjudged to pay a fine to the Treasury and to find surety for their good behavior.

elections to General Assembly
Last Monday being Freemen's Meeting in this colony, we hear the following gentlemen were chosen members of the General Assembly:

for New London: Richard Law and William Hillhouse;

for Norwich: Samuel Huntington and Benjamin Huntington;
for Groton: Thomas Mumford and Nathan Gallup;
for Stonington: Major Charles Phelps and Nathaniel Miner;
for Lyme: Marshfield Parsons and Ezra Selden;
for Windham: Jedidiah Elderkin and Ebenezer Devotion;
Lebanon: Col. William Williams and Johnathan Trumbull, Jr;.
Hartford: Col. John Pitkin and Col. Samuel Wyllys;
Wethersfield: Silas Deane and Maj. Thomas Belden;
Haddam: Joseph Brooks and Joseph Smith;
Durham: Col. James Wadsworth

died
at Hatfield, Mrs. Sarah Porter, wife of – Porter of that place and daughter of the Rev. David Jewett of this Town.

funds for mission work
Whereas, the General Assembly at their meeting September last, appointed me to receive and transmit to the Committee by them appointed, those monies which should be collected in the county of Windham in order to send missionaries to the new settlements etc., this is to desire the gentlemen entrusted with the collection to transmit the money collected so that I may send it on to the Committee with speed, as they desire.
                    James Cogwell

to stand stud
Young Wildair, property of John McCurdy at Lyme. As this horse gets fine colts and now is so well known, a description of his properties or pedigrees is needless.

to be sold
by Alexander Merrell in New London, two Moses built boats, one 13 feet log, the other 14; also two cedar boats suitable for Gaspee fishing; one of them has masts and sails.

                    ****

From The Gazette, April 21, 1775

land in Lyme for sale
about 200 acres of land lying in the First Society of Lyme, about 4 miles north of the Meeting House, with a dwelling house and barn thereon, lately the estate of Reynold Marvin of Litchfield; notice by Abraham Bradley, Miles Beach and Moses Seymour of Litchfield.

to be sold
by Moses Morsee, an assortment of English and West Indies goods.

please pay
Notice by Richard Law, Russell Hubbard and Guy Richards, Committee, to all those indebted to the First Ecclesiastical Society in New London that they must come and pay the interest due on their obligations at the house of Capt. Palmes at 5th of May at 2 o'clock

sloop for sale
on reasonable terms (or exchange for a larger one) a sloop upwards of 80 tons; inquire of William Stewart of New London.

condemnation of the community
It appearing to the Committee of Inspection of the Town of Norwich, that Ebenezer Punderson of that place has repeatedly drank tea since the first of March last, in open contempt and defiance of the Continental Association (and has been requested to appear before the Committee to clear up his conduct, but utterly refuses to pay any regard to their requests) and endeavours to discard and vilify the doings of the Continental Congress and, by every means, to persuade and induce mankind to disregard the Continental Association, and, to use his own words, that he has and means to continue in the practice of tea drinking, that the Congress was an unlawful association and that the petition from the Congress to His

Majesty was haughty, insolent and rascally.
The Committee therefore ordered the above conduct of said Punderson to be published and that no trade, commerce, dealings or intercourse whatsoever be carried on with him but that he ought to be held as unworthy of the rights of Freemen and as inimical to the Liberties of his Country.
by order of the Committee, Dudley Woodbridge, Clerk

warning
by Thomas Allen, given under his hand at the London Coffee House, to the people of all denominations that:
Whereas, he pays a large rent annually for a lot, called and known as Hills Lot, which people have and do continue to make a thoroughfare, which greatly hinders the growth and increase thereof to his detriment;
Therefore, he desires all those who have been thus practising, to consider for the future and turn from that evil way –and follow the Golden Rule. Otherwise in justice to himself, those found trespassing through said lot, after this date, may depend upon being prosecuted to the utmost severity of the law.

****

From *The Gazette,* April 28, 1775

Battles of Lexington and Concord
Early on Wednesday morning, the 19th instant, a brigade of 1300 men marched from Boston in order to destroy one of the provinces magazines at Concord about 20 miles distance. On the way, soon after sunrise, at Lexington, about 14 miles distance, they fell in with a company of soldiers exercising their arms, who, in the most insulting way, ordered them to disperse, which they very soon did. However, the Kings troops fired on them and killed eight on the spot; then marched forward and there destroyed a small magazine and then began to retreat. The Provincials rallied immediately and 150 men attacked them in front. Many killed on both sides. The Provincials, increasing to 400, followed them briefly and attacked , wherein there fell 33 of the Provincial troops and 150 of the Kings troops. The Regulars continued retreating,

being closely pursued by no more than 500 Provincials (as fast as possible) towards Charlestown and before they arrived, they were reinforced by another brigade of 500 men and that night encamped on a hill in Charlestown, within a mile of Boston under the protection of the King's ships and before sunrise the next morning, embarked for Boston.

The King's troops committed great barbarities. Accounts vary as to the number of prisoners taken by the Provincials, but it thought to be about 30. The Americans on the first alarm marched immediately for Boston and now are about 26,000 strong and have formed three encampments at Cambridge, Charlestown and Dorchester Point, opposite Castle William. The Kings troops in Boston at that time were supposed to be about 4,000.

General Haldiman and Col. Hodgson are said to be among the dead.

ship and cargo for Boston seized
Last Tuesday, 400 barrels of flour, which were purchased at Newport by Mr. Brown of Providence for the use of our Army and shipped aboard two of the Providence Packets, were seized and the two packets carried alongside a man of war in the harbor. The above Mr. Brown was on board one of the packets.

died
On the 8th instant, departed this life at Colchester, Mr. Robert Ransom in the 86th year of his age. He lived with his wife near 67 years, by whom he had eleven children and had 106 grandchildren, 177 great grandchildren and three of the fourth generation.

for stud
Notice by Zephaniah Rude in the First Society in Hebron that offered for stud is famous black horse *Flying Buck*. He is the same horse which Ensign Benjamin Morgan had of Mr. John Buckley of Colchester;

Notice by Joshua Randal of Stonington he has an excellent horse to cover mares; also a jack ass, lately owned by Mr. Denison Palmer. He has excellent pastures for mares and good care will be taken of them.

response
by Elizabeth Green to charge by James Green of Enfield that she had eloped from his bed and board: "That cannot be because he has neither of them, without whatever he begs or borrows."

****

From *The Gazette,* May 5, 1775

wool spinning
A number of married and unmarried ladies of the First Society in Woodstock, to the amount of seventy seven, on the 4th day of April, met at the Rev. Mr. Leonard. to spin wool. In the afternoon they presented Mr. Leonard with 145 score of linen yarn. One married lady spun on that day three score. After which, they were elegantly treated with American produce without any addition of foreign superficialities and the ears were entertained with the most excellent vocal music which enlivened the whole.

to whom it may concern
This is to certify that Capt. Robert Avery, having taken on board his sloop a quantity of provisions (Indian Corn and Pork) for Nova Scotia, and being approached by the Committee of Inspection here (Norwich) at their desire, cheerfully unloaded the same and said Avery made a present of four barrels of said corn for the benefit of the Poor in Boston: Committee: Jonathan Lester, Samuel Peabody, Benajab Leffingwell and William Coit.

for stud
Notice by Charles Eldridge of Groton that his famous sorrel horse will stand stud.

to be sold
by the Printer *CRISIS* Number 1.[16]

farm for sale
to be sold by Uriah Smith and – Overton, Executors, a small farm in New London on Jordan Plain about a mile and a half from the town plat and on the Post Road, lately the property of the Rev. Noah Hammond, deceased; it contains about 40 acres of choice land, well proportioned into mowing, pasturing arable and wood land. There is also on the premises a convenient dwelling house and barn, an excellent well of water a good orchard and a variety of other fruit trees. It is almost all enclosed with a good stone wall, the rest well fenced; inquire of Elisha Hammond on the premises for particulars; notice by Marvin Wait.

taken up
by Phineas Abby in Windham, a large black horse.

for stud
Notice by John Watson of famous English horses *Paolini* to stand stud in East Windsor.

administration of estates
Notice to creditors by Thomas Hempsted and William Hempsted, Executors of the estate of Stephen Hempsted of New London, deceased, to file claims and settle accounts.

Notice to creditors that John Hale has been appointed Administrator of the estate of Elijah Ripley, late of Coventry and that a meeting will be held at the house of Ephraim Root of Coventry.
****
From *The Gazette,* May 12, 1775

news from Boston
By the best accounts of the late action and the most accurate computation, it appears, considering the number engaged on

each side, the fire of the Americans did at least four times more execution as that of the Regulars.[17]

It is said that the British troops are done playing the Yankee tune[18] and give the Americans a great character for courage and humanity.

We learn that only two persons were permitted to leave Boston on Monday last and that no more of the inhabitants of Boston will be permitted to leave town for the present. At the same time a town meeting was called for Boston when the inhabitants were determine to have the arms deposited with the select men or have liberty to leave the town.

A number of troops (about 300) arrived in Boston a few days ago from Halifax.

A printing press is being set up in Cambridge. (Note the first printing press in New England was set up by in that place by Captain Samuel Greene, great grandfather to the printer of this paper).

exoneration
Obidiah Platt and Ebenezer Hall of Fairfield convinced the Committee of Inspection that they were wrongfully accused and they are now fully restored to the Friendship of the Friends of the Country. Notice given by Thaddeus Burr, Committee Clerk.

new mail route to Boston
Nathan Bushnell, Jr., mail rider, proposes with Elijah Willoughby to ride once a week to the camps at Roxbury, Cambridge, and, as often as possible, to Boston to convey letters.

died
of the small pox in Norwich, Dr. Joseph Perkins of that Town.
****

From *The Gazette,* May 19, 1775

murder
On the 22nd day of April a murder was committed in

Westmoreland by the widow, Lavina Hawkins, upon the body of Abial West. The widow Hawkins had gotten possession of a house belonging to William Williams, formerly of Groton, and some attempts had been made to dispossess her. On the 22nd of April some people had gathered at the house and among the rest, this Mr. West who had come to grind an ax. As it seems she had a long grudge against him, she fired a gun loaded with some shot and beans into his head and he died within half an hour. The said Lavina Hawkins was committed to goal at Litchfield.

all clear
There has been no appearance of any men of war, cutters, tenders or cruisers within the limits of this port (New London).
****
From *The Gazette,* May 26, 1775

troops to Boston
We hear that five regiments of Regular troops arrived at Boston in the last several days.

hops
Thomas Mumford of Groton want to buy a large quantity of hops, for which he will pay cash.

taken up
in the Sound, near Bartletts Reef, a large canoe, pettiaugre built, by David Rogers in New London, Great Neck.

lottery
Notice from Managers of the Stonington Point Meeting House lottery, Nathaniel Miner, Joseph Denison II and John Denison IV.
****
From *The Gazette*, June 2, 1775

administration of estates
Notice to creditors by J. Robinson, Samuel Hyde Jr., and

Beriah Southworth, Commissioners of the estate of Nathaniel Porter, deceased, late of Lebanon, that a meeting will be held at the house of Elizabeth Alden in Lebanon.

seize the rogue
Notice by John Holbrook of Pomfret that a watch was stolen from his house.

calf skins wanted
Nathan Chapman of Colchester pays cash for any number of calf skins and would take it as a favor of his customers, if they would procure and supply him with what calf skins they can.

****

From *The Gazette*, June 9, 1775

British ships sent to Boston
We learn that all the Men of War, which were in the harbors near Boston, have been called to that place and evident methods are taken to strengthen the town. The entrenchment and fortification is now extended quite across the Neck, by which the Town has become an island. General Gage by all his late conduct appears to be greatly alarmed.

christening
Last Lord's Day, a child of Ebenezer Ledyard of Groton, a seventh son, was baptized by the name of William Pitt.[19]

died
Thursday morning May 25th departed this life at Plainfield, Mrs. Abigail Warren, widow of Jacob Warren, in the 85th year of her age;

Last Monday morning died here in New London, Miss Polly Proctor, aged 18, youngest daughter of John Proctor, late of Boston, deceased;

On Wednesday, died, Mrs. Holt, widow of William Holt.

notification
Whereas the General Assembly has resolved that all charges occasioned by the march of inhabitants of this colony toward Lexington on the late alarm should be paid,
Therefore, all persons in New London that marched or supplied arms, ammunition, provisions, horses, carriages or any other articles of service are desired to lodge their accounts, particularly stated, to John Hempsted or William Hilllhouse, two of the Selectmen of New London.

strayed
from Mr. Nathaniel Shaw's wharf in New London, a sorrel mare, in good order for shipment.

small pox inoculations
Notice by Elisha Ely that the hospital on Duck Island is now open for inoculation.

please settle accounts
Notice by Abijah Jones of Colchester that he requests all those indebted to him to settle the same immediately with Capt. Jabez Jones.

leather for sale
Choice neat leather to be sold by Solomon Perkins of Groton.
****
From *The Gazette*, June 16, 1775

more British troop arrive at Boston
Saturday and Sunday last three transports, being a part of 36 sails, arrived at Boston from Ireland with troops. In the transport are a number of horses - 14 of them - died in passage.

died
Last Saturday morning, died in Boston being on a journey into the country for the recovery of her health, died Mrs. Mary Woodbridge, consort of the Rev. Mr. Woodbridge of this place, New London. Her remains were brought to Town and interred

here the next day.

taken up
by Elisha Lay in Lyme, a black mare.

found
in New London on the road between Capt. Jonathan Latimer's and Mr. Jeremiah Richards' on the third instant, a draught chain which the owner may have by applying to Thomas Jones in New London and paying charges.

strayed
from William Smith 2d of Groton, a two year old black horse.

****

From *The Gazette*, June 23, 1775

blown off course
Wednesday se'nnight in the afternoon, a squaw, belonging to Niantic, went in a canoe to carry some brooms to a vessel anchored off Black Point. On her putting off from the vessel to return, it being very windy, she drove out into the Sound, where she remained until the next day, where she luckily got on shore at Plum Island.

cash given
for wheat by Elijah Lathrop 3rd at his mills in Norwich.

administration of estates
Notice to creditors by Simeon Smith, Gilbert Smith and Jabez Smith, Jr, Commissioners appointed by the Probate Court of Stonington on the estate of John Willworth, late of Groton, that a meeting will be held at the house of Silas Burrows of said Groton.

too many sheep?
Notice by G. Saltonstall that the Committee on Inspection met at the house of Thomas Allen in New London to consider what was proper to be done relative to the increase in sheep duly

observed. As representative of the towns were not present, it was resolved to meet again later in the month.

****

From *The Gazette*, June 30, 1775

Battle of Bunker Hill
On Friday evening the 16th instant, a detachment of men from the camp at Cambridge were ordered to take possession of Charlestown Hill, just back of the town, in order to prevent the excursions of the enemy in that quarter. On 8 p.m., we marched from the parade, observing a profound silence lest the enemy should suspect our design and annoy us. The night was very still and we laboured incessantly till day without being discovered by the enemy, when we had enclosed about a quarter of an acre with a very good breast work for defense. A little before sunrise, the enemy discovered us, which they announced by an immediate discharge of cannon upon us from the *Lively* Frigate, lying in the ferry way. We continued our preparations, notwithstanding the continual flight of cannon shot, bombs etc. from their shipping and batteries in Boston, until about 12 o'clock, when we discovered the enemy landing at a place below us, to the number of about 3,000 with six field pieces and advancing to attack us. We immediately made dispositions for defense. Capt. Knowlton, Lieuts. Hyde and Dane, were ordered with a party to take a fence upon a marsh below us, to prevent them from surrounding us. At about 2 o'clock, the firing became general with small arms on both sides and, although greatly superior to us in number and supported by an incessant fire from several ships drawn up on all sides of us and from the batteries of Boston, yet we plied them so warmly from the left wing of our battery, that they retreated with the greatest precipitations and confusion. They advanced briefly upon our front where they were so well received that instead of their usual erect posture of fighting, they endeavoured to evade death by skulking in the grass, behind trees and fences till our ammunition being nearly exhausted and our fire slackened they advanced swiftly upon us in the breast working which was then scarcely defended by 20

rounds; upon which we retreated, but not before several of them met their fate upon the breastwork. They had us surrounded on all sides and had gotten within a rod of the gateway. We retreated from Charlestown Hill to Bunkers Hill, about a mile, fatigued with incessant toil, and closely pursued by the enemy, when a small party under Captain Coit and Lunt arrived to our relief and put a stop to their farther progress. The loss on our side was about 150 killed, wounded or missing and, from letters from Boston and by people who escaped from there after the battle, we are assured that the loss of the regular army amounted to 1,500 killed or wounded. [20]

died
Last Wednesday, died here New London, Mrs. Mary Dare, wife of Mr. Thomas Dare;

at New Haven, Mrs. Margaret Arnold, wife of Col. Benedict Arnold.[21]

butter wanted
Church and Hallam will pay cash for good butter at their shop in New London.

****

From *The Gazette*, July 6, 1775

strayed
from Charles Decalph near the Meeting House in the Province of Brookline, Pomfret, a black mare.

sorry
Notice by John Branford that he has realized he has wrongfully accused Isaac Bates of Saybrook, who operated a boat from New York to Brandford, of stealing a dollar from him. Apology witnessed by Daniel Olds and Robert Olds.

more troops to be raised
The General Assembly of this Colony met in Hartford on Friday last and have ordered two more regiments to be raised in

the Colony to consist of 700 men each, exclusive of officers. We hear the following Gentlemen have been appointed Field Officers of those regiments.
Jedidiah Huntington of Norwich, Colonel
John Douglass of Plainfield, Lt. Colonel
Jonathan Latimer, Jr. of New London, Major
Charles Webb of Stamford, Colonel
Street Hall of Wallingford, Major
Joel Clark of Farmington, Major

died
at New Haven, Samuel Mansfield, Esq.

denial
Notice by Charles Phelps of Stonington, denying the accusation that he had supplied the Kings troops with provisions, blaming Samuel Prentice of lying about him because of a prior disagreement with him.

ship stopped
On the 4th at five o'clock pm, appeared of this harbor (New London) His Majesty's frigate *Nautilus*, in chase of a brig, which, after some time chasing and firing seven shots, the brig brought to. After the barge had visited the brig, she was acquitted and stood her course westward, supposed for New Haven. Next day, the *Nautilus* appeared in Newport where there were two Men of War, the *Rose* and *Swan* with a tender. "The Season comes on. Hawks catch chickens, so keep a look out."

lost
Notice by William Wheeler 3rd, of New London that a chestnut canoe was found between New London Ferry and Gales Ferry
****
From *The Gazette,* July 14, 1775

exchange of gunfire on the Connecticut River
Last Lord's day, a barge was sent with two swishes and a

number of smaller arms from the *King Fisher* Man of War, which was lying in the Sound off the mouth of the Connecticut River, in chase of a schooner belonging to Rocky Hill, which was bound into the River. The schooner grounding on Saybrook bar, she was boarded by the people from the Barge, who attempted to get her afloat, but finding they could not, left her. On sight of the barge, numbers of armed persons immediately collected on points on each side of the River, when a number of shots were exchanged on both sides. Our people received no damage, What damage was done to the people on the barge we did not learn, but upon receiving our fire they immediately moved with great haste from the shore.

to the owners and masters of all vessels
New Orders received last evening. Be it known from this day and after this day, no vessel is permitted to begin any loading for any port whatever, until the owner himself of such vessel and Master appear in the Custom House and there give bond.

for sale
a quantity of choice Spanish hides, cocoa and iron to be sold at the Still House in New London.

cash
given by Thomas Jones at the house of the widow Colfax in New London for butter and tow cloth.
****
From *The Gazette*, July 21, 1775

lightning strikes
Last Monday, Mr. Giles Ellsworth, Jr. was killed by lightning in Windsor. The same day a young man at East Hartford was struck by lightning, but likely to recover. The same day also a cow was killed by lightning at Marlborough Society.

mail detained
The Rhode Island Post was stopped by a Man of War in Newport harbor, last Wednesday morning in passing the ferry

on his way to this place, New London, the Ferry Boat was carried alongside the Man of War where she was detained till near Night. The post arrived here yesterday in the forenoon.

died
Last Lord's Day morning, died very suddenly in a fit of apoplexy, Mr. Stephen Fox of this town, New London.

wants to buy
Thomas Mumford of Groton wants to buy a quantity of tow cloth and yard stockings.

hats
Thomas Tileston, Hat Maker from Boston, begs leave to inform the Public that he has taken a shop in Windham, near the Golden Ball, where he intends to carry on his business in all of its branches with fidelity and dispatch. He now has for sale the best of beaver, beaverett, castor and felt hats.

reading, writing and arithmetic
Notice by William Harris that he has opened a school at the house of Mr. Jonathan Douglas, next to the London Coffee House, to teach in the most easy and soft manner, the branches above mentioned. The school will be open for the instruction of misses from 5 to 7 o'clock in the morning and from five to six o'clock in the evening. The time that will be devoted to boys will be from 8 to 11 in the morning and from 2 to 5 o'clock in the afternoon.

for sale
A general assortment of drugs and medicines to be sold by Simon Wolcott at his shop in New London, on the most reasonable terms for cash only.
****

From *The Gazette*, July 28, 1775

day of prayer
Thursday of last week, agreeable to the recommendation of the

Delegates to the Honorable Continental Congress, was observed with the utmost solemnity, fasting and devotion in the religious societies in this and neighboring colonies.

cannons spiked
Yesterday some men were sent from the Man of War in this harbor, New London, who spiked up three cannons which had for years laid on the western point of the harbor.

died
at Newport, Mr. John Coit, late of this town, New London.

ran away
from John Harris 3rd, an apprentice girl named Charity Rogers in the 17th year of her age.
****

From *The Gazette,* August 4, 1775

passage boat
Henry Bates' passage boat plies weekly between New London and New Haven. His boat is a fast sailor and has good accommodations for passenger. When in New London, he can be found at Mr. Eliott's at the Town Wharf and, when in New Haven, at Mr. Thatchers at the Long Wharf.

runaways
from Hannah S. Park of Stonington, a Scotch servant man named John McDonald, aged 20; speaks broken English; stutters some; wears short hair; small of stature;

from John Skinner in Colchester, an apprentice girl named Susanna Taylor; in the 18th year of her age; short and stocky made; has black eyes and black hair; is very comely.

strayed or stolen
from John Gorton in New London, North Parish, a large chestnut colored mare
****

From *The Gazette,* August 11, 1775

feared attack on New London
Yesterday morning at six o'clock, we discovered nine ships, one brig, one Snow, one schooner and two sloops beating up this harbor New London with the wind at North East which greatly alarmed the inhabitants of this town, New London, and they immediately sent an express off to warn the neighboring towns so that they may get themselves into readiness to go wherever they might be needed. But in a few hours, it was determined that they were bound to Fishers Island to take off the stock, which they effected next morning. It consisted of 30 sheep, three milch cows, one pair of working oxen, about 25 young cattle and ten hogs. All the beef that was fit for market had been taken off the day before. As soon as they came to anchor, an express was sent to the towns that had been before notified, to let them know the function of the fleet and to recommend their being in readiness as it was uncertain as to where they would proceed next. On Tuesday morning, they sailed for Gardiners Island and anchored on the East side and were yesterday there taking off the stock.
The inhabitants of the Town of New London return their sincere thanks to those gentlemen in the neighboring towns who so readily came to their assistance and, if ever occasion should require it, will return them the like favor.

fire
On Saturday morning, the 5th instant, the house of Mr. Thomas Gattes of Colchester took fire and was consumed with all the furniture. His loss is computed to be upwards of 500 pounds.

a senior company
We hear from Middletown that some time since, a number of the respectable, senior gentlemen formed themselves into a company for attaining the military art. They have met every Monday since and have gotten themselves to a degree of perfection in the art and are determined and resolute to preserve the liberty of their country at the hazard of their lives. What is

still more remarkable is that their drummer is upwards of 80 years old and is much alert and engaged as any young lad.

deserters
from Col. Samuel H. Parsons Regiment of the Continental Army, stationed at Camp Roxbury:
David Beebe Pratt of Captain Ely's Company; he belonged to Saybrook in Connecticut and is 21 years old; middling stature, pale faced, by trade a goldsmith;
from Captain's Chapman's Company, Thomas Cary (alias Roach) a foreigner, deserted from the Regular service; between 25 and 30 years old; about five feet ten inches high; full faced, marked with the small pox; very expert in the use of a flint lock and has taught the Manual Exercise in New London;
Joshua Pain, a transient person; about 35, well set, about five feet ten inches high; black curled hair, very loquacious; pretends he has been a preacher; is a foreigner;
Thomas Grover, has been in the Regular service; about 25 years old; is a stout well made fellow about five feet ten inches high; wears his own brown hair;
Levi Lee of Col. Parson's Regiment; 32 or 33 years of age; about five feet ten inches high; light complexion; blue eyes; commonly resides in Lyme, Connecticut and some years since sat in the pillory in New London;
from Capt. Prentice's Company Jonathan Jacquies of Stonington.

****

From *The Gazette*, August 18, 1775

young horses
William Stewart wants immediately a few young shipping horses.

taken up
by Joseph Tyler Jr. of Preston, a white mare.

runaway
from Jabez Beebe of New London, Great Neck, an apprentice

girl named Bet Shackmaple, 17 years of age; is short and very well set; of a light complexion; fresh colored and has yellow hair.

real estate
to be sold by Thomas Johnson, Jr. Executor of the estate of Thomas Johnson, Sr., deceased, of Chatam, a convenient dwelling house in Middletown; Upper Houses; about 15 rods northward of the Meeting House, with a good garden spot, a small barn and a piece of plow land about 3/4 of an acre.

for sale, a good grist mill, saw mill and grind house standing on the Willimanic River; on the road leading from Windham to Hartford; also a farm containing about 80 acres under good improvement with a dwelling house, two barns and three orchards thereon; the stream upon which the mills stand are constant streams; inquire of Jonathan Martin on the premises.

British plunder
The fleet of men of war and transports which plundered Fishers Island etc, as mentioned in our last, sailed from Gardiner's island on Saturday last for Boston. It is said that they took about 50 head of cattle and about 800 sheep from Gardiner's Island and 11 head of cattle from Plum Island. General Wooster arrived from New York to Oyster Pond, last Wednesday se'nninght, with 400 troops. He took the remaining stock from Gardiner's and Plum Island and we learn that all the grain on those islands is to be immediately threshed and sent to New York. Upon the arrival of the fleet at Fisher's Island, Mr. Brown, the owner of the stock, was applied to and was offered payments, but he was reluctant to dispose of them. And he then was threatened that they would be taken from him without pay, when it appears he reluctantly complied. The stock was feloniously taken from the other two islands without payment.

Continental troop assemble
Since our last, seven companies of the troops last raised in our

Colony have arrived in town of New London, when they received orders to rendevous here.

post rider stopped, detained and searched
Mr. Benjamin Mumford, post rider between New London and Newport was, last Friday in crossing the Rhode Island ferry, ordered by Capt. Wallace onto the *Rose* Man of War where he was detained until Monday and had his mail broke open and examined.[22]

died
Mr. George Williams of New London, Inn holder.

horses wanted
George Eldridge of Groton wants to buy 50 young sprightly horses (not large). They must be delivered by September 8 next.

deserted
from Capt. Rowlee's Company at New London in Col. Huntington's Regiment, a soldier named John Thayer, a transient person; about 22 years of age; light complexion; red hair and somewhat freckled; light eyes; about six feet and one inch high; well proportioned, walks a little bit stooping and rather leggy; talks but little and slow; shows his teeth and gums when he laughs; he is not though to be of quick apprehension.

land for sale
to be sold by Order of the General Assembly, various tracts of land in New London and Lyme; apply to Samuel Latimer in New London.

for sale
by T. Green, printer, *Edwards' Life and Sermons*.

****

From *The Gazette*, August 25, 1775

investigations by Committee of Inspection
Last Thursday Roger Gibson and John Friend, both of New London, were examined before the Committee of Inspection for violation of the third article of the Continental Association for purchasing a quantity of tea in violation of that Association and were found guilty. But, upon a showing of penitence for their past conduct and sincerely promising not to transgress in the future, they agreed to have the tea delivered up (two barrels of 100 pounds each) to be publicly burnt, as it was. The troops that were here paraded and attended upon the occasion with a great number of spectators. While that noxious and obnoxious tea was being consumed by fire, music (drums, fifes and French horn) were playing and, at the conclusion, three *Huzzas* were given, the whole conducted with order and decorum and to the general satisfaction of the well wishers to their country.

At a meeting of the Committee of Inspection of the Town of Groton convened in order to examine the conduct of John Gates of Groton with respect to his selling and importing tea from New York since last March 3, contrary to Article Three of the Association, William Avery Esq., Moderator. Gates appearing before this meeting on examination, freely acknowledge and confesses that he purchased from John Friend of New London, ten pounds of East India tea and purchased and sold the same which he now confessed, being sensible to his error, was inimical to the rights of American Liberty and therefore has forfeited his rights to and exposed himself to the resentment by the true Sons of Liberty. He promised to do no more in the future and said confession was accepted by the Committee.

strayed
from Hugh McMaster of Enfield, a white mare.

clothing store
Elias Peck carries on the clothing business in Colchester at the

place lately improved by Abidiah Jones.
****

From *The Gazette,* September 1, 1775

British attack Stonington
Wednesday morning a tender carried two small sloops into Stonington harbor, which had a number of people on board bound for Block Island. And they just had time enough to get on shore before the tender came in, and after making a tack, they came close alongside of Denison's Wharf and discharged a full broadside into stores, houses etc. and sailed out again and, in a little time, returned with the *Rose* Man of War and another tender and ,as soon as the *Rose* could get her broadside to bear on the Town, he began a very heavy fire; also the tenders which were under sail and continued firing the whole day with very little intermission during the time a flag was send from shore, desiring Captain Wallace of the *Rose* to let them know what he meant by firing on the Town. His answer was that he did it in his own self defense. We have one man mortally wounded, houses, stores etc. very much shattered. Yesterday morning they sailed out and anchored at the North side of the West End of Fisher's Island, where they remain at this publication. There were five or six people killed on board the tenders by the inhabitants who gathered and were under arms the whole day. They have carried off a schooner loaded with molasses belonging to Patuxet in Providence from the West Indies and the two small sloops that landed the people.

died
Last Friday died at Rev. Mr. Whitman's house in Hartford, Rev. Joseph Howe, late pastor of the New South Meeting in Boston.

escape
Notice by Ephraim Miner, Goaler in New London, that a certain Nathan Parent broke out of the goal in New London, who was committed by virtue of an advertisement in the *New*

York Mercury, on suspicion of having robbed the store of Messrs. Morrells in Elizabeth Town; he is about five feet eight inches tall; thin visaged; pretty spare, very talkative and apt to get drunk. He can talk Dutch, French, Spanish and Portugese.

horse left behind
Notice by Thomas Allen of the London Coffee House that a white mare was left at his stable. The person who rode her here was the French Doctor, who called himself Lewis, who said he was from the camp in Cambridge.

deserted
from the Seventh Company in the Seventh Regiment, a soldier named Reuben Bellamy; he is six feet high; black eyes and hair; notice given by Capt. Isaac Bostwick.
****
From *The Gazette,* September 8, 1775

Rose continues to harass
We mentioned in our last the *Rose* man of war and some of her tenders were anchored on the west end of Fisher's Island. On Friday between 3 and 4 o' clock pm, the whole, ten in number, made sail, stretched across the mouth of this harbor and then bore away and went around the west end of Fishers Island. About an hour before they came to sail, they took a sloop (Capt. McGibbin) bound out from this harbor (New London) with a cargo of horses regularly cleared for Jamaica, whom they carried to Newport where they still remain. On Saturday night, one of the tenders got on Shagwogonneck reef, when her guns were taken off by another tender and afterwards drifted on Plum Island.

youth seized by British
Last Wednesday night, a two masted boat with a number of young men and women in her, went from New London to Fishers Island, where they landed. Soon after, a tender came alongside the boat, when three of the men, who had been in her, came back on board for the protection of some things they

had left in her but they were carried on board the *Rose* Man of War and the boat pillaged of everything in her (among which was a parcel of women clothes). They also stole from the one of the men two 40 shilling bills and five dollars. Upon application being made by the father of one of the young men and another for their discharge, they were only answered by Capt. Wallace with oaths and threatened with being detained on board themselves.

American troops deployed
Three companies of the troop last raised in the Colony are ordered to Stonington and one company to Lyme, where they are stationed for the protection of those places.

runaway
notice by David Richards, Jr. a Negro Servant boy, Cudgo, has run away. He is about 17 years old; of middling stature; his middle finger on his right hand is somewhat stiff.

****

From *The Gazette,* September 15, 1775

poisoned cattle
At Lebanon North Parish, near the house of Zerubbabel Collins and by the highway, on the 22nd of August, in the afternoon, the limbs of a small cherry tree were cut off for the convenience of getting the cherries and, before night, there came to said tree, six or eight young cattle, who ate the leaves which were somewhat wilted, when two of said cattle died instantly. Some others were of the appearance of being very sick, but got well. Certified to by Zerubbabel Collins, James Crocker, Elezer Richardson, and Henchman Bennet.

died
at Guadalupe, Mr. Eleazer Pomeroy, late of Hartford;

Last Lord's Day morning, Mr. James Luce, in the 34th year of his life, after 11 days of distressing sickness of an ardent nervous fever. He left not a child, nor a brother or sister, but a very sorrowful widow and mother to lament;

at Pomfret, Lieut. Asa Kingsbury.

foundering vessel saved
Last week was observed a sloop laying on the rocks on the South side of Plum Island without any person on board. A number of men on two vessels went from Sag Harbor, took her off and towed her into the harbor. She was entirely stripped of sails and rigging. Her name, *Prosperity,* is painted on her white stern. We suppose her to have been taken unjustly from her rightful owner and employed in the service of our enemy as she has had four swivels mounted on her gunwales and is somewhat marked with musket balls. The owner is desired to call upon Capt. Daniel Fordham or John Foster, Jr at Sag Harbor with proof of his ownership and he may receive his vessel again.

choice molasses
to be sold by the hogshead or larger quantity by William Stewart in New London; he also has for sale a few hogsheads of the best West India rum.

taken
Notice by Aaron Hawley, that a man with a pack consisting of five Holland shirts, one silk vest and one pair of breeches, when examined, confessed they were not his own.

runaway
from Samuel Hassard, a Negro servant man named Jack, a well built fellow about five foot seven or eight inches high. He had a fiddle with him which he much delights in. He has had the hair cut off the top of his head.

strayed
from Mary Marshall of Providence, a dark chestnut colored mare. Please return to Charles Keen in Providence or Jesse Pease in Enfield.

****

From *The Gazette,* September 22, 1775

Committee of Inspection
At a meeting of the Committee of Inspection of the Towns of Saybrook, Killingworth and Lyme, on the 5th day of September, 1775, Benjamin Williams Chairman.
This meeting, taking into consideration the necessity we are under at this critical day to preserve all the gunpowder we have (and all further supplies we might obtain) to use in our defense against our common enemies. And, as there are a number in the aforesaid towns who do frequently make use of this necessary article for fowling and other game, which practice, in the opinion of this meeting, ought to be laid aside for the present;
Therefore, it is resolved that it is recommended to all the inhabitants in the Towns of Saybrook, Killingworth and Lyme, not to make use of any gun powder for fowling or any other game, from and after the date hereof, until the first of April next, as they would preserve to themselves the honorable character of being Friends to their county.

an inspired invalid
Mr. Robert Herrick of Canterbury, a true Friend of Liberty, who for some year has been afflicted with gout, to such a degree as to almost lose the use of his hands, though in the 75th year of his age, has mowed and cured with his own hands, twelve tons of hay this past summer, his grandson, on whose labors he depended, being in the Army. A good example of industry. He says it is God who gives him strength and activity.

married
at Westmoreland, Col. Zebulon Butler to Miss Lydia Johnson, daughter of the Rev. Jacob Johnson.

died
at Norwich, Mr. Simon Tracy, aged 97 years. He went to bed

in good health and was found dead the next morning;

Mr. Daniel Bishop, only son of Mr. Nathaniel Bishop;

Mr. Ezra Bingham, oldest son of Mr. John Bingham;

At Colchester, Lieutenant David Day, aged 65.

runaway
Notice by Christopher Leffingwell of Norwich that Abimelect Uncas, a likely Indian boy of about 15 years of age, well set, comely, sensible, handsome spoken and ingenious, who has lived with him for the past 8 years, took it in his head to elope last evening.

strayed
from a pasture in Stonington, a mare belonging to Thomas Rogers of New London, Great Neck; please return to him or to Widow Green in Stonington.

administration estates
Notice by Elisha Latrhop of Norwich, Administrator of the estate of Mr. Robert Avery, late of Lebanon, deceased, to creditors that a meeting will be held at the house of Mr. Gamaliel Little in Lebanon, North Society;

Notice by Benj. Bill, Silas Phelps, James Thomas, appointed by the Probate Court of Windham as Commissioners of the estate of Capt. Joseph Fitch, late of Lebanon, deceased, to creditors that a meeting will be held at the dwelling house of Mr. Simeon Gray in Lebanon.

****

From *The Gazette,* September 29, 1775

fire
on the 14th instant, the dwelling house of Mr. Samuel Dunk of Saybrook took fire and was burnt down with all his personal estate, except the little clothing he had on.

administration of estates
Jedidiah Balie is appointed Administrator of the estate of Jonas Woodward of Stonington, lately deceased.

found
Notice by John Hurlbut of Groton that a black horse, without brand, broke into his corn field.

****

From *The Gazette*, October 6, 1775

British demand of Rhode Island farmers
Four men of war, nine tenders and six transports are now at Newport.
Last Monday, Captain Wallace of the *Rose* Man of War issued a demand of all the stock of Rhode Island and has threatened to destroy the town of Newport in case of refusal. A committee was sent to Capt. Wallace to discuss the matter with him; nothing has transpired from that meeting at our last account. However, we hear that it has been determined that there would be no consideration to deliver up the stock.
We hear a large party of citizens have gone from Providence to secure and protect the stock of Rhode Island.

sloop escapes
A sloop arrived here New London from Providence. The Master says he was chased by a Man of War from Newport, who carried sail until he broke his top mast and shrouds and got clear.

died
In Mansfield, Shubael Conant, 65 years old; was born in Windham, a descendant of Roger Conant, one of the first settlers in Massachusetts Bay colony. His father was Josiah Conant, one of the deacons of the First Church of Mansfield to which he had removed shortly before the birth of his only son and child; His mother was the daughter of Mrs. Joanna Dimock and of Shubael Dimock. He early received a liberal education and was designed for the ministry; but, on the advise of his best

friends, he chose the political life. He was made a Justice of the Peace and a member of the Quorum of Windham and Colonel of the First Regiment. His first wife was Mrs. Eunice Williams, daughter of the Rev. Eleazer Williams, pastor of the church in Windham; his second wife was Ruth Conant, daughter of Caleb Conant, a relation; this third and last wife was the widow of Zebulon West; he left four sons and three daughters, all by his second wife and the late Mrs. Eunice Storrs, daughter of his first wife, who left two sons and one daughter by her first marriage to Dr. Samuel Howe and one son by her second husband Rev. John Storrs of Southold, Long Island. The disorder from which he died was hidden and complicated. It first destroyed his memory and invention and almost imperceptively to himself destroyed all his mental powers. He had fits of paralysis long before his death and, for many weeks before his death, he conversed little; had neither pain nor fever during his illness until his last fit that he was seized on the Wednesday before his death when he was struck speechless; thrown into a violent and agonies of death until God saw fit to release him and, we hope, take him to the rewards of the faithful. His funeral was preached by the Rev Richard Salter.

administration of estates
Notice to creditors from Abraham Brooks and Nehemiah Brainers, Commissioners appointed by the Probate Court of Middletown, to the estate of Col. Hezekiah Brainerd, late of Haddam; that there will b a meeting at the house of David Brainerd of Haddam.

strays
Notice by Peter Crary Jun., Stonington, Long Point, of a lost or stolen horse;

Notice by Solomon Wolcott of Colchester of a lost or stolen horse.

****

From *The Gazette*, October 13, 1775

lightning strike
Last night a cow was killed by lightning at the door of Deacon Nathaniel Bushnell at Newent in Norwich.

price controls
At a meeting of the Committees of Inspection of the Towns of Saybrook, Killingworth and Lyme, Benjamin Williams, Chairman, taking into consideration the late rise of goods or merchandise, do resolve that at this critical day it is absolutely necessary that every article of the Association entered into at the Continental Congress should be strictly adhered to and, whereas in the ninth article of said Association, it was agreed that the vendors of goods or merchandise shall not sell their goods or merchandise at a price higher that they were accustomed to for the last twelve months past; and, lately, it has been alleged that traders and vendors of such merchandise and goods have raised the price and, when they are questioned about it, they offer as a reason that they were obliged to give higher for these goods in the Head Markets than which they were accustomed to, which in the opinion of the meeting was not a reasonable excuse. It is therefore resolved that all such vendors of goods or merchandise who shall sell their goods or merchandise at a price higher that they were accustomed to the for the last twelve months past; ought to be held up in the public view in such disagreeable light as being enemies of American Liberty.

Lackaway Purchase
Notice by James Stedman and John Brewster, Committee, chosen by the Proprietors of the town of Thurlow of the Lackaway Purchase to meet at the dwelling house of Jacob Simons, Inn holder of Canada, Windham.

administration of estates
Notice by Hannah Mumford, *Administratrix* to the estate of Captain George Mumford, late of New London, that his

personal estate will be sold at the house of William Stewart in New London;

Notice to creditors by John Dyar, Jedidiah Calkins and Marvin Wait, Commissioners appointed by the Court of Probate of New London to the estate of Amos Calkins, deceased, that a meeting will be held at he house of Thomas Dursey of New London;

Notice by Elisha Lathrop 3d of Norwich, *Administrator* of the estate of Robert Avery, late of Lebanon, deceased, to all those indebted to the estate to come to the houe of Gamaliel Little of Lebanon to settle up.

runaway
from David Jewtt of New London, North Parish, on last Sabbath Day, a Negro servant man named Jordan; 19 years of age with a view towards his joining the Regulars, as is supposed by his frequently wishing to be among them; he is of middle stature; speaks quickly and with stammering.

stray
Notice by John Williams of Lebanon of a lost mare.

farm for sale
a farm lying in Newent in Norwich, 30 acres; having a fulling mill and shop on premises; also a dwelling house and a barn; there is a fine stream running through the property as any in the colony with a good dam; inquire of Capt. Jeremiah Kinsman, living near the premises.

****

From *The Gazette*, October 20, 1775

leather breeches
Notice by William Terrett, breeches maker and glover from London, that he has for sale the best of buck and doe skin leather, next door to John Denison 5th, Merchant, at Stonington, Long Point.

strayed
from Jeremiah Halsey of Preston, a black mare;

Notice by David Beebe that a stray heifer broke into his orchard in Lyme North Society;

from by Jonathan Latimer, Jr. of New London, a horse;

broke into the pasture of Pain Turner of New London, Great Neck, a strayed cow.

****

From *The Gazette*, October 27, 1775

just published and to be sold
by T. Green and several post riders and by shop owners in the Town and County *Freebetters New England Almanac* for the year 1776.

denouncements
At a meeting of the Committee of Inspection of the Town of East Haddam made against Jonathan Beebee for justifying and approving the late tyrannical acts of the British Parliament and saying that he hoped that Gage and his men would have success and prevail for they were in the Right. The said Beebee, being notified of the meeting, did not appears, and the Committee continued to take evidence. On the adjourned date, Jonathan Beebe appeared with his counsel Breckway Beebee and Abner Beebee, arguing that the opposition to the late acts of Parliament were treason; that those who opposed them would have their bowels cut out and quartered and would be hung up on a public corner; that opposing Gage was wrong and Hancock's head, he hoped, would be cut off; that the Regulars had a right to fire on our people if they did not deliver up their ammunition; and calling the Congress a parcel of mob men and they were chosen by Tom, Dick and Harry etc;
After hearing the evidence, this committee is unanimously of the opinion that the said Jonathan Beebee is guilty as set forth in the complaint and that it be made public in the *Connecticut*

Gazette that said Beebee may be treated as an enemy to his country and all persons may break off dealing and commerce with him.
William Beebee was also set forth as an enemy of this country by dealing with Abner Beebee, a known enemy.
By order of Daniel Brainerd and Capt. Jabez Chapman.

appointment
Col. Gurdon Saltonsall is appointed Deputy Post Master of New London.

died
Last Thursday died here (New London) Christopher Christophers, Sheriff of New London;

in Fairfield, Hon. Ebenezer Silliman;

at Bethlem, Mrs. Esther Pruddin, relict of late Rev. Pruddin of Milford in the 62nd year of her life.
****
From *The Gazette,* November 3, 1775

representatives to Congress
The following five gentlemen have been nominated by the General Assembly to be delegates at the next Continental Congress: Roger Sherman, Oliver Wolcot, Samuel Huntington, William Williams and Titus Hosmer. The first three named to attend.

Benjamin Franklin passes through
Last Wednesday evening, Dr Benjamin Franklin arrived in Town from Cambridge and, next morning, set out for Philadelphia.

shoes for sale
Women's black callamanca shoes and Barcelona Handkerchief to be sold; inquire of E. Palmes at home in New London.

school master wanted
The Proprietors of the School house in Groton, South Ferry want to hire a school master who is well versed in reading, writing and arithmetic; any person so qualified will be met with encouragement by Thomas Mumford.

settle accounts
Any person having any demands on Thomas Mumford of Groton, one of these colonies commissaries, are desired to apply to him without delay with their accounts and receive their monies.

runaway
from Shubael Abbe of Windham, a Negro man named Prince; about 34 year old; is short and thick and has a high forehead; the toes of each foot froze off; speaks plain English and is given to pilfering.

administration of estates
Notice that Samuel Brown ha been appointed Administrator of the estate of Lt. Samuel Brown, late of Westerly.
****
From *The Gazette,* November 10, 1775

died
Departed this life in the Second Society in Lebanon, Capt. Seth Wright in the 48th year of his age; he was a man of quiet demeanor, sound judgment and uncommon prudence.

for sale
to be sold by Davis Belton of East Haddam choice molasses, indigo, cotton, wool, paper, coffee, all spice, ginger and white holland; he wants to buy a quantity of check flannel.
****
From *The Gazette,* November 17, 1775

child dies in accident
Last Sunday in New London, the only son of Dr. Joseph Baker

of Brookline, Pomfret, about 18 months old. He fell backwards into a small dish kettle of boiling water and died a few hours afterwards.

died
Thomas Manwaring, aged 97 years old;

at Plainfield, Mr. Richard Fanninn, aged 76;

John Plumbe, aged 83;

at South Brimfield departed this life after a lingering illness, Mrs. Mary Rieve, consort of the Rev. Ezra Rieve, 40 years old; she left a disconsolate husband and six children to mourn her

evening school opens
Next Monday will be opened an evening school at the school house in New London for the instruction of writing and arithmetic.

cannons to be tested
Notice by G. Saltonstall, to prevent alarm, let it be known that the cannon at the fort in New London will be sealed in the beginning of next week by firing them in succession every half hour and the remainder will be sealed in like manner as soon as they are mounted.

war casualty
Notice by Thomas Allen of the London Coffee House in New London, instituted in the year 1770 for the reception and benefit of gentlemen traveling by land and sea, is now being closed by the Subscriber.[23] He begs leave to return to his friends his hearty thanks for their past favors, not doubting that, whenever the unhappy dispute between Great Britain and her colonies are settled, he shall resume that office and character he now declines.

whale bone for sale
Notice by Ebenezer Backus Jr. of Norwich that he has for sale split whale bones.

for sale
a likely spry, stout, healthy Negro fellow, 29 years old. He is well calculated for a farmer as he is a master of every brand of husbandry in a practical way; he is sold for no fault save a too great fondness for a Negro wench in his old neighborhood; inquire of the Printer or Messrs. Joseph or Caleb Knight, post riders.

strayed
from William Coit of New London, Great Neck, a black heifer; please return to Mrs. Sarah Coit of New London or Morris Fowler in Great Neck.

taken up
by Edward Dixon of Hadlyme of East Haddam, a pair of steers.

please submit accounts
Notice by William Pitkin, Thomas Seymour, Ez'l Williams and Oliver Ellsworth, Committee of "Pay Table" that, whereas it is absolutely necessary that a speedy adjustment be made of the expenses heretofore incurred in this colony by raising, equipping and supplying the militia, hereby require that all accounts of said expense be submitted for proper settlement.

****

From *The Gazette,* November 24, 1775

fire
Last Friday, a fire broke out in a joiner's shop in East Haddam belonging to Mr. Nathan Goodfield which, together with all his tools and a considerable portion of his stock, was entirely destroyed. The fire communicated itself to his barn, full of hay, which was almost contingent and reduced it to ashes. His loss is estimated at 120 pounds.

strayed
from Jacob Brown of Preston, a bay mare;

From Roger Sterry of Preston, a mare.
****
From *The Gazette,* December 1, 1775

new sheriff
Prosper Wetmore has been appointed Sheriff of New London County.

runaway
from William Gorton of New London, an indentured girl named Mary Hewit, 11 years old.

wanted
by Christopher Leffingwell, a quantity of good combed hog bristles in a bunch for which he will pay 8 pence per pound, delivered to his shop in Norwich.

leather for sale
Thomas Topping Jr., at his shop near Capt. Hulbert's in Bridgehampton, has for sale a large quantity of sole leather and upper leather, which he would dispose of for a reasonable price for cash.

strays
taken up by Thomas Treat of Glastonbury, a sorrel horse colt, two years of age; such horse is in the custody of C. Edwards Jr. of Middletown Upper House

notice by Turner Miner of New London that a yearling broke into his enclosure.
****
From *The Gazette,* December 8, 1775

arrests
We hear a number of Tories in Woodbury have lately been

committed to Litchfield Goal for refusing to resign up their arms when demanded by the Sons of Liberty.

Dr. Church who was lately convicted of carrying on an illicit correspondence with the enemies is confined in Norwich goal.

died
On the morning of the 24th of November last, departed this world, Mrs. Faith Huntington, amiable consort of Col. Jedidiah Huntington of Norwich at Dedham in the 33rd year of her life. She was a lovely and greatly beloved daughter of Gov. Trumbull.

seamen and marines wanted
Notice by Dudley Saltonstall that all gentlemen seamen and marines willing to serve their county in the glorious cause of Liberty are desired to call upon him in New London.

split whalebone
to be sold by Josiah Waters in Windham.

small pox shots
Notice by Silas Halsey Jr. that inoculations for small pox is constantly carried on the hospital in Sag Harbor at 10 dollars each.

whale oil and blubber
to be sold by Jeremiah Clement in Norwich, whale oil and blubber for curriers and skinners, home made good cloth, women's shoes of all kinds, good hard soap.

administration of estates
All persons having demands on the estate of Deacon Thomas Gustin of Hartford county are desired to make payment to Thomas Gustin of Colchester, Administrator.

found
Notice by John Gelston of Sag Harbor that left at his shop was a sack containing a quantity of wood and wooden ware, owner

unknown.

strays
Notice by Lemeuel Lamb of Stonington that broke into his enclosure were two one year old heifers;

from Thomas Gardner in Stonington, a mare; reward offered by Benajah Gardner.

****

From *The Gazette,* December 15, 1775

fire
Last Monday, the dwelling house of Nathan Smith of Groton took fire under the chamber hearth and, as the wind was very high, the house was soon consumed with almost everything therein, among which was a large quantity of household furniture and weaving apparel which had been deposited there for safety by people living near Groton Ferry. One gentleman, we learn, has a loss of 250 pounds.

ship wreck
Capt. James Perkins of the sloop *Lydia,* who sailed from this port (New London) for the West Indies, foundered and was stranded for six days during which time three persons perished. Himself and the rest of the crew were taken off the wreck and carried to the West Indies.

died
very suddenly at Paquanak Wednesday evening, Mr. Patrick Robertson of this Town, New London.

curriers and skinners oil
to be sold by John Bolles 3rd at his shop in New London.

strays
Notice by James Sherman of New London that a steer came into his enclosure;

Notice by Benjamin Jerom of New London, Great Neck that six sheep came into his enclosure.

administration of estates
Notice by William Beebe, Executor of the estate of William Beebe of New London to make immediate payment.

****

From *The Gazette,* December 22, 1775

premature babies die
Last Tuesday and Wednesday night, the wife of James Robinson, shoemaker of this town (New London) was delivered of four perfect children, two boys and two girls; two of them were born alive but soon expired; the other two were still born. We hear she did not go out her proper time occasioned by her having a fright. The woman is likely to do well.

new store
Edward Taylor, a tailor from Boston, has opened a shop in the Parish of Scotland in Windham.

strays
Notice by John Raymond of New London of a stray 2 year old heifer that broke into his pasture;

Notice by Daniel Chandler of Enfield of a stolen horse;

Notice by Jabez Richards of New London of a stray steer;

Notice by Lemuel Chapman of a stray in New London.

please settle accounts
Notice by Ebenezer Hovey that those who owe for newspapers for one year must settle their accounts.

estate sale
Notice by Williams Manawaring that, pursuant to an order of

the Probate Court of New London, the personal estate of Amos Calkins of New London , consisting of household goods, farming utensils, wearing apparel, two horses, two oxen, a cow and a calf, will be sold at public sale.

died
Capt. Jonathan Latimer, aged 78;

at Voluntown, at 80 years of age, the Rev. Samuel Dronance, who for upwards of 59 years had been the pastor in that Town.

****

From *The Gazette,* December 29, 1775

died
in Mansfield in the 41th year of her age, Mrs. Martha Welch, consort of the Rev. Daniel Welch.

currier
Notice by Thomas Dennys of London that he is carrying on the currying business in New London, next to the tan yard of J. Dershon.

strays
strayed from Lemuel Griffing of East Haddam, two heifers;

Notice by Benjamin Brainerd of Middle Haddam in Haddam that he has taken up a steer and a heifer;

Notice of stray heifer taken up in Lyme;

Notice by James Douglass of New London of stray mare which broke into his enclosure.

medicine for sale
Dr. Yeldall's medicines may be had of Joseph Knight, post rider.

****

ABSTRACTS FROM 1776

From *The Gazette,* January 5, 1776
day of fasting and prayer
Wednesday next is appointed by the General Assembly a Day of Fasting and Prayer.

married
at Chatham, Dr. Thomas Mosely of Glastonbury to Mrs. Mary Hurlbut, widow of Joseph Hurlbut, late of New London.

sugar for sale
best Muscavado sugars by hogs head, barrel or retail, also English goods at John Baker Brimmer of Norwich.

Delaware Companies
Notice by Elisha Tracy, Clerk for the Proprietors of the Delaware Companies of upcoming meeting at townhouse in Norwich.

strays
Notice by Timothy Clark of East Society of Norwich of a stray horse coming into his enclosure.

Notice by Joseph Gates Jr. of East Haddam of red bull breaking coming into his enclosure.

administration of estates
Notice by George Williams, Executor of estate of Gerge Williams of New London, to creditors to make payment.

****

From *The Gazette,* January 12, 1776

shortened paper
The want of paper leads us to publish only a half sheet this

week in which, however, is digested every material article come to hand.

wanted
a number of journeymen nail smiths by John Herttell in New London.

died
at Lyme at age 73, Mr. John Lord.

taken up adrift
in the Sound, near Faulkner Island, by William Harris of New London, a Moses built long boat.

****

From *The Gazette,* January 19, 1776

war efforts
A number of hands are now employed in working a lead mine in Middletown of this Colony where several hundred tons of that necessary article will be ready in a short time. The salt petre works are likewise are likewise going on there with great success, the bounty having already paid upon near 1000 weight.[24]

blankets for soldiers
Notice by John Durkee, Lt. Colonel in Norwich, to the recruiting officers of the 20th Regiment at Cambridge and all the recruits who may have enlisted that the officers are to very careful that each man be supplied with a good blanket before he marches.

administration of estates
Notice to the creditors of to the estate of Capt. John Wattles, deceased and late of Lebanon, that a meeting will be held at he dwelling house of Charles Hinckley in Lebanon, Inn holder.

tanner and currier
Notice by Patrick. Grant Pemberton, Tanner and Currier from

Newport Rhode Island, that he proposes to carry on all the branches of his business in the North Parish of the Town of Preston.

****

From *The Gazette,* January 26, 1776

died
at Lyme, David Gardiner, late of New London, aged 58.

list of letters at New London Post Office

John Black - Southhold
John Conklin - Southhold
Edward S. Colemen - Stonington
John Crampton - New London
William Clayton - New London
Hannah Dolbeare - Colchester
Joseph Gallup - Groton
Samuel Griffing - Southhold
Thomas Grenell, Norwich
Nabby Gotten - New London
John Heath - Groton
Daniel Hunt - Norwich
Elizabeth Hern - New London
John Ledyard - Groton
Joseph Lee - New London
Nathaniel Miner - Stonington
William Noyes - Groton
Benjamin Prince - Southhold
Nathaniel Rogers - New London
Nathan Scovel - Colchester
Oliver Smith - Stonington
Thomas Stoddard - New London
James Thompson - New London
Stephen Tinker - New London
Richard Weeden - New London

Committee of Inspection
The Committee of Inspection for the Town of New London are desired to meet at the Court House on Tuesday next at 2 o'clock pm.

just imported
by Jabez Perkins and to sold at this store in Norwich Landing, a quantity of choice good cod fish, fit for any gentleman; also a few barrels of liver oil.
N.B. Wheat, rye or Indian corn will be received in payment for fish.

runaway
from Amos Lyon of Wodstock, a Negro servant man named Jeff; about 26 years of age; short and middling thick for his height, straight built, a flat nose and a scar over his left eye.

administration of estates
Notice by Archibald Robertson, Administrator, to the creditors of the estate of Patrick Robertson, late of New London , to file claims and make payments;

Notice by Shubael Conant, Administrator, to the creditors of the estate of Shubael Conant of Mansfield to file claims and make payments;

Notice by Gideon Ackley, Administrator, to the creditors of the estate of Giles Gilbert, late of East Haddam, to file claims and make payments.

strays
Notice by Edward Badger of Windham that a bay horse five or six years old, broke into his enclosure;

Notice by Edward Chapman of East Haddam that a red heifer broke into his enclosure;

Taken up by Thomas Park of Groton, a white shoat.[25]
****
From *The Gazette,* February 2, 1776

taxes waived for soldiers
Whereas, the non commissioned officers and soldiers of this

Colony, who have employed for the year past in the Continental armies, stand liable and are obligated by law to pay taxes at their respective polls, yet considering the fatigue and importance of the service and being desirous to encourage the future services and to show some gratuitous token of the approbation to those who have behaved so well and served out faithfully the stipulated time entered into by them;
Therefore, be there enacted by the Governor, Council and Representatives in General Court assembled and by authority of same, that those non commissioned officers and soldiers who have faithfully discharged their obligations and duties as soldiers in the campaign just past shall be exempted for paying any taxes in their respective polls in the list given in for the year 1775; and for those who have already enlisted or will be enlisting in the Continental army for the ensuing campaign succeeding shall be exempted from paying any taxes in their respective polls in the list given in for the year 1776; and the persons who shall enlist or have already enlisted shall be exempt from arrest for debt until the term of their service is expired.
by order of George Wyllys, Sec.

settle accounts
Notice by Josiah Huntington of Haddam that, as he intends to locate in Wethersfield, he appoints as the days, February 19 and 20, for him to meet with those who have accounts with him at the home of Lt. Phineas Brainerd in Haddam which will save them the time of going to Rocky Hill.

runaways
from Mortimer Stodard, a Negro girl named Cloes; she is thick set; about 16 or 17 years old, has a scar on a foot occasioned by a burn; also a scar on her nose and on her ear.

from Abraham Hodges, living on the Mohawk River in Tryon county, a Negro man named Harry; about 38 years old; speaks good English; five feet ten inches tall; a wagon maker by trade; can also do carpentry.

premature quadruplets die
Last Tuesday and Wednesday night, the wife of James Robinson, shoemaker of this town (New London) was delivered of four perfect children, two boys and two girls; two of them were born alive but soon expired; the other two were still born. We hear she did not go out her proper time, occasioned by her having a fright. The woman is likely to do well.

blubber for sale
by the barrel or retail, by Joshua Starr, Jr.
****
From *The Gazette,* February 9, 1776

strays
Broke into the enclosure of Edward Chapman of East Haddam, a stray red heifer.

died
Richard Christophers of East Haddam, aged 31.

rags
Cash given for clean rags of any kind and old sail cloth by Nathaniel Patten, Bookbinder and Stationer at the East End of the Green in Norwich.
As paper is one of the most necessary articles now made use of, it is hoped that all true friends of America will exert their utmost efforts to encourage and promote the collection.[26]

adjourned court session
Notice by the Hon. Charles Phelps, Judge of the Probate Court, was so indisposed and unwell as not to be at the recent term of the court, but that court will be held at Charles Smith's in Groton on the 20th next.
****

From *The Gazette,* February 16, 1776

warning as to waste of gun powder
Whereas sundry complaints have been made to the Committees of Observation and Inspection of the Town of Groton that some of the inhabitants, through a lack of the proper knowledge as to the necessity of preserving the necessary article of gunpowder, which in this calamitous times is the necessary means of repelling the attempts of an unnatural foe, have made imprudent use of same, gunning and fowling. Charity would induce us to suppose that it was not because of a willful waste of this useful article and, as we the Committee of Inspection of the said Town are particularly instructed and advised to regulate the matters aforesaid do desire and request all persons who prize Life, Liberty and Property for themselves and their children to desist in any unnecessary use of the same, until there is a surplus as may be spared without injuring the public cause. Otherwise, they must expect to be looked upon as inimical to the cause and to be proceeded against accordingly.
      John Elderkin

died
Capt. John Simpson at St. Vincent who, for some years, had been a resident of New London.
    ****

From *The Gazette,* February 23, 1776

murder
Last Thursday night a most shocking murder was committed in Niantic in Lyme upon Mary Cuish, an Indian, by her husband Jacob Cuish, as appears partly by his own confession. Her head and shoulders were mangled in a horrible manner by a hatchet. Last Saturday, he was committed in the goal of this Town (New London). He appears to be very penitent. It is said they lived in utmost harmony until this affair.

enemy attack in Newport Harbor
By a gentleman from Rhode Island, we learn that last Saturday,

Captain Wallace, granted a permit for a Brig to sail from Newport harbor with one or two families and their effects. But before the vessel go clear of the harbor, the Men of War fired upon her, which occasioned the people to run the vessel on shore, when she was set on fire by the enemy and consumed with all her cargo, which was very valuable.

departed this life
at Coventry, Deacon Samuel Parker in the 94th year of his age.

found
in Enfield, a quantity of flax.[27] The owner may have it by applying to John Scott of Enfield, proving his property and paying charges.

not responsible
Notice by Joseph Robinson of Windham that "as I am going to remove some distance from this place and as Rebecca, my wife refuses for some reason or other, as she saith, to go with me, I now forbid any person trusting her on my account as I shall not pay any debt of her contracting from this time on."

deserted
from Ensign John Buell of Capt. John Kyes company in the 20th regiment, one John Carter, a transient person, who enlisted in Hebron and received two dollars advanced pay; he is about 30 years old, has short black hair and dark complexion.

came into the enclosure
of Noah Smith of the East Society of Norwich, ten sheep.

****

From *The Gazette*, March 1, 1776

died here
in New London, John Penniman;

at Groton, David Lester, ship carpenter.

Common Sense
Tomorrow will be published and sold by the printer hereof, and by J. P. Spooner in Norwich *Common Sense,* addressed to the Inhabitants of America on the following interesting subjects:
I. of the origin and design of Government in general, with concise remarks on the English Constitution;
II. of Monarchy tomorrow and Hereditary Succession;
III. thoughts on the present state of American affairs;
IV. of the present ability of America, with some miscellaneous reflections;
Written by an Englishman
"Man knows no Master, save creating heaven or those whom choice or common good ordains."
Such has been the demand for this pamphlet that eight editions of it has been printed in different colonies in the course of a few weeks only.[28]

swords for sale
Two silver hilted swords to be sold; inquire of the Printer.

to be sold
about fourteen acres and a half of choice land lying in New London, Great Neck with a small dwelling house and barn thereon; very convenient, being near a highway and within a 100 rods of a school house; for further particulars apply to Absalom Beckwith, living on the premises.

administration of estates
Notice by Henry Latimer, Administrator of the estate of Christopher Christophers, late Sheriff of New London County, to creditors to file claims and debtors to settle accounts;

Notice by Peter Strickland 2d and John Prentis, 2d, Commissioners appointed by the Court of Probate of New London to the creditors of the estate of Elisha Man, a transient person, lately deceased and represented insolvent, that a meeting will be held at he house of Capt. Zacchus Wheeler in said New London.

the salt petre business
Notice by Alpheus Billings, of Chelsea in Norwich that he has for some considerable time been employed in making salt petre in all its particular branches at the Works in Norwich. While employed at that place, he has been favored with the knowledge of a mystery in that art by a foreigner, who had served seven year in that business in Germany, by which particular art, I believe, I can be consistently serviceable to my country, myself and my friends in particular. I intend to give up my time wholly to that employment for a living. I shall be ready to assist and instruct any person or persons who are inclined to manufacture it in their own houses, which may be done with little trouble and expense and to great profit.

deserted
William Fargo, about 20 years of age, five foot seven inches; well set; born in New London, North Parish; notice by Lt. James Holt.

****

From *The Gazette*, March 8, 1776

administration of estates
Notice by John Hunt, Administrator appointed by the Court of Probate of Windam, to the creditors of the estate of John Hunt of Mansfield, deceased and represented insolvent; that a meeting will be held at the dwelling house of the late deceased.

to be sold
a dwelling house, barn, chaise house with about six acres of excellent land having a number of choice fruit tree and two wells of good water thereon and also a living spring running through the land, the whole nearly enclosed with a good stone wall and properly divided into convenient apartments for plowing, pasturing or mowing. The said premises are pleasantly situated in Chelsea Society in Norwich on the Great Road leading from the Landing to Norwich Town, about three quarters of a mile from said Landing. It is presently in the occupation of William

Philips; inquire of Hugh Ledlie of Hartford and Dudley Woodbridgr in Norwich;
also to be sold by said Ledlie, four dwelling houses, two barns and sundry valuable lots of land in Windham.

Committee of Inspection
Notice that the Committee of Inspection for the Town of New London, by desire of the Committee of the Town of Lyme, hereby request the Committees of Inspection in the respective towns in this County to meet at the Court House in said New London on Thursday the 14th instant, at 10 o'clock in the forenoon, and there to take into consideration the alarming rise of European and West India goods for sale and to transact any other matters that may be thought proper.

please pay
William Stewart desires all those indebted to him, either by book or note, to make speedy payment as thereby they will avoid trouble.

****

From *The Gazette*, March 15, 1776

died
At Lebanon, departed this life on the 28th of February at midnight, the Rev. Dr. Solomon Williams of that place in the 76th year of his age and the 54th year of his ministry. He was the son of the late Rev. William Williams of Hatfield, and grandson of the late Rev. Venerable Stoddard of North Hampton. He was born on January 3, 1701 educated at Harvard College where he was remarkably studious and circumspect in his behaviour; he was ordained a minister of Christ at Lebanon on December 16, 1722 where he has been a faithful laborer in his vineyard above half a century;

Last Lord's day, died at Hebron, Mrs. Darby, wife Nathaniel Darby of that place. Mr. Darby in the 56th year of his age; he has had five wives all of whom were young women when they married him. He buried four of them in the course of eight years.

Three of them died in child bed with their having their first child.

Mrs. Lucy Osgood of Stoneham in Massachusetts, but late of New London; wife of John Fisk Osgood.

In Middletown, Benjamin Rawson, the youngest son of Eliot Rawson; he was seized by the canker and malignant fever last Monday, from which he died in the third year of his life.

ship seized
Tuesday se'nnight, a castaway near East Hampton on the South Shore of Long Island, was taken by the men of war at New York on her passage to Boston. She was loaded with salt. Some of the people, we hear, are sent to the Southhampton goal.

bring receipts
Christopher Leffingwell of Norwich requests all persons who have received flour, pork, butter, peas, shot, shells or other kinds of provisions of war, to bring him their receipts.

cash given
for small furs, beeswax, old copper and pewter by John Baker Brimmer at his store in Norwich Landing.

runaway
From Jeremiah Kufman of Norwich, a slave Peter (sometimes calls himself Peter Pond) about 30 years old; five foot, seven or eight inches high; pretty thick set; turns his toes in when he walks.

breeches maker
John Saltmarsh, leather breeches maker from London, makes and sells all sorts of doe and buckskin breeches in the neatest and best manner and will warrant them to fit properly; he likewise informs those, who have breeches already made for them which do not fit well, that he can alter them and make them fit well or demand nothing for his trouble. And those persons, who have skins, may have them made up suitable to their request by

applying to him at Jabez Avery's, living near the Court House in Norwich.

administration of estates
Notice by Jonathan Latimer and Daniel Latimer, Administrators, to creditors of the estate of Capt. Jonathan Latimer, late of New London, that they should submit their claims to him

****

From *The Gazette*, March 22, 1776

died
in Lyme, Capt. Elijah Smith, 59 years of age, leaving a sorrowful widow and seven children;

last Monday died here in New London, after a short illness, David Gardiner, aged 53.

continental currency
The Constables and Collectors of the Colony Taxes are hereby informed that continental currency will be received by the Treasurer of the Colony in all payments to the Treasury.

administration of estates
Ruth Case appointed Administrator of the estate of Joseph Case late of Mansfield, deceased.

Notice by Daniel Foot, John Watrous and Dudley Wright, Commissioners appointed by the Court of Probate of East Haddam of the creditors of the estate of Charles Clark, late of Colchester, deceased and represented insolvent, that a meeting will be held at the house of Capt. Dudley Wright of Colchester; all people owing estate are desired to make payments to Administrators Ezra Clark and Elihu Clark.

deserted
Notice by Joshua Elderkin, that William Backer, a New London enlisted soldier in the Continental army, has deserted.

price regulations
At a meeting of the Committee of Inspection of the several towns of New London county, held in New London, on the 19th of March, 1774, Captain Ebenezer Baldwin, Chairman.
VOTED
That this meeting advises the several towns and Committees of Inspection of this County that the following items ought not to be sold higher than the following prices, *viz*
West India rum at 3sh/6p per gal. by the hogshead;
New England rum at 2sh/4p per gal. by the hogshead;
molasses at 1sh/11p per gal. by the hogshead;
Sugar of the best quality at 50 sh per hundred by the hogshead and a less price in proportion to the deficiency of the quality;
Salt as 3sh/4 pper bushel, by the cart load or less quantity;
coffee at 10 d per pound by the by the bask or cask;
wool at 1 sh/6 p per pound;
Cotton wool at 2 sh/4 p per pound by the bag;
flax at 9 d per pound;
Hay at 3 pounds 10 sh per ton at the usual places of delivery in the towns of New London and Norwich;
And that the several towns in this County either in town meetings or Committees of Inspection, as they think fit, should make further alterations in the price of the above enumerated articles in case they judge an alternation reasonable or necessary;
And that the town or Committees of Inspection, should regulate the prices at what the above articles shall be sold by retail in their respective towns and they should make further regulations as to such other articles as not enumerated above, as they may judge necessary or expedient;
And that a committee be appointed to refer a Memorial to the next General Assembly to encourage the raising and manufacturing of flax and wool by giving a bounty thereon;
        R. Mumford, Clerk

passage boat
Springer's New London and Norwich passage boat continues every day of the week to ply between Norwich and New London, wind and weather permitting. Said Spinger may be found in New

London at his own house or Eliots Tavern and ,when at at Norwich Landing, at Ebenezer's Backus' Tavern.

ran away
from Joshua Powers of Lyme, a mulatto fellow named Sy; about five feet, five inches high; about 35 years of age; has a curled head, well built.

****

From *The Gazette*, March 29, 1776

fatal accident
On the 17th instant, the only son of Mr. Benadam Denison of Norwich Landing, an amicable and promising child about 6 years old, being at play with some children at a neighbor's house, he fell into a kettle of hot water which put an end to his life 23 hours later.

died
Last Saturday died here in New London , Alexander M'Neil, aged 51 years;

On Tuesday the 12th instant, at 2 o'clock in the morning, died at the house of Benjamin Clark of Stonington, Mrs. Mary Tanner, the virtuous consort of John Tanners, late of Newport, in the 65 year of her age and yesterday her remains were decently interred near the Sabbatian Baptist meeting house in Hopkinton;

John Gardiner of New London, aged 42 years

fatal illness in Preston
It has pleased the Holy God of late to visit the North Society of Preston with a distressing and mortal sickness by which a number of useful and valuable citizens are numbered among the dead. Nine heads of families have been called off the stage in the space of month and seven of them in less than a fortnight, although some of them were far advanced in life and one or to of them nearly worn out with age and infirmity, yet most of them were in the midst of life and usefulness. Among these much

lamented deaths is that of Mrs. Lester, the worthy and excellent wife of Timothy Lester of Preston.

London Coffeehouse
To the Public:
Being moved by the gratitude for many favors bestowed on me by gentlemen travellers and noticing the want of a place for Reception, Ease and Quiet of my old friends and customers. I now give notice that, on the 10th of April, will be opened by the subscriber, the London Coffee house lately occupied by Capt. Freeman Crocker on Jordan Plain adjoining the Brook; very pleasantly situated on the Post Road leading to New York over the Rope Ferry and within two miles and three fourths of New London Court House where every convenience possible for such a place will be erected in order for the accommodation of gentlemen travellers.
Good attendance will be given and the best liquors etc. to be had at the usual reasonable prices; also, for the weak and sickly, they may be had, by the bottle or smaller quantity: Choice Genuine London Madeira; New York Madeira, Choice Old Lisbon , Old Malagra, Frontenac and Red Port.
      T. Allen
Note well: a generous price will be given at the London Coffee House for all sorts of fresh provisions; also for fresh salmon, trout, fish, lobsters etc.

notice of freed slave
This is to inform the Public that, whereas Dick, a Negro man, of late a servant to Mr. Stephen Bacon of Middletown, but is now made free of slavery by the charity of the People and, by virtue of his freedom, has liberty to pursue the necessaries of life by his own industry as other free born subjects have, therefore, any and all persons who do, or shall, trade, bargain or make contact with him, will be liable themselves to bear all the loss that he or they do sustain by so doing:
    Zacccheus Higbe
    Joseph Graves, Middletown

wanted
a quantity of mustard seed for which cash will be given by Azariah Lathrop, near the Meeting House in Norwich.

taken up
in Uxbridge in the latter end of 1775 and left with Samuel Read, Inn holder in said Uxbridge, a soldier's pack.

slave for sale
at a reasonable price, a Negro man about 32 years of age. Inquire of Joshua Hempsted, Post Rider.

farm for sale in Norwich, West Farms
an excellent farm, containing 70 acres with a beautiful large new house, square in the crotch of two main roads from Norwich Town to Windham, and four miles from said Norwich; also a good barn and corn house. Inquire of Nathan Stedman, living on the premises.

deserters
Notice by Capt Peter Perit that deserted from his company in Col. Webb's Regiment were:
John Hill; about 20 years of age; light complexion; short and well built;
Samull Belcher, about 22 years of age; short and thick set; has a sore on one foot;
Edward Mofatt, about 18 years old; small made; very much pitted with the small pox;

Notice by Lt. Ezra Selden that John Burges, a transient person about 22 years, well Het; of a light complexion and short dark brown hair; he was prior enlisted in Farmington in Capt. Hart's Company, Col. Wolcott's Regiment, under the name John Coles; speaks broken English.

****

From *The Gazette,* April 5, 1776

murderer convicted and sentenced
At the Superior Court last week, held at Norwich in the County of New London, one Jacob Cuise, an Indian of the Niantik Tribe, was convicted of the crime of manslaughter and was sentenced to be branded on the hand, whipped 39 stripes, to forfeit all of his estate to the Colony and rendered incapable of giving evidence as a witness forever hereafter.

list of letters at New London post office

Silas Church, New London
John Chapman, New London
William Corlis, Norwich
Esther Fowler, Groton
Henry hill, Connecticut
Robert Holliday, Groton
David Hair, Norwich
Hannah Keeny, New London
Shaddrick Kelly, Brook Haven
Ann Lay, Lyme
Nathaniel Miner, Stonington
Mary Occum, Mohegin
Jermiah Page, New London
Andrew Palmer, Stonington
William Phelps, Stonington
Bliis Ransom, Colchester
Smith & Denison, Stonington
Gabriel Sistar, New London
William Stewart, Groton
Phineas Stanton, Stonington
Stephen Tinker, New London
Alexander Whaley, New London

passage boat to New Haven
Henry Bates's New London and New Haven passage boat; plies weekly between said places; his boat is a fast sailor and has good accommodations for passengers; he sails from Norwich to New London on Mondays and proceeds to New Haven on Tuesdays and sails on thence on his return on Thursday, wind and weather permitting.
When in New London he may be found at Mr. Elliot's at the Town Wharf and, when in New Haven, at Mr. Thatcher's at the Long Wharf.

passage boat
Notice for Braddick's Passage Boat between Norwich and New London. She is an exceptionally fine sailor and is new and large and has excellent accommodations for passengers. For passage or freight, agree with Braddick at this house in Chelsea or at the *Golden Ball* in New London.

settle up
Notice by Jonathan Brooks to all persons having any bonds, notes or books of account with him to settle same. He also has for sale a few gallons of spirits of turpentine, a quantity of lampblack, a few thousand pine and cedar shingles and a good frame, 26 by 16 feet, fit for a dwelling house or store.

charity to the poor
Notice is hereby given that the United Company to desire relief for the poor are desired to meet at the house of Mr. Jonathan Nobles in Norwich on Thursday next.
****
From *The Gazette,* April 12, 1776

escape at sea
Last Saturday, Capt. Samuel Champlin arrived here (New London) in 27 days with a quantity of powder and warlike stores. Off the Capes of Virginia, he was brought to by a schooner tender of six carriages and 12 swivel guns and ordered to lie under her stern, until some people could be put on board (there being at the time a heavy sea). The wind shifting and blowing a hard gale, he got clear of them after being nine hours under the their care. Three days thereafter , off the middle of Long Island, he was attacked by a tender of 12 swivel guns and between 20 and 30 men. The Tender discharged about 40 swivels and 60 small arms at Capt. Champlin, who with swivel guns and 16 men, beat them off. They chased her for 30 hours, but could not get up with her. When Camplin was attacked by the first mentioned vessel, he threw over some letters he had for the Members of the Continental Congress.

troops arrive in New London
Since our last, eleven regiments of the Continental troops from the encampment near Boston have arrived in town *viz.* Col. Read's, Nixon's, Poor's, Baldwin's, Durkee's, Prescott's, Baley's, Read's, Hitchcock's, Vernon's and Little's and also a detachment of four companies from the train of artillery under the Command of Maj. Crane. Almost the whole of the above troops have embarked and sailed for New York.

prizes taken
On last Monday, Commodore Hopkins with the Continental Fleet under his command, arrived here from New Providence. He had sailed from Philadelphia the 17th last, at which time four of his fleet was infected with small pox, which made it imprudent to cruise along this coast. The Fleet sailed for New Providence where they arrived the 1st of March and on the 4th, they took possession of His Majesty' ports and stores on that island
On the 17th of March, the fleet sailed again from thence and on 4th instant made the East end of Long Island where they fell in with His Majesty's armed Schooner *Belona*, of 6 carriage guns, 8 swivels and 25 five men, commanded by --Wallace, a nephew of the noted Captain Wallace, which vessel they took possession of and the next day they fell in with the Brig *Bolton* (employed by Captain Wallace as a bomb vesel) which they also took possession of. The next morning at two o'clock they spied His majesty's Ship *Glasgow*, commanded by Timingham Howe and engaged her with part of the fleet, for three glasses, when the *Glasgow* bore away for Newport and was chased for three glasses longer, when the commander gave a signal to discontinue the chase as he had a number of his sailors on board the prizes he had taken before.

died
Last Wednesday morning at Middletown , Richard Alsop, an eminent merchant of that place.

Loyalist recants
Whereas I, Jonathan Beebe of East Hampton, having formerly held sentiments inimical to the just rights and privileges of the United Colonies of North America, for which said principles, I was complained of to the Committee of Inspection of that town, being formally notified by said Committee and having a formal trial of the same, still holding such principles, I was judged by said Committee to be published as an enemy of the people in *the New London Gazette*, No. 624 and since said time of trial etc, having then discovered I was in error particularly in holding that the King and Parliament had the right to bind us in all cases whatever, and being desirous to be restored to my former situation, I applied to the now Committee of Inspection for the Town for relief, upon this, my new sentiments.
Accordingly the Committee met, before which I declared, that I wholly disavow such sentiments, aforesaid, and hold that the King and Parliament have no right to bind us in any case of taxation whatever. I desire wherein the forgiveness of all good people and a desire to be restored to the friendship of my neighbors and acquaintances, whom I have offended and of all the good people in the colonies, hoping that the glorious struggle for the Liberties and Privileges, both Civil and Sacred of these United Colonies, may be crowned with success and vindicate us and ours from the hands of Tyranny to the last posterity.
                    Jonathan Beebe
The above was presented to the Committee who approved the same and judged that Beebe should be restored to favor.
        Humphrey Lyon Chairman, Gibbons Jewett, Clerk

submit orders for payment
Notice by Marvin Wait to all persons who have any orders on the Treasurer of the Town of New London, to submit same to him for payments.

administration of estates
Notice by Daniel Fish, James Palmer and Charles Chesebrough, Commissioners appointed by the Court of Probate of Stonington, to the creditors of the estate of James Loyde, deceased and

represented insolvent; that a meeting will be held at he house of Elijah Palmer in Stonington.

****

From *The Gazette,* April 19, 1776

warning of enemy warships
Wednesday last, the town (New London) was alarmed with an account that four men of war had sailed frm New York to this place. But, as they are not yet arrived, it is believed that they went to some other port.

bandages needed for casualties
Clean white linen rags wanted for the use of wounded seamen and marine at the hospital in New London . The smallest favor that way from the charitable will be thankfully received. Baum, sage etc wanted for the sick at said hospital.

deserted
from Capt. Joseph Jewett's Company of Col. Huntington's Regiment, Parce Mobs; middling stature; very talkative when intoxicated with liquor;
It is expected that John Palmer and William Butler, soldiers of the same company, who were left at home sick, that, as soon as they recover, they immediately rejoin their Company without delay;
from Capt. Isaac Boster's Company of Col. Learned's Regiment, David Rawon; 35 years old, five feet ten inches high; dark complexion; straight black hair.
Notice by Lt. Solomon Orcutt that deserted from Capt. Tyler's Company of Col. Huntington's Regiment, Daniel Warner of Stafford; aged 55 years; dark complexion; five feet eight inches high; thin featured.

for sale
by David Belding at his house in East Haddam choice indigo, coffee, chocolate, onions, allspice and ginger;

Watt's Psalms by the quantity or retail T. Green.

please settle accounts
As Jedidiah Huntington of Norwich is in the army and cannot continue with his trade, all his customers are asked to settle accounts with Benjamin Backus of Norwich.

administration of estates
All persons having any demand on the estate of Asa Kingsbury, late of Norwich, deceased, should bring accounts to Obidiah Kingsbury Administrator;

Notice by Amos Main, Administrator, to the debtors to the estate of Stephen Main, late of Stonington, deceased, to make speedy payments.

lost
Notice by Benjamin Babbit of Captain Sumner's Company in the 22nd Regiment that he lost and thought was taken by mistake a pack containing a home made blanket, a red duffel Great Coat and a regimental coat with red facings.

stud services
Notice by Zaphanaiah Rude of the First Society of Hebron that his horse *Flying Buck* will cover this season

inheritance
If Mr. John Hughes, a blacksmith by trade, who came to this country from the neighborhood of Swansey in Glamororganshire, Wales in company with one Mr. Compson and is said to have married and settled in Connecticut, will apply to Mr. George Chapman , merchant in Stratford in Fairfield county, he will hear of something greatly to his advantage.

pay up
Lee & Jones want all persons obligate to it to make payments as soon as possible to Thomas Lee at Norwich or to Jones in Newbury port.

women demonstrate
The following odd affair happened at Stratford on the 10th of last. A child of Mr. Edwards of that place was baptized by the Rev. Mr. Leaming of that place and named Thomas Gage[29]. This alarmed the neighborhood and, on the 13th, a 170 young ladies formed themselves into a battalion and, with some solemn ceremony, appointed a general and the other proper officers to lead them on. . Then the petticoat army marched in the greatest good order to pay their compliments to Thomas Gage and present his mother with a suit of tars and feathers. But Thomas senior having intelligence stopped the female soldier from entering his house. The female soldiers gave three *huzzas,* returned to their headquarters without effecting what they intended and disbanded themselves. Col. Whiting's wife headed them.

died
here in New London after a few days illness, Dr. Thomas Fosdick aged 51 years;

at Lyme Mrs. Esther Plumbe, wife of Mr. Nathaniel Plumbe, late of New London;

in Hebron, Capt. Jonathan White in the 76th year of his age

strayed
from Jacob Perkins of Newent in Norwich, a black Dutch horse.
****
From *The Gazette,* April 26, 1776

harbor protection
We hear that it is the determination of the Continental Congress to fortify New London harbor in the best and most effectual manner; it being judged a good and convenient rendezvous for the Continental fleet.

hog killed
On the 1st instant, Mr. Joseph Palmer Jr. of Voluntown killed a hog, which, when dressed, weighted 559 lb. He was but one year, ten months and a half old.

recovered
Notice by John Hallam that a large silver spoon was taken from a soldier. Under the circumstances, it is supposed to be stolen.

price restrictions
At a meeting of the Committee of Inspection for Town of Groton, Benadam Gallop , chairman, noted the prices of certain goods were restricted and the Committee remarked that it does what may be thought proper to encourage and enforce a uniform adherence to the Association of the colonies or Estates of America and the preservation of our Liberty ever to be desired and the Civil Constitution against the attacks of most unnatural Tyrants, abroad and at home.

At a meeting of the Committee of Inspection for Town of Windham, Samuel Gray, Chairman, the prices of certain goods were restricted and the Committee noted that there was great complaint as to the general rise of the price of English and West Indies goods, which, if continued, will be greatly distressing to the members of the country, especially the industrious poor.

****

From *The Gazette,* May 3, 1776

runaway
Taken up in Lyme, East Society, by John Miller Tubbs and William Rolland, a Negro man named Dick; 20 to 30 years of age; five foot six inches high; much scarred in the face; turns his feet outward when he walks; speaks broken English; presently in New London Goal.

farm for rent
In the west part of New Hartford, county of Litchfield, 250 acres, 100 under improvement. Inquire of Benjamin Henshaw in Middletown.

notice of death
Notice by Joseph Smith of Middletown to the relatives of James Bennet, who shipped on the Brig *Middletown* from New London to Jamaica, that he was taken sick after arriving at Jamaica and, after some weeks of a long and tedious fit of sickness, died and was decently interred. After paying his charges, there was something left for wife or heirs. He had formerly sailed with one Capt. Colyer from some part of Boston where he married his wife.

settle accounts
Joel Sweetland of Hebron wants all indebted to him to settle their accounts.

administration of estates
Notice by Commissioners Joseph Palmer, Gershom Palmer, Sanford Longworthy, appointed by the Court of Probate of Stonington, to the creditors of to the estate of Daniel Campbell, late of Groton, deceased and represented insolvent, that a meeting will be held at he house of Sandford Longworthy.
****
From *The Gazette,* May 10, 1776

patriotism and charity
in Scotland, in Windham, the freeborn Daughters of America, met at the house of Mr. John Tileston, formerly of Boston, refugees in this place and spun for Mrs. Tileston 1202 skeins of linen yarn. The greatest amount spun by one person was 62 skeins. They retired after a genteel and plentiful repast with that heartfelt satisfaction that is always attendant on good actions. May a laudable emulation to exceed each other in acts of liberality and munificence to those unhappy sufferers warm every American heart.

American ship escapes
Last Monday a New York Privateer that was bound out of this port (New London) was chased for several hours by the *Cerebus* Frigate and a brig, her consort, from Montauk Point to the westward, but the privateer, by making short tacks close to shore, stayed out of the reach of their shot and got clear. Meanwhile several sundry vessels, which for some weeks had been waiting an opportunity to get to sea, ran by Montauk Point and got out.

Union School
The Proprietors of the Union School in New London are desired to meet at the schoolhouse Monday next. As some matters of importance to said school will be laid out before them, a general attendance is greatly desired.
Those gentlemen proprietors or others who desire to send their children the next quarter are desired to give their names before or at said meeting.

administration of estates
Notice by Thomas Boutineau and Benjamin Henshaw, Administrators, to those obligated to the estate of Thomas Walker of Middletown, to make payment;

Notice by Elisha Harvey, Executor of estate of John Harvey of East Haddam, to those owing the estate to settle up;

Notice by Catherine Geer, *Administratrix* of the estate of Samuel Geer, late of Stonington, deceased, to creditors to file claim and settle accounts.

runaway
from Daniel Troop, a Negro man named Newport, 15 years of age and a slave for life; is a smart active fellow of middling stature; one of his eyes smaller than the other;

from Mark Newton of Groton, an apprentice girl, named Sarah Fiss, 14 years of age.

rope for sale
good cordage to be sold in either large or smaller quantity by Nathaniel Hempsted in New London.

farms for sale
In the parish of Brooklyne, part of Canterbury, about a mile from meeting house, a large dwelling house and out houses of almost every kind; a stream runs through and is capable of water works of every kind and a number of small rivulets that run in every direction; has ana orchard that can produce 200 barrels of cider a year, capable of keeping 30 to 40 cows; inquire of Daniel Tyler on premises.
Another farm in the south part of Pomfret adjoining the above farm, about half a mile from the Brooklyne meeting house; inquire of James Tyler.
Another farm, also adjoining, 65 acres, inquire of James Cleveland.

to stand stud
Notice by Daniel Hyde of Woodstock that his horse will stand stud at the the stable of Capt. Walter Hyde in Lebanon;

Notice by George Denison 4th of the North Society of Stonington that his horse *Jolly Buck* will stand stud;

Notice by Joshua Randal of Stonington that his horse *Jolly* will stand stud.

taken up
by Zabadiah Holt, Second Society, Windham, a dark bay mare;

by Nathan Douglas, Inn holder in New London, a dark bay mare.

please settle accounts
Notice by David Safford of Stonington, post rider, to those indebted to him, to settle accounts.

All those whose accounts to the *Gazette*, which are more than a year overdue, are asked to make payment to the Printer

****

From *The Gazette,* May 16, 1776

a day early
The *Gazette is* published these week on day earlier than usual because of public fast ordered by the Authorities for tomorrow.

elections
Last Thursday, being the annual election, the following gentlemen were selected for the General Assembly and other positions.
Jonathan Trumbull, Governor
Matthew Griswold, Deputy Governor
General Assembly, Jabez Hamlin; Elisha Shelden; Eliphalet Dyer; Jabez Huntington; William Pitkin; Roger Sherman, Abraham Davenport; Joseph Spencer; Oliver Wolcott; Samuel Huntington; Richard Law; William Williams; Joseph Lawrence, Treasurer
George Wyllys, Sec.

In New London County, those elected to their town's government were:
New London - Richard Law, William Hillhouse
Norwich - Benjamin Huntington, Rufus Lothrop
Lyme - Maj. Samuel Selden, Marshfield Parsons
Killingworth - Stephen Wilcox, Hezekiah Lane
Groton - Capt. William Ledyard, Capt. Bendam Gallup
Stonington - John Deane, Major Charles Phelps
Saybrook - Capt Samuel Shipman, Col. Wm. Worthington
Preston - Capt. Jeremiah Halley and Samuel Taylor

In the County of Windham, those elected to their town's government were:
Windham - Jed. Elderkin, Amariah Williams
Lebanon - Col. William Williams, Capt. Jeremiah Mason
Mansfield - Col. Experience Storrs, Col. Amariah Williams

Canterbury - David Pain, John Herrick
Pompret - Thomas Williams, Nathan Frink
Ashford - Capt. Benjamin Sumners, Ezra Smith
Voluntown - Capt. John Gordon, Ezra Crary
Woodstock - Capt. Elisha Child, William Skinner
Killingly - Capt. Stephen Crosby, Daniel Watrous
Plainfield - Capt Andrew Beckus, Joshua Dunlap
Coventry - Elisha Kingsbury, Ephraim Root

died
Isaac Coit of Plainfield; 62, for many years Justice of the Peace at that place;
P
Abel Merrill of New Hartford. He had been for many years a member of the General Assembly;

Capt. Christopher Allen, aged 45, of Groton;

At Lyme, of small pox, Zechariah Paddock, formerly of Middleborough of Massachusetts Bay Colony.

for sale
A neat hanger and lare pistol to be sold; inquire of the Printer.

administration of estates
Notice by John Deshon, Winthrop Saltonstall and Marvin Wait, Commissioners appointed by the Probate Court of New London to estate of Christopher Christophers, late of New London; deceased, that a meeting will be held at Marvin Wait's Writing office in New London;

Notice by Jeremiah Shelby of East Haddam, Administrator of the estate of Timothy Fuller of East Haddam, to all persons to settle accounts or make claims.

taken up
by George Williams of New London, near Gales Ferry, a sorrel mare.

cover
Notice by John Watson of East Windsor that his horse *Paoli* will stand stud;

Notice by William Williams in Stoningotn that his horse *Liberty* will stand stud.

deserted
Notice by Ensign Waters Clark of 20th Regiment of desertion of Jared Baley; a sturdy Fellow; age 21 years; short hair; round favored.

shop moving
John Saltmarsh, Breeches Maker, has moved from Jabez Avery, in Norwich to the house of comb maker, Noah Haiden in Norwich, opposite the Coffee House.

cash
Cash given for clean cotton and linen rags of Printer's office; quantity desired not less than 4 or 5 pounds at one time.
****

From *The Gazette,* May 24, 1776

war news
The *Cerberus* frigate watered at Block Island. On the 12th instant the brig, which was for some time with her, sailed for Halifax with two or three prizes.

Wednesday se'nnight, one of the new Continental ships was launched at Providence. [30]

We hear that Capt. Harding, in an armed brig belonging to this colony, a few days since took a vessel loaded with Tories, bound from the western part o this colony to Long Island, who are since properly secured.

rum boycott by tavern owners
In consequence of the sudden and enormous rise in price of rum, which within the compass of a few months has risen to a price beyond all proportion high and unreasonable, we the subscribers, Inn holders in the Town of Windam, do promise among ourselves, that we will not, after the 10th day of June, purchase any more rum to retail in our Houses; nor will we suffer any to be sold in our House after that time, until the iniquitous price of that commodity is reduced in some measure to the rules of Justice and Equity and we look upon those persons who have monopolized such quantities of this article for the purpose of exorbitant gain, not only to be guilty of a glaring violation of the Resolves of Congress and Committee, but also to be destitute of that public spirit which ought to influence every honest man. We are willing to pay generously for all extraordinary but we are not willing that a few avaricious men should pinch out from the great necessities of Mankind, a Fortune which in prosperous times they could not have gained.[31]

We hope this publication will induce the Inn holders and retailers of the neighboring towns to likewise exert themselves at this critical juncture; for we had better be subdued by the Enemies from abroad than be devoured by the Friends at Home, by Inn holders.

Paul Hebrard   Solomon Lord
Eleazer Carey   Nat. Hebard
Edmund Badger

to stand stud
to cover at stable of Daniel Hyde in Woodstock a horse of beauty, swiftness, courage and resolution by the name of *TRIALL*;

notice by Thomas Branch Jr at Capt. Eaton's in Plainfield, the famous one eyed horse called *Leopard*.

general merchandise
Advertisement by Amos Palmer of his store in the house of Charles Chesebrough, about 2 miles from Long Point, opposite Capt Daniel Fish's, in Stonington.

stolen
from Christopher Darrow, Jr. of New London, North Parish, pieces of tow cloth, one of six yards, one of five and one of one yard.

Enfield, New Hampshire
Notice Nathan Bicknell to the proprietors of the Town of Enfield in New Hampshire that they pay up their respective rate at a meeting to be held at the house of Capt. John Lasells in Ashford.

please pay
Notice by Ebenzer Backus of Windham to creditors to settle accounts.

just published
and to be sold Judah P. Spooner at Norwich CIVIL PRUDENCE recommended to the Thirteen United Colonies of North America, a discourse.

strayed
from Joseph Gale and Nathaniel Townsend of Norwich, two cows

****

From *The Gazette,* May 31, 1776

war news
Last Wednesday afternoon, Capt Niles in the *Spy* Privateer, being out on a cruise between Montauk Point and Block Island came across the *Cerebrus* Frigate who chased him as far as the Race and then left him. Capt Niles lost his top mast in the chase. Capt. Jones in a privateer (one of the Continental Fleet) and Captain Brooks in a New Haven privateer, who sailed from this port in company with Captain Niles, put into Newport.

177

Canterbury town meeting
We hear that the Town of Canterbury, in a full meeting, have unanimously adopted the principles of independence contained in the *Common Sense* book, and also voted that the delegates to the next Continental Convention should be elected by the freemen of the colony and not by their representatives.

bad bet
Last Friday the armed brig of this colony commanded by Capt Harding, arrived here as did Capt. Brooks in a New Haven privateer. He had sailed from New London, put in at Newport, and the western part of the colony. While this vessel was coming into the harbor, one Robert Dunlap, a transient person, by trade a leather breeches maker, attempted to swim from Groton shore, and board said vessel for a wager, but he sunk before he reached and was drowned.

fire
On Thursday se'nnight, a large dwelling house, belonging to Samuel Lord of Saybrook, together with his salt petre works and about 400 pounds of salt petre, which was put up in barrels, was entirely consumed by fire.

cash given
for pot ash and salts of lye by Henry DeWitt at his shop in Windam;

for Red and Gray Fox and Musquath skins by Aaron Cleveland at the upper end of Norwich.

wanted
A quantity of green lamb skins with the wool on, for which cash or good felt hats will be given in payment by Abiezer Smith at his shop at Norwich Landing.

lost or stolen
Notice by William Coit in Norwich that was lost within a few miles eastward or westward of Say Brook Bar, in about five or

six fathoms of water, two anchors, belong to the Brig *Royal*, Elisha Lathrop , Master. If found, deliver to Thomas Harris at New London harbor.

A sealed gold ring was lately sold to a Goldsmith in Colchester for 28 shilling, which was the value of the gold. By some circumstances, it is suspected that the ring was stolen in Roxbury or on the road from thence to Colchester; apply to John Breed, Goldsmith in Colchester.

administration of estates
Notice by Elijah Whiton, Ezra Smith, Joseph Woodward, Commissioners appointed by the Court of Probate of Pomfret to the creditors of the estate of John Preston, late of Ashford, deceased and represented insolvent; that a meeting will held at the house of Benjamin Clark, Inn holder at Ashford.

to stand stud
Notice b Elias Irish of Stonington of his steed, *Lycurgus*.
****

From *The Gazette,* June 7, 1776

Connecticut warship
We hear that a war ship of the Colony is to be launched next Thursday at Saybrook.[32]

died
Lady Ann Miller, widow of Jeremiah Miller, late of New London, aged 92 years;

Capt. Edward Palmes, aged 58 years;

Mrs. Phepe Shackmaple, widow of Capt John Shackmaple;

in New London, Great Neck, Mrs. Sarah Crocker, aged 95;

at Norwich Dr. Kingsbury;

in Lebanon, Benjamin Bill, in the 66th year of his life; he left a widow and three children.

administration of estates
Notice by Executors John Lord and John Way of the estate of John Lord of Lyme, to all creditors of, and debtors to, the estate to come forward and settle accounts.

Notice by Administrators William Avery and Thomas Lester, of the estate of David Lester of Groton to all creditors of, and debtors to, the estate to come forward and settle accounts.

runways
from James Rogers, late of New London Great Neck, a fellow named Sy; a Mestee[33]; about 5 feet, five inches high; about 25 years of age; five foot five inches; short curled hair nearly resembling a Negro's; well built;

Notice by Peter Spencer of Millington Society in East Haddam that his son, a distracted man, absented himself from his father's house about 8 weeks ago; he is about 25 years of age and of middling stature.

from Peter Bulkley in Colchester, a Negro man named Cyrus; about 28 years old; his right eye is perished; five feet, eleven inches high; large built and very strong.

to be sold
at the steel furnace in Killingsworth by Aaron Eliot, various metal objects;

Barcelona handkerchiefs, women and children's stays, currants and Indigo to be sold nearly opposite the Printing Office in New London.

taken up
Notice by Silvanus Seaman that a scow was taken up adrift in the Sound between Saybrook and Gull Island;

by William Welch of Colchester, a bright bay mare;

by William Banning of Lyme, a red mare.

****

From *The Gazette,* June 14, 1776

arrived
A French vessel arrived at Stonington a few days ago from the West Indies.

died
in New London, John Still Winthrop;

Mrs. Elizabeth Sheriff in an advanced age, widow of Maj. Sheriff, late of Boston;

The public was some time since informed by the channel of your paper of the distressing sickness and mortality in the North Society of this town (Preston). Numbers have been carried off, most of them heads of families; many of whom were in the most useful stage of their life to their families and to others, among them Mrs. Billings, the wife of Capt. Roger Billingson, the 24th of May, aged 66 years, of which she had lived with her husband 47; she has been the mother of eleven children of which only six are now living.

meeting of Committee of Observation and Inspection
The Committee of Observation and Inspection of Groton was called to meet at the house of Charles Smith, Inn holder in Groton on June 19th instant regarding the issue of whether the Committee should regulate the price of salt.

new court
A Court is erected to try and condemn all vessels found infesting the sea coast of the Americas.

libels of taken vessels
Libels[34] are filed before me against the armed Brigadine *Bolton*, mounting 14 guns with 40 men, Edward Sneid, Commander; the armed Schooner *Hawk*, mounting 6 guns with 20 men, John Wallace, commander, and a small sloop, lately a tender to the Ship *Glasgow,* with three men on board. These vessels are said to have been armed and set forth to infest the sea of the United Colonies of North America and were taken by the Continental Fleet and brought into the county of New London. The court erected to try and condemn all vessels found infesting the seacoast of Americas and brought into this county will be held at the Courthouse in New London on the 5th day of July next at nine o'clock in the forenoon to try the justice of said captures, of which this notice is given pursuant tot he laws of this Colony that the owners of said vessels or any person concerned therein may appear and show cause, if any, they have, why the said vessels, with their guns, stores, tackle and furniture should not be condemned.
    Richard Law. Judge of said Court

deserted
from Capt. Joseph Jewett of the 17th . Regiment, Jonathan Kane of Norwich; a short, well set man; supposed to be upwards of 30 years; he is of a brown complexion and wears short hair.

strays taken up
Notice by Bennet Munro of Norwich West Farms that a roan mare has broken into his enclosure.

administration of estates
Notice by Executor Esther Smith s of the estate of Capt. Elijah Smith, late of Lyme, to all creditors and debtors to come forward and settle accounts.
                   ****
From *The Gazette,* June 21, 1776

naval activity
We hear that Captain Harding in the privateer brig *Defense*

has taken a transport ship in Boston Bay from Europe after an engagement of two hours and brought her into Boston and, at about the same time, Capt. Harding drove ashore a transport brig, consort to the above vessel.

Capt. Niles advices that he saw last Wednesday three vessels off Block Island and that this coast is so infested with them that it is almost impossible for any vessel to get in or out without falling into their hands.
The same afternoon Capt. Niles came up and spoke with a sloop from this port (New London), Captain Bulkley outward bound, whom Captain Niles warned of the danger and recommended returning to port but as she is not yet arrived ,it is feared she fell prey those ministerial plundering pirates.

taken up
by George Williams of New London, two cows.

found
in the house of Nathaniel Linken in Windham, a bill of public credit in a sizeable amount.

runaway slaves captured
Taken up by Richard Pritkin of Hartford, a mestee and a Negro man; the former is about 23 years of age, well built, five foot five inches high; has short curled hair and is supposed to belong to Caleb Gardner of Little Rest; the other is 20 years of age, five foot two inches high; thick set and very black; he is supposed to belong to Manuel Case of Little Rest; they are confined in New London goal.

to stand stud
Notice by Amos Brown that Joshua Swan's of Stonington horse *Okshirener* will stand stud.

****

From *The Gazette,* June 28, 1776

naval activity
Since our last, the brig *Cabot,* Captain Hinman, the brig *Andrea Doria,* Captain Biddle and the *Fly* tender, part of the Continental Fleet, has arrived here New London.
A considerable number of vessels bound for foreign ports, are now lying New London Harbor waiting for a favorable opportunity to put to sea.

died
Mananssa Leach;

Mrs. Fox, wife of Ezekiel Fox in New London, North Parish.

deserted
from 20th Regiment, William Quirk, an Irishman; five feet ten inches high; well set; light complexion; dresses poorly; says he lived in Worchester the past 17 years. Notice given by Lt. Nathaniel Bishop;

from Abraham Waterhouse's Company of Col. Parson's Regiment, William Baker; appears to be a man of about 30 years of age., five foot ten inches. Said Baker has passed through the country under the name Smith in pretense of pursuing deserters.

from the Brig *Cabot,* Capt Hinman, and supposed to have taken a yawl, oars, a compass and a top gallant studding sail, three seamen James Wilkeson, Abel Jones and Joseph Mains. Wilkeson is a thick set man about 45 years old and five foot six inches tall; wears his own short hair; Jones is a Dutchman about 40 years of age; five feet, seven inches tall, a sandy complexion; short light hair; Mains is a carpenter by trade, five feet seven inches high; fair complexion; born in Philadelphia; likewise was stolen at the same time from William Bunting, cook, two twenty and one ten dollar bills.

for sale
Woods, shingles, iron ware, hats, soap, chocolate at the store of Jeremiah Clement at Norwich Landing.

administration of estates
Notice by Mary Palmer, *Administratrix of* the estate of William Palmer to all creditor of, and debtors to, the estate to come forward and settle accounts;

Notice by Executors Jabez Perkins, Executor of the estate of David Lamb of Norwich, to all creditors of, and debtors to, the estate to come forward and settle accounts;

Notice of the sale of all the moveables of the estate of Capt. Jonathan Latimer of New London at his former house.

strayed
from Joseph Arnold of East Haddam, a bay mare.

from William Fanning of Groton, a dark sorrel mare.

runaway
from Abistai Bushnell of Norwich, an apprentice boy named Beriah Hartshorn, a well set man; about 19 years old; five foot nine inches; black hair and black eyes; is somewhat fancy and not a stranger to pride.

found
a parcel of cordage in New London harbor and a few tools; apply to the Printer.

taken up
Notice by Ezra Hall of Lyme that a white sow swine broke into his enclosure some three months past.

to be sold reasonably
A very likely Negro wench; about 27 years of age; a good cook; can wash, iron and do all kinds of housework in the best manner. Inquire of the Printer.

****

From *The Gazette*, July 5, 1776

medical war preparations
The public may be assured that Major John Ely has been ordered by the Governor and Council of Safety of this Colony to remove himself forthwith to the Continental Army, North Department and to take special care of the soldiers there who are sick or exposed to small pox and to take all prudent measures to prevent the spreading of that contagion among the troops.

The Council of Safety has given immediate orders for the taking of stock etc. from the islands lying off New London.

married
in Mansfield, Mr. Luke Flint to Miss Mary Slate, daughter of Ezekiel Slate; an agreeable and happy pair.

died
William Stewart for many years, a merchant in New London;

Mrs. Elizabeth Smith, wife of Nathan Smith of New London, North Parish. She made an early protection of religion and lived in the enjoyment of it all her years. Her death is greatly lamented.

administration of estates
Notice by Judah Storrs, Executor of the estate of Jabez Cleveland of Mansfield to all creditors of, and debtors to, the estate to come forward and settle accounts.

strayed
from Jordan Dodge of Pompret, a mare.

for sale
a few neat muskets suitable for officers in the army to be sold by the Printer.

****

From *The Gazette*, July 12, 1776

In Congress July 4th, 1776
A Declaration
by the Representatives of
The United States of America
Assembled in General Session

When in the Course of human events it becomes necessary for one people to dissolve the political bands which have connected them with another and to assume among the powers of the earth, the separate and equal station to which the Laws of Nature and of Nature's God entitle them, a decent respect to the opinions of mankind requires that they should declare the causes which impel them to the separation.
We hold these truths to be self-evident, that all men are created equal, that they are endowed by their Creator with certain unalienable Rights, that among these are Life, Liberty and the pursuit of Happiness. — That to secure these rights, Governments are instituted among Men, deriving their just powers from the consent of the governed, — That whenever any Form of Government becomes destructive of these ends, it is the Right of the People to alter or to abolish it, and to institute new Government, laying its foundation on such principles and organizing its powers in such form, as to them shall seem most likely to effect their Safety and Happiness. Prudence, indeed, will dictate that Governments long established should not be changed for light and transient causes; and accordingly all experience hath shewn that mankind are more disposed to suffer, while evils are sufferable than to right themselves by abolishing the forms to which they are accustomed. But when a long train of abuses and usurpations, pursuing invariably the same Object evinces a design to reduce them under absolute Despotism, it is their right, it is their duty, to throw off such Government, and to provide new Guards for their future security. — Such has been the patient

sufferance of these Colonies; and such is now the necessity which constrains them to alter their former Systems of Government. The history of the present King of Great Britain is a history of repeated injuries and usurpations, all having in direct object the establishment of an absolute Tyranny over these States. To prove this, let Facts be submitted to a candid world.

He has refused his Assent to Laws, the most wholesome and necessary for the public good.

He has forbidden his Governors to pass Laws of immediate and pressing importance, unless suspended in their operation till his Assent should be obtained; and when so suspended, he has utterly neglected to attend to them.

He has refused to pass other Laws for the accommodation of large districts of people, unless those people would relinquish the right of Representation in the Legislature, a right inestimable to them and formidable to tyrants only.

He has called together legislative bodies at places unusual, uncomfortable, and distant from the depository of their Public Records, for the sole purpose of fatiguing them into compliance with his measures.

He has dissolved Representative Houses repeatedly, for opposing with manly firmness his invasions on the rights of the people.

He has refused for a long time, after such dissolutions, to cause others to be elected, whereby the Legislative Powers, incapable of Annihilation, have returned to the People at large for their exercise; the State remaining in the mean time exposed to all the dangers of invasion from without, and convulsions within.

He has endeavoured to prevent the population of these States; for that purpose obstructing the Laws for Naturalization of Foreigners; refusing to pass others to encourage their migrations hither, and raising the conditions of new Appropriations of Lands.

He has obstructed the Administration of Justice by refusing his Assent to Laws for establishing Judiciary Powers.

He has made Judges dependent on his Will alone for the tenure of their offices, and the amount and payment of their salaries.

He has erected a multitude of New Offices, and sent hither swarms of Officers to harass our people and eat out their substance.

He has kept among us, in times of peace, Standing Armies without the Consent of our legislatures.

He has affected to render the Military independent of and superior to the Civil Power.

He has combined with others to subject us to a jurisdiction foreign to our constitution, and unacknowledged by our laws; giving his Assent to their Acts of pretended Legislation:

For quartering large bodies of armed troops among us:

For protecting them, by a mock Trial from punishment for any Murders which they should commit on the Inhabitants of these States:

For cutting off our Trade with all parts of the world:

For imposing Taxes on us without our Consent:

For depriving us in many cases, of the benefit of Trial by Jury:

For transporting us beyond Seas to be tried for pretended offences:

For abolishing the free System of English Laws in a neighbouring Province, establishing therein an Arbitrary government, and enlarging its Boundaries so as to render it at once an example and fit instrument for introducing the same absolute rule into these Colonies

For taking away our Charters, abolishing our most valuable Laws and altering fundamentally the Forms of our Governments:

For suspending our own Legislatures, and declaring themselves invested with power to legislate for us in all cases whatsoever.

He has abdicated Government here, by declaring us out of his Protection and waging War against us.

He has plundered our seas, ravaged our coasts, burnt our towns, and destroyed the lives of our people.

He is at this time transporting large Armies of foreign Mercenaries to complete the works of death, desolation, and tyranny, already begun with circumstances of Cruelty & Perfidy scarcely paralleled in the most barbarous ages, and totally unworthy the Head of a civilized nation.

He has constrained our fellow Citizens taken Captive on the high Seas to bear Arms against their Country, to become the executioners of their friends and Brethren, or to fall themselves by their Hands.

He has excited domestic insurrections amongst us, and has endeavored to bring on the inhabitants of our frontiers, the merciless Indian Savages whose known rule of warfare, is an undistinguished destruction of all ages, sexes and conditions.

In every stage of these Oppressions We have Petitioned for Redress in the most humble terms: Our repeated Petitions have been answered only by repeated injury. A Prince, whose character is thus marked by every act which may define a Tyrant, is unfit to be the ruler of a free people.

Nor have We been wanting in attentions to our British brethren. We have warned them from time to time of attempts by their legislature to extend an unwarrantable jurisdiction over us. We have reminded them of the circumstances of our emigration and settlement here. We have appealed to their native justice and magnanimity, and we have conjured them by the ties of our common kindred to disavow these usurpations, which would inevitably interrupt our connections and correspondence. They too have been deaf to the voice of justice and of consanguinity. We must, therefore, acquiesce in the necessity, which denounces our Separation, and hold them, as we hold the rest of mankind, Enemies in War, in Peace Friends.

We, therefore, the Representatives of the united States of America, in General Congress, Assembled, appealing to the Supreme Judge of the world for the rectitude of our intentions, do, in the Name, and by Authority of the good People of these Colonies, solemnly publish and declare, That these united Colonies are, and of Right ought to be Free and Independent States, that they are Absolved from all Allegiance to the British Crown, and that all political connection between them and the State of Great Britain, is and ought to be totally dissolved; and that as Free and Independent States, they have full Power to levy War, conclude Peace, contract Alliances, establish Commerce, and to do all other Acts and Things which Independent States may of right do. — And for the support of this Declaration, with

a firm reliance on the protection of Divine Providence, we mutually pledge to each other our Lives, our Fortunes, and our sacred Honor.
Signed on the order of and behalf of the Congress
    John Hancock President
    attest :Charles Thomson Secretary

fire
Last Friday afternoon, a barn belonging to Joseph Witter of Hopkinton, was consumed by lightning.

sloop taken
the sloop *Macaroni* from this town New London to the West Indies has been taken and carried into Halifax.

died
Pygan Adams of New London;

Mrs. Philenach Whiting, widow of Col. John Whiting, late of New London.

strayed
from John Wood, North Quarter of Lyme, a pair of oxen.

stop thief
Notice by Thomas Hall 2d of East Haddam that was stolen from him a horse. The thief has passed by the name of Peter Smith; he also passed under the name Ichabod Peve; he is a young man; of middling stature, of dark complexion with several dark moles on his face.

runaway
from Joseph Farnham, Jr. of Canterbury, a Negro servant man Jack; remarkably well limbed, 29 years of age; five foot seven inches.

               ****

From *The Gazette*, July 19, 1776

died
Mrs. Jervina Estabrook of Millington; 62 years of age, daughter of Isaac Chauncey of Hadley and relict of Rev. Hobart Estabrook; the sermon was preached by Rev. Mr. Parsons of East Haddam.

administration of estates
Notice by John Hempsted, Joseph Hurlbut and Silas Church, Commissioners appointed by the Court of Probate of New London to the creditors of the estate of Patrick Robertson of New London, deceased and represented insolvent; that a meeting will be held at the house where the Edward Palmes, deceased, lived.

strayed
from Jonah Crone of East Haddam, a mare colt.

cash
given for pork by Christopher Leffingwell.

wanted
by Ebenezer and William Ledyard to purchase, a number of yarn stockings for the use of the army.

administration of estates
Notice by William Avery and Thomas Lester, Administrators of the estate of David Lester of Groton, to all creditors of, and debtors to, the estate to come forward and settle accounts.

deserted
Notice by Silas Walker that, from Capt. Butler's Company, Col. Nixon's Regiment, of a Negro deserter named Jack Straing; light complexion; about 36 years old; middling stature; walks clumsy.

letters left at New London post office

Jane Appleby - New London	Israel Ashley - Westbrook

David Barrel - Killingly
E. Bushnell - New London
William Clark - Stonington
Ann Carpenter - New London
Elisha Comstock - New London
Silas Church - New London
Sydney - Norwich -
Molly Dixon - New London
John Fitch - Norwich
Joseph Fitch - Stonington
Thomas Grennel Jr - Norwich
Clement Hayden - Norwich
Jonathan Hakes - Stonington
W. Henderson - New London
Thomas Jones - New London
Lawrence Martin - New London
Joseph Otney - New London
Ichabod Powers - New London
Jeremiah Page - New London
Dr. Perkins - Norwich
-- Shackmaple, - New London
Samuel Smedley - New London
John Sandford - New London
Eleaser Stockwell - Killingly
Oliver Smith - Stonington
Joseph Waterman - New London
William Wheeler - New London
Ephraim Wilcox – Lebanon
Caleb Whitley - Norwich

to be sold
by Joseph Hurlbut and Robinson Mumford, a number of milch cows and yearling cattle lately from Fishers Island.

general merchandise to be sold by Roswell Saltonstall, next to Joseph Hurlbut's in New London.
****

From *The Gazette*, July 26, 1776

Committee of Inspection and Observation
Notice by John Elderkin, Clerk, that the Committee of Inspection and Observation of Groton is to meet ast the house of Jonas Belton Inn holder, in Groton.

New London ship taken
The sloop *Commerce*, Capt. Watrous of this port of New London was seized in her passage from Montserrat. The Captain, who arrived here on last Wednesday, via Nantucket, informs that very few northern vessels escape the vigilance of the British cruisers.

deserted
from Capt. Baldwin's Company of Col. Morris' Regiment, Jonathan Bayh, an old countryman; about 35 years of age; 6 feet high; well built; has been shot through one his sides with a musket ball and has sundry scars on his shins; notice by Ensign Stephen Billings Jr.

eloped
Notice by William Fairfield of Woodstock that his wife Eleanor has, without just cause, left his bed and board and that he is no longer responsible for debts of her contracting.

administration of estates
Notice by James Jones and Susanna Loveland, Administrators to the estate of Capt. John Loveland of Middletown to all creditors of, and debtors to, the estate to come forward and settle accounts.

Notice by John Howard, Samuel Morgan and Jonah Palmer, Commissioners appointed by the Court of Probate of Windham to the creditors of the estate of John Cary of Windham, deceased and represented insolvent; that a meeting will be held at the house of Deacon John Cary in Windham.

for sale
wool and cotton cards, made and sold by John Gates in Groton.

runaway
from Peleg Williams in Groton, an apprentice boy named John Sholes, small of stature; black complexion and black hair and eyes.

****

From *The Gazette,* August 2, 1776

escape from the Cerebrus ,
Since our last arrived here (New London), Capt. Joseph Packwood in an armed sloop from the West Indies with ten tons of powder and between 300 and 400 stands of arms and a quantity of English goods. Last Tuesday arrived here also, Capt. Bigelow from the West Indies. Both vessels were chased by Frigate *Cerebrus,*[35] Capt Simmonds, but had the good fortune to get in safe.

prize taken
Last Friday morning, the vessel *Nathaniel & Elizabeth,* Capt. Hoar, a fine vessel of 250 tons burthen (taken by the brig *Andrea Doria,* Captain Biddle) was chased on the rocks near Watch Hill by the frigate *Cerebrus.* She had on board about 300 hogshead of sugar and about 100 hogshead of rum. , most of the latter is saved, but the sugar, except for six hogsheads, and the vessel is lost.

died
at Newbury Port, the Rev. Jonathan Parsons, one of the ministers of that town;

Mrs. Sarah Holt, wife of John Holt.

to prevent alarm
Notice is hereby given that the cannons of Fort Trumbull in New London Harbor will be proved on Thursday next.

please pay up
Debtors to Jabez Chapman, in co partnership with Richard Christopher of East Haddam, deceased, are desired to make speedy payment.

new tavern
Travelers notified by Christopher Darrow of a house of entertainment, about nine miles from New London on the road to Colchester.

weapons to be sold
at public vendue on Wednesday next, fourteen cannon, three and four pounders, 17 swivels and a number of muskets, pistols cutlasses etc.

administration of estates
Notice by Lohn Leray, Executor of the estate of Nicholas Longfeffis of Stonington to all creditors of, and debtors to, the estate to come forward and settle accounts.

deserted
from Capt. Baldwin's Company in Col. Mott's Regiment; John Noles, a well built fellow; 23 years of age; five feet ten inches high; notice given by Lt. William Calkins;

from Capt Rowley's Company of Col. Swift's Regiment, Joseph Moory, belonging to Colchester; he is about five feet, ten inches high; middling well set; light complexion; one of his ankles crooked.; notice given by Lt. Samuel Hassard Jr.;

from Capt Richard Deshon's Company in Col. Selden Regiment; a man who calls himself John Homes; said to belong to Westerly or South Kingston and lately dismissed from the Northern Department; he enlisted at Mr. Horton's in the North Parish of New London in another company under the name Williams; five nine or ten inches high; well set; has short black curled hair, something gray; pretty bald; 41 years of age.

****

From *The Gazette,* August 9, 1776

lightning hit
On Thursday night, the new ship of war for the colony, which was being built at Saybrook, was struck by lighting which did considerable damage to her main and mizzen mast.

prize taken
Capt. William Chace sent to Newport a ship from Dominica ,bound for England, with 300 hogsheads of sugar and 100 barrels of oil.

patriotic older men
Last Monday was viewed in this Town (Southampton) a very agreeable prospect. The old gentlemen, grandfathers to the age of 70 and upwards met, by prior agreement, and formed themselves into an independent company. Each man was well equipped with a good musket, powder, ball , cartridges etc. and unanimously made choice of Elias Pelletreau for their leader (with other suitable officers) who made an very animating address of the necessity keeping themselves in readiness to call into the field in time of readiness. They all cheerfully agreed to it and determined at the risk of their lives to defend the free and independent states of America. May such a stirring example inspire every other father in Long Island in particular and in America in general to follow their aged brethren here.

trial, conviction and recantation
Mr. Ira Bushnell of Saybrook, being complained of by the Committee of Inspection of that town for refusing to take in tender bills issued by the Continental Congress and saying that "they were not of legal tender and were such the stuff that Congress called money" and several other sundry expressions tending to depreciate those bills. The witnessers being heard in support of the allegations, the Committee deemed them fully proved and adjourned the meeting until the 25th of July. At such adjourned meeting, Ira Bushnell submitted his confession to the Committee . He acknowledged himself at blame and is heartedly

sorry for it and in then future always endeavor to keep up the credit of those bills in every way withing his power, meaning in all respects to conform to the regulations and establishment of the honorable Congress.

to be sold
at the store of Nathaniel Shaw, Jr of New London, coffee, ginger, sugar, cotton and pimento – also a number of cannon.

warning
To give notice and prevent an alarm, notice is hereby given that the cannons of the fort at Trumbull in Groton will be proved on Thursday next, if the weather permits and, if not, the first proper day thereafter.

tax collection
Notice to those in New London who have not paid their taxes for 1776 that Collector of Taxes, George Douglas, will be at the at the houses of the following on the dates stated.:
Nathan Douglas, Monday the 2nd next
James Houghton, Tuesday the 3rd next
Joshua Raymond, Wednesday the 4th
Jason Allen Thursday the 5th
Nicholas Bishop, Friday the 6th
Thomas Durfey Saturday the 7th

administration of estates
Notice by Daniel Clark, Executor of the estate of Roger Clark of Colchester to all creditors of, and debtors to, the estate to come forward and settle accounts; a meeting to be held at house of Darius Clark in Colchester.

General Hospital in New York
Wanted for the use of the army a large supply of dried herbs particularly balm, hyssop, wormwood and mallows for which a good price will be given; also clean linen for the use of the sick and wounded. From principles of humanity and benevolence, it is presumed that many will attend to the matter. And as soon

medicine s will be very scarce, the collecting and curing of various herbs will greatly help and promote the health of the arms and considerable benefit themselves as the best prices will be given.

strayed
from John Beckwith of Lyme, a dark brown mare.
****

From *The Gazette,* August 16, 1776

emancipation of slaves
Lately published and selling by Judah P. Spooner at his printing office near Christopher Leffingwell's in Norwich, a dialogue of the slavery of the Africans showing it to be the duty and interest of the American colonies to emancipate all their African slaves; with an address to the owners of said slaves dedicated to the Continental Congress.

died
At Preston last Sabbath, Mrs. Abigail Mott, consort of Samuel Mott;

In East Haddam, Joseph Sluman, Justice of the Probate Court, Westmoreland.

wanted
by Andrew Huntington of Norwich, for the use of the army, a quantity of wool and home made cloths for soldiers coats.

administration of estates
Notice by David West, Executor of the estate of Amos Randall, late of East Haddam to all creditors of, and debtors to, the estate to come forward and settle accounts.

Notice by Ralph Stoddard, Nathan Gallup, Amos Geer, Commissioners appointed by the Court of Probate of Stonington, to the creditors of to the estate of David Lester, late of Groton, deceased and represented insolvent, that a meeting will be held at the house of Jonas Belton of Groton.

no longer responsible
William Bradford of Canterbury will no longer be responsible for any obligations by his wife, Abigail, who has left his bed and board.

cash given for feathers
by Nathan Douglas at the *Sign of the Golden Ball* in New London.

soap for sale
hard and soft soaps and candles made and sold, retail or wholesale, by Archibald Robertson. Cash given for ashes.[36]

printing
All types of printing on types and copper plating, done with neatness and expedition. Inquire of the Printer.

****

From *The Gazette,* August 23, 1776

war ship launched
Last Lord's Day, the new ship of war of the State of Connecticut, built in Saybrook and captained by William Coit, came out of the river and arrived here in New London on Tuesday. She is the largest vessel ever to come over the Saybrook bar and was piloted by Capt. James Harris.

neighbors' support
This may certify to all persons that the advertisement in the *Connecticut Gazette* against Eleanor Fairfield by William Fairfield of Woodstock is unjust and cruel, that her leaving him was of his cruelty, that her swearing the peace against him was for her own safety, that she is a dutiful wife when used with humanity, a kind and tender mother and a good neighbor, who sustains a good character, although now abject and miserable by her husband's conduct.

signed by 18 credible persons in the neighbor where she lives

David Williams	Abigail Griggs
Thomas Shapely	Sarah Griggs
Ephraim Griggs	Hannah Griggs
Stephen Griggs	Mary Holmes
William Holmes	Bulah Holmes
Thomas Fox	Mary Fox
Joseph Ormsbee	Lucretia Smith
Elizabeth Williams	Mahetabel Bowen
Abigail Williams	
Joanne Shapely	

died
Mrs. Hannah Harris, widow Capt Peter Harris.

administration of estates
Notice by Silas Church Jr., Administrator of the estate of Capt. Edward Palmes of New London to all creditors of, and debtors to, the estate to come forward and settle accounts.

blacksmith's shop to be sold
a convenient blacksmith's shop in New London, well situated for a tradesman at the lower end of the New London town plot; a small convenient barn, standing a few rods from said shop; a complete set of blacksmith's tools including an anvil, vise, bink, iron, bellows sedges, hammers, tongs, pincers etc; inquire of Marvin Wait.

liver oil
for curriers and skinners to be sold by Joshua Starr in New London.

raisins, indigo, nutmeg
to be sold at the Printer's Office; also women shoes, Barcelona handkerchiefs, silk, calico, needles; also writing paper, fine and superfine.

taken up
by Samuel Androws of Groton, a sorrel horse.
****

From *The Gazette,* August 30, 1776

married
Capt, John Welch of Philadelphia to Nancy Hurlbot, daughter of Capt. Joseph Hurlbot of New London.

died
David Harris of New London.

taken up
by Widow Grace Fosdick in New London, a stray horse.

two men broke out of goal in New London
Notice by Ephraim Miner that John Evins, a short, thick set, man, about 40 years old, dark complexion, black hair large scar on face and very large scar on nose; very bold; and Matthew Thomison; tall, light complexion, black hair, looks pale, 30 to 40 years of age.
****

From *The Gazette,* September 6, 1776

the Battle of Long Island
On Tuesday se'nnight, a number of ships with troops on board sailed from the British Fleet at Staten Island through the Narrows and, the next day, were followed by many more. Next morning, a number of troops, thought to be 10,000, landed between New Utrecht and Gravesend on Long Island.[37] On Friday, an advanced party took possession of Flatbush, where our people having possession of the surrounding heights, kept a continued, although irregular, fire upon them, but at too great a distance to do much execution. However, some were killed and wounded on both sides, the enemy keeping up an almost constant fire upon our people from mortars and field pieces loaded with grape shot. On Sunday, they covered the landing of more men on Long

island, when a great number of our people went over to strengthen our posts and oppose the enemy.

Monday night, our people began to throw up entrenchments on the highest hill near Flatbush, which would have commanded the town, but the enemy the same night have formed a plan to take the hill. It is said that both parties met and a smart engagement between then began at about 4 am in the morning with severe skirmishes, between many detached parties, and continued Tuesday and Wednesday, during which many were killed, wounded, taken prisoner on both sides and several are missing. Who kept possession of the hill at Flatbush where the flag is still flying, we have not heard. The enemy attempted several times to force our lines but were always repulsed with considerable slaughter, notwithstanding their superiority in point of disciple and an extended front.

From the best accounts, we learn that the force of the Ministerial army on Staten island and Long Island is about 23,500 men, number of Marines unknown. The fleet consists oft the following Ships *Asia* and *Eagle*, of 64 guns, the *Roebuck* and *Phoenix* of 44, one bomb and about 20 frigates and sloops of war. They also have about 300 sail of transports, store ships and prizes

We learn Col. Huntington's Regiment from Connecticut suffered greatly at the engagement at Long Island.

Council of Safety
Last Wednesday, the Council of Safety of the State of Connecticut met in this town (New London) on some affairs of importance.

refugees from Long Island
Numbers of the distressed inhabitants who are friendly to America have arrived at this place (New London)and other towns on the seacoast.

privateers
Last Tuesday three privateers - two sloops and a schooner - commanded by the Captains Rogers, Pond and Clarke, arrived

here in New London from Fire Island inlet on the south side of Long Island, where they had at different times carried in eleven prizes - one ship, two brigs, one schooner and seven sloops. The cargoes of these vessels had been carried to Huntington and is now in the possession of the enemy.

died
Mrs. Elizabeth Latimer, widow of Mr. Samuel Latimer;

died, at the house of James Tiley of Hartford, Miss Hannah Sanford, aged 26, daughter of Thoms Sanford of Bridgehamton on Long Island.

lost
Notice by Robert Herrick of Canterbury that he lost last Tuesday between Norwich Landing and Christopher Leffingewell's Tavern on the Plain, a plain leather, double folded pocketbook.

tea, snuff
and sundry sorts of dry goods to be sold by Asa Spaulding in Stonington.

****

From *The Gazette,* September 13, 1776

company of seniors
We hear from Canterbury that a number of aged and respectable gentlemen of that town have agreeable to the advice of the Honorable General Assembly of the State, formed themselves into a body or military company and have made choice unanimously of Timothy Backus for their leader. One thing worthy of notice is that the Hon. Jabez Fitch, has enlisted as a private in that company. May all the gentlemen of this State follow their noble and patriotic example.

prize taken
Yesterday, returned here (New London) from a cruise , the armed schooner *Spy*, Capt. Robert Niles, belonging to the State of

Connecticut, and he brought in with him the schooner *Mary and Elizabeth,* bound for Halifax from Barbados.

help in evacuation
All persons who have any demands for supplying vessels etc. in bringing the inhabitants from Long Island, we desire to bring them to the subscibers, a sub committee appointed by the several committees of Correspondence and Inspection of New London and Groton.
Thomas Mumford, Robinson Mumford and Marvin Wait

died
at Preston, Mrs. Abigail Rosseter, consort to the Rev. Rosseter of that place.

deserted
from Col. Selden's Regiment, William Sherman; he uses the alias Samuel Sherman; aged 40 years, well built; about five feet six inches high; his ear locks something gray; notice given by Ens. Asa Strong.

runaway
from Francis Clark of the lower part of Middletown, a Negro servant man called Dick; 21 years of age; five foot six inches high; had a scar on the instep of one foot occasioned by a cut; return to subscriber or Deacon Joseph Clark in Middletown.

administration of estates
Notice by Amos Stack and William Stack, Executors of the estate of Samuel Stack of Stonington, to all creditors of, and debtors to, the estate to come forward and settle accounts;

Notice by Amos Stack and William Stack, Executors of the estate of William Stack of Stonington, to all creditors of, and debtors to, the estate to come forward and settle accounts.

to be sold
a vessel 165 tons , a good molded vessel for fishing; also a sloop of 65 ton well built for sailing. Apply to George Sheffield in Stonington or James Sheffield in Westerly.

wanted
by William Cox of Hebron to lease a house and small farm, suitably situated for a cooper and land sufficient to keep two cows and a score of sheep, for which payment will be made at year end.

came into
the enclosure of Martin Cone of East Haddam, six sheep, three of which are white and three black.

****

From *The Gazette, S*eptember 20, 1776

sale of cattle and sheep taken from Long Island
We, the subscribers, having been appointed to make sale of the cattle and sheep which have lately been taken off Long Island, which are now in this town (New London.) All said cattle for which no owner shall appear before October next will be sold at public vendue at Mr. Winthrop's, by order of the Committee of Inspection.
John Hempsted and Joseph Hurlbut

better communication needed
In consequence of the resolution of Congress, for more frequent and speedy communication of Intelligence, William Goddard , Surveyor of the General Post Office, arrived here in New London on his way to those Northern states in order to carry it into immediate execution.

off on assignment
Last Friday, the Hon. Gurdun Saltonstall of this Town (New London), who is appointed Brigadier General of the Militia of this State, set out for New York, accompanied by Gilbert Saltonstall, who is appointed Brigadier Major in said Militia.

new postal rider
Jeremiah Pollard advises the public that he intends to ride Post from New England to New York and will deliver and receive letters from Groton at Lt. Nehamiah's Smith's; in Preston, at Dr Joshua Downes and at this own house at Poquonnock.

strayed
from Ebenezer Witter 2d in Preston, a 3 year old heifer;

from Oliver Spicer in Groton, about a month ago, two bulls.

Suttonian Inoculation
Mr. Latham, inoculator for the small pox, acquaints the public that accommodations are ready in this Town, New London, for the reception of strangers.
As small pox has prevailed so much lately and seems likely to spread, Mr. Latham informs the public that, if any town having leave from the General Court to set up inoculating, that he or one of his partners will wait on their application; Mr. Latham is at Capt. Wheeler's of New London or Timothy Hubbard's in Sheffield.

excellent claret
to be sold by the bottle; inquire of the Printing office.

runaway
from Pember Calkins of New London, an apprentice girl named Lucretia Crocker; well set; between 16 and 17 years old; light complexion; sandy hair and freckled.

stockings and shoes needed
Thomas Mumford of Groton pays a good price in cash for any quantity of good yarn stockings and well made men's shoes; also for striped and checked flannel.

clothier
Elias Peck of Colchester carries on the clothier business and weaving and dressing of plaid.

deserted
from Capt. Vincent Elderkin's Comapny in Col. Mott's Regiment Jonathan Mansfield; of middling stature; light complexion; down look with eyes.

****

From *The Gazette,* September 27, 1776

soldier slain and captured
Maj. James Chapman of this Town (New London) a worthy and good gentleman fell in the late battle near New York.
Col. Samuel Selden of Lyme was taken prisoner in New York, the day the City was evacuated by our troops.

New York City burned
At 11 o'clock last Friday, a fire broke out in the city of New York, which is said to have consumed near a third part of the City. We hear it was seen to take fire in twelve different places at nearly the same time.[38]

strayed
from John Robinson in New London, a large sorrel mare.

meeting
Notice by John Elderkin, Clerk, that a meeting of the Committee of Inspection and Observation for the Town of Groton will be held at the house of Charles Smith, Inn holder in said Groton.

****

From *The Gazette,* October 4, 1776

duel at sea
Yesterday noon, Capt. Harding in the *Defense* privateer arrived from a cruise. The same morning at Naraganset Bay, he fell in with two British frigates who fired 60 or 70 shots at him and he returned a like number. At about two o'clock yesterday, the frigates came to anchor off Goshen Reef about five miles westward of this harbor (New London).

to be sold
by Zabdiel Rogers & Co. 500 bushels of good salt by small quantities.

strayed
from Obidiah Havens, late of Shelter Island, a dark brown horse; if found, it is requested that it be brought to the Green Plumb;

from John Gates of Groton, a chestnut sorrel mare.

****

From *The Gazette,* October 11 1776

sale of prize vessels and cargo
Notice given by Winthrop Saltonstall, Register, that the libel filed before Richard Law against the schooner *Hannah and Elizabeth*, about 45 tons, lately commanded by Ronald Bruce, said vessel belonging to subjects of the King of Great Britain, taken as it sailed from the island of Barbados loaded with rum and sugar and bound for Halifax; and brought to New London by Robert Niles in the armed schooner *Spy;* that a hearing will be held on the 6th of November.

notice by Tax Collector
Ichabod Eccleston, Tax Collector, advises all the inhabitants of Groton that he will meet with them at the following places at the times specified to receive their taxes:
at Capt. John Denison's, Long Pointon on Monday, the 21$^{s;t}$
at Col. Giles Russel's on Tuesday, the 22nd;
at Asa Champlin's on Wednesday, the 23rd;
at John York's on Monday, the 4th of November
at Charles Wheeler's on Tuesday, the 5$^{th;}$
at Capt. Robert Swan's on Wednesday, the 6th;
at Capt. Richard Hewit's on Thursday, the 7

sale of cargo of prize
Notice by Prosper Wetmore that a parcel of Jamaican spirits and sugar, part of the ship *Nathaniel & Elizabeth's* cargo will be sold in New London, per the order of the Maritime Court; Winthrop. Saltontall, Register

cash
to given for flak seed and oats by William Hubbard at his store at Norwich Landing.

lost
on the road from Westfield in the Massachusetts Bay colony to New London, a lease and release from Daniel Whipple of Brattleborough to William Rogers of New London for 134 acres of land.

deserted
from the ship *Oliver Cromwell* lying in the New London harbor, an Indian named Oliver Blossom; said he was born at Montauk; he is tall and straight limbed; pitted with small pox; pretty talkative; notice by William Coit.

meeting called
Committees of Correspondence and Inspection are desired to meet at the Courthouse in New London on some matters of importance
M. Wait, Clerk

administration of estates
Notice by Lois Hillard, Executrix of the estate of Lt. Joseph Hillard, late of Stonington, to all creditors of, and debtors to, the estate to come forward and settle accounts;

Notice by Ephraim Kingsbury and Sarah Kingsbury Executors of the estate of Dr. Obidiah Kingsbury, late of Norwich, to all creditors of, and debtors to, the estate to come forward and settle accounts.

prizes retaken
Last Tuesday, two prize snows were retaken by two British Men of War in a fight in Stonington harbor. One of them had been a prize that had been taken by a Providence privateer, captained by James Munro; the other had been taken by a privateer of the State of Rhode Island. We learn that the people got to shore in their boats.

rum and molasses
to be sold by Rufus Tuthill, back of the Church in New London.

slave for sale
to be sold by Silas Church Jr. of New London, a likely Negro wench, about 22 years old, and her child, about six months old.

taken up
by Joseph Wait of Lyme, a cow.

strayed
from Jonathan Minard of Lyme, a pale red cow.

****

From *The Gazette,* October 18, 1776

troops arrive
Last Monday, a regiment of Continental Army troops, commanded by Col. Richmond, arrived here (New London) from Rhode Island.

spies caught
Last Saturday, the wife and daughter of one John Hill, confined as a prisoner in Boston for being concerned with Cream Brush and others in robbing the inhabitants of Boston, when that place was evacuated, came to this town (New London) from Providence by water and were endeavoring to get a passage to the west end of Long Island, but were stopped by the Committee of this town and, upon examination, were found to have upon them, sundry papers concerning matters of intelligence respecting the people and state of that country, send by said Hill and others, to be communicated with General Howe. It appeared from the papers found that they had been other papers in their possession which they either secured or destroyed. They were both sent back with the papers, under a proper convoy to the place from whence they came.

fire in Killingsworth
Last week, a large dwelling house in Killingsworth, which belonged to the late Maj. Buell of that Town took fire and was consumed.

died
Last Saturday, at Middletown, Edward Eells, Pastor of the Church of that Town.

evacuation
From *The New York Mercury*, we are informed from a gentleman, just escaped from New England, that it was learned that the rebels lately carried hundreds of head of cattle from the eastern end of Long Island to New London in Connecticut and that their privateers are very business in negotiating this kind of business.

new members of General Assembly
The following gentlemen were chosen members of the General Assembly:

for New London: Nathaniel Shaw, Jr. and William Hillhouse;
for Norwich: Rufus Lathrop and Benjamin Huntington;
for Groton :P. Avery and John Hurlbut;
for Killingsorth: Hezekiah Lane and Capt. Samuel Gale;
for Stonington: Capt..Daniel Fish and Joshua Prentice;
for Lyme: John Lay and Marshfield Parsons;
for Saybrook: Samuel Field and Capt. Benj. Williams;
for Windham: Jabez Huntington and Capt. Ebenezer Mosely;
Lebanon: John Clark and Capt. Joshua West;
for Plainfield: Elisha Perkins and Joshua Dunap;
for Pomfret: Thomas Williams and Nathan Frink;
forCanterbury: David Pain and Eliasha Adams;
for Woodstock: Samuel M'Lallen and Capt. Timothy Perrin;
for Mansfield: Constant Southward and Edmund Freeman
for Killingly: Simon Learned and Benjamin Leavings;
for Coventry: Ebenezer Kingsbury and Abraham Burr;
for Ashford: Capt. Benjamin Clark and Capt. Elisha Wales.

permits required
Whereas the frequent passing of vessels, boats or other water craft between this and the neighboring States and Towns may serve the purpose of conveying person inimical and Intelligence and Effects detrimental to the United Stayes of America, unless care be taken to prevent it, for which purpose the several Committees of Correspondence and Inspection for the Towns of New London and Groton have directed that the owner of vessels, boats or other water craft that shall convey any persons, effects, letters or Intelligence to any other of the States or to any other Towns in this state without first applying for and receiving a permit from two or more of us the subscribers, a subcommittees appointed for that purpose

Nathaniel Shaw Jr.
MarvinWait
Robinson Mumford
Thomas Harris
Griswold Avery

William Ledyard,
Thomas Mumford
David Avery
Joseph Packer

libels filed
Notice given by Winthrop Saltonstall, Register that a hearing will be held on the libel filed before Richard Law against the ship *Adventure*, lately commanded by Richard Chapman, 210 tons, and said to belong to subjects of the Kings of Great Britain, not of Bermuda or the Bahama islands, loaded with rum and sugar; said vessel was taken and brought to Stonington by Thomas Nickelson of the armed brig *Defense*.

Notice given by Winthrop Saltonstall, Register that a hearing will be held on November 4 next on the libel filed before Richard Law against the ship *Sally,* 250 tons, commanded by William Jackson, and said to belong to subjects of the Kings of Great Britain, not of Bermuda or the Bahama islands, loaded with rum and sugar; said vessel was taken and brought to New London by Capt. Seth Harding in the armed sloop *America*.

Notice given by Winthrop Saltonstall, Register that a hearing will be held on the second Monday of November next on the libel filed before Richard Law against the ship *John*, James Dunbar, Master, and said to belong to subjects of the Kings of Great Britain, not of Bermuda or the Bahama islands, loaded with rum and sugar; said vessel was taken and brought to New London by Capt. Seth Harding in the armed Brig *Defense*.

strayed
from Samuel Wolcott of New London a sorrel mare;

from Orange Webb, late of Long Island, two swine.

slave for sale
Likely Negro boy, about 16 years old, to be sold by Orange Webb, late of Long Island.

deserted
from the 5th Company in the 3d Regiment, Samuel Billings, belonging to New London; notice given by Ensign Benj. Atwell.

administration of estates
Notice by John Hempsted, Joseph Hurlbut, and Silas Church, Commissioners to all creditors of, and debtors to, the estate of Patrick Robertson of New London, that a meeting to be held at the house of Capt. Edward Palmes, deceased, in said New London.

wanted
A journey man at the goldsmith's business; such a person may have constant employment and receive punctual pay; inquire of the Printer.

****

From *The Gazette,* October 25, 1776

book store opened
Samuel Loudon, late printer and bookseller in New York, has just opened in Norwich at the store of Capt. Jedidiah Huntington to be sold there by Eliphalet Huntington, maps of the world including Africa, Europe, South and North America; pictures and a large assortment of books.

cash given
for feathers or feather beds by Noble Hinman in New London; he would be glad to hire 5 or 6 beds and allow a good price for their use; also excellent claret by the bottle to be sold by said Hinman.

for good sheep skins, well tanned and curried, by Ebenezer Loomis, Card Maker at Norwich.

administration of estates
Notice by David Gardner, Executor of the estate of Benjamin Gardner of Norwich, to all creditors of, and debtors to, the estate to come forward and settle accounts.

taken up
in Colchester by James Kelly, a two year old steer.

found
a man's hunting saddle on the Meeting House hill in New London; apply to the Green Plumb in New London.

strays
from Christopher Leffingwell of Norwich, a black horse;

list of strayed cattle from people from Long Island in the care of Robert Denison in Stonington, John Burrows in Groton and Joseph Packer in Groton.

****

From *The Gazette*, November 1, 1776

to be sold
by David Beldings at the house of the widow Martha Hosmer in East Haddam, choice sugar, coffee and chocolate. Said Beldings gives cash for checked flannel, bees wax, yarn stockings and clean linen or cotton rags.

wanted
by Azariah Lathrop, near the meeting house in Norwich, a quantity of mustard seed.

appointment
The. Hon. Richard Law is appointed a delegate to represent the state in the Continental Congress in addition to those chosen last year, who are reelected to that important trust.

died
Wednesday evening died here suddenly, Mrs. Rebecca Saltonstall, consort to the Hon. Gurdon Saltonstall of New London.

wanted
Zabiel Rogers & Co. pay cash for pork and oats and a generous price at their store in Norwich.

oil and curry
by the barrel to be sold by Joshua Starrs in New London.

taken up
by David Rogers of New London, Great Neck, a red heifer;

by Gideon Southward of Chester in Saybrook, a white hog;

by John Parsons of New London, a chestnut colored cow;

by Peter Crary on Stonington Long Point, a sorrel horse.

strayed or stolen
from the pasture of Robinson Mumford of New London, a sorrel mare; notice by Samuel Tozer, Colchester;

from Jonathan Tuthill living on Stewart's Wharf in New London, a large white hog.

deserted
from Capt. Deshon's Company of the late Col. Shelden's Regiment, James Taylor, belonging to Somers, Connecticut; he is a large well set man; notice given by Lt. Edward Hallam.

notice of moving business
These are to inform the public that John Hudson, late of Sag Harbor, Tanner and Currier, has removed to Long Point in Stonington where he carries on the business of currying and making women's heels. He also takes this method to inform Thomas Deering of Sag Harbor and Reil Howell of Southampton that they can have their leather by sending for it

****

From *The Gazette*, November 8, 1776

enemy off shore
Four of the enemy ships are cruising near Block Island *viz*. *Lark*, 32 guns, Smith, Master; *Cerebrus* 28 guns, Symonds; Master; *Merlin* 18 guns and another ship of 28 guns.

died
Lately died, at his house on Long Island, Cadwalader Golden for many years Lt. Governor.

to be sold
cargo of ship *John* to be sold at Norwich Landing.

cash and a good generous price
will be given by Christopher Leffingwell at his store in Norwich for good hogsheads, hoops, white oak and barrel staves.

to be sold
by David Palmer of Groton a farm lying in Westerly in Rhode Island.

taken up
by Daniel Ashcraft on Fisher's Island, a spar, supposed intended for a ship.

costs for moving refugees from Long Island
The sub committee chosen to adjust the accounts for removing inhabitants and affects from Long Island to New London and Groton will meet for the last time at Mr. Wait's Writing Room.

wanted
two or three journeyman cordwainers who can be well recommended; apply to Consider Chase at Stonington Long Point.

runaway
from Thomas Avery of Groton a boy named Nathan Smith; about 13 years old; short and thick set; four feet, three inches high.

broke out of goal
in Windham five prisoners of the Continental Army:
David Wardrop surgeon, a Scotchman, speaks broad, about five feet ten inches high; between 20 and 30 years old; of a sandy complexion; wears his own hair and walks with his knees wide asunder;
Richard Tillage, a midshipman between 20 and 30 years old; wears his own hair of a light brown color and long; is an Englishman; he is a well set man;
Samuel George a marine; a lusty well set man about 30 years old;
James Bussel; has a bushy head of hair, long foretop small legs and thighs; is a worsted comber;
Joseph Reed, a short thick set fellow; about 22 years old; walks quick and nimble, wears his own hair of light brown color; notice by Nathaniel Hebard, Goal keeper.

Long Island sheep
brought from Southold in the schooner *Sally* , by Capt. Oliver Coit and left in the care of Thoms Mumford of Groton, sixty sheep. The owners are desired to call for them in ten days or they will be sold.

taken up
by John Perkins a white hog in Lyme.
****

From *The Gazette*, November 15, 1776

list of letters at New London Post Office

Joshua Bradley - New London	Mary Bowers - Stonington
	Capt. Samuel Chew - New

London
Dr. Benjamin Chapin - New London
Ann Carpenter - New London
Alpheus Chapman - North Parish, New London
Abram Chapman - New London
William Clark - New London
Widow Sarah Copp - Stonington
Sarah Chancy - New London
Molly Dimon - New London
Jacob Fowler - Groton
Jonathan Foster - New London
Wm Fargo - New London
Obadiah Gildersleeve - Sag Harbor
Thomas Gatt - Groton
Abraham Gardner - Stonington
Chrisitian Gosner - New London
Monsieur Girand - New London
William Henderson - New London
School Master - New London
William Harris - New London
Alex Hopkins - New London
Amos Hallam Jr - Stonington
Joseph Jeffrey - New London
Capt. Wiiliam Knot - New London
Capt. Thomas Kennedy - New London
Eliphalet Lester - New London
Matthew McFee - New London
Robert McClury - New London
Mrs. McNeil - New London
Alex. McKenzie - New London
Zebediah Mix - New London
Nathaniel Miner - Stonington
Daniel Newbury - New London
Joseph Olney - New London
Capt. Nathan - Palmer Stonington
Lemeul Pierson - Stonington
Joseph Packwood - New London
Abigail Potter - New London
Benjamin Paine - Southhold
Capt. Daniel Starr - New London
Elizabeth Sullivan - New London
Edward Tinker - New London
William Wheeler - New London
Thomas Worrell - New London

James Willson - New - London
Georg Wils - New London

Charles Wheeler - Stonington

left
at Sag harbor wharf and brought to Groton, a small bed and some wearing apparel: a red cloak; inquire Robert Sheffield.

embargo
An embargo is laid against the exportation out of this State provisions as woolen clothes suitable for clothing for the army.

to be sold
by Marvin Wait, the *Bachelor*, being a schooner of 25 tons burthen with her appurtenances, sails etc.

broke out of the goal
Notice by Nathaniel Hebard, goal keeper at Windham, that two Continental Army prisoners, Lt. Edward Sneyd; about 22 years of age; of middling stature; slim built; wears his own brown hair; has a little fuzz beard on his upper lip and stutters; and William Cook, a tall young man about 20 years of age; wears his own hair of a dark brown color; many pimples on his face. There also escaped with them two other prisoners. One, John Russel, is of a dark complexion, with dark colored hair which curls; the other is John Coggin, a rough looking fellow; both seamen.

sale of seized cargos
The public are desired to take notice that on Thursday the 21 instant, will begin the sale of the ship *Adventurer* and her cargo of rum, sugar, molasses, cotton wool, mahogany and wines as per Prosper Wetmore, Marshal;

The public are desired to take notice that on the 27th instant, will begin the sale of the ship *John* and her and cargo of rum, sugar molasses, cotton and wool, as per Prosper Wetmore, Marshall;

The public are desired to take notice that on the 3rd of December 27th instant, will begin the sale of the ship *Sally*, her appurtenances and cargo as per Prosper Wetmore, Marshall.

strayed
from Thomas Williams in Groton, a two year old steer.

cash and a good price
given for hides by Mark Newton in Groton.

items stolen
Notice by Ephraim Whitmore of Canterbury that stolen from him were assorted personal items and some notes from others including one on Daniel Davis in Killingly for 6 pounds seven shillings and another on Ebenezer Blancher; on the sale of a score of sheep; thief's name unknown but was of rather small stature; light complexion and had on a sailor's dress of green trousers.

wanted
William Stewart wants to buy a quantity of hoops and staves for which he will pay cash.

monies due
Notice by Capt. Theo. Standon that there are several open accounts on the *Shark* galley and would ask they be paid at the house of Abiel Cheneny in Norwich or at Capt. Denison's in Stonington or at Capt. Douglass' in Norwich Landing.

libel filed
Notice given Winthrop Saltonstall, Register, that the libel filed before Richard Law against the ship *Claredon*, her tackle appurtenances, cargo etc , John Denison, Master, and belonging to subjects of the King of Great Britain and not of Bermuda or the Bahama Island; she was taken by the *Brig Cabot*, Elisha Hinman Master and brought to New London.

pills to be sold
Anderson's Pills to be sold at six shillings a box by Nobel Hinman in New London.

administration of estates
Notice by Commissioners A. Adams and Isaac Stevens, appointed by the Court of Probate of Plainfield, to the creditors of the estate of T. Ensworth, late of Canterbury; deceased and represented insolvent, that a meeting will be held at the house of Timothy Backus, Inn holder at Canterbury.

****

From *The Gazette*, November 22, 1776

corn husking
On the 18th of September last, several of the most respectable ladies in the Town of East Haddam, to the number of 30, met in the afternoon at Jabez Chapman's and husked, in about four or five hours, about 240 bushels of corn. A noble example and worthy of imitation by the ladies of other towns and societies around us. I hope that examples of this kind will animate some, who perhaps would think it beneath them to stoop so low as to assist the farmer in tilling the ground and gathering the fruits of the earth, which is so necessary to do for the salvation of our bleeding country.

mother and infant son die
The amiable and virtuous wife of Dr. Eliot Rawson of Middletown was seized with a faint turn, last Friday about 5 o'clock and expired a little after six the next morning in the 39th year of her age, leaving three promising sons, three pretty daughters.
Her youngest son of three days old died about Noon.

an Act for the punishment of High Treason
At a General Assembly, held in New Haven, an Act was passed entitled "An Act for the punishment of High Treason and other atrocious conduct."
If any persons belonging to or residing within the state and under the protection of its laws, shall levy war against the State or

government thereof and knowingly aid or assist any enemies to open war against this State or the United States of America by joining their armies or by enlisting, procuring, persuading others to enlist for that purpose or by furnishing such enemies with arms, ammunition or of any other article for their aid and comfort or by carrying on traitorous correspondence with them or shall form, or in any way be concerned in forming of, any combination, plot or conspiracy for betraying this State and shall give attempt to give or send intelligence to the enemies of this State for that purpose; every person s so offending and being thereof convicted, shall suffer death.

to be sold or let
a large dwelling house with a good cellar, garden and being in being in the East Society of Norwich, about two miles from the Landing Place on the road that leads to Preston. Inquire of Joseph Wight on the premises or Phineas Holden at said Landing.

strayed
from Joshua Stanton of Stonington, a black mare.

taken up
by Nathan Douglass, a black horse;

by Daniel Holt of New London, a dark red cow;

by Collins Corton of New London, Great Neck, a reddish cow.

stolen
from Joseph Waterman Inn holder in New London, a large silver spoon marked with the maker's name "J. Copp"–.

found
by Thomas Jones in New London, a bay mare.

wanted
at the stocking factory at Norwich, a quantity of single worsted and linen yarn, likewise coarse woolen yarn; cash will be given at

the store of Christopher Leffingwell or at said Factory by William Russel.

two journeymen cordwainers. Inquire of Nathaniel Rogers in New London.

slave for sale
to be sold a likely Negro wench, healthy and strong, used to all kinds of housework with her male child, about 4 years of age. The above wench is sold for no fault, the owner at present having no employ for her. Inquire of Obadiah Haven, late of Shelter Island now residing at Pechanga in Saybrook or James Havens in New London.

administration of estates
Notice by Ralph Stoddard, Nathan Gallup and Amos Geer, Commissioners appointed by the Court of Probate of Stonington, to the creditors of to the estate of David Lester, deceased and represented insolvent, that a meeting will be held at the house of Jonas Belton, Inn holder at Groton.
****

From *The Gazette*, November 29, 1776

RESOLVED
at the General Assembly, held in New Haven, that there be provided in this Town as soon as possible for the use of the Militia thereof when called into actual service, the following articles of camp equipage and utensils – namely, two thousand tents, two thousand iron pots containing two gallons each, 4,000 wooden bowls and 6,000 canteens or wooden bottles;
Resolved further that each tent contain the quantity of 27 yards of cloth , one yard wide, well manufactured of yarn not scarcer than 30 knot to the pound
George Wyllys, Sec.

apprehended
Tuesday night last, one John Coggin, late boatswain of the *Bomb Brig* (who with three other prisoners broke out of Windham goal) was found on board a brig in this harbor. He gives the following

account of said prisoners *viz*; that the night after breaking out of goal, they, with the help of one Lewis, who was taken in a prize vessel, stole a canoe near Norwich Landing with which they attempted to cross the Sound to Long Island but at the entrance to the Race near Gull Island, the canoe overset, when all of them, except Coggin, were drowned. The names are Edward Sneyd (late commander of the *Bomb* Brig), William Cook, John Russel, and –Lewis.

died
Mrs. Elizabeth Starr, widow of Captain Daniel Starr;

Miss Sarah Belden, eldest daughter of Samuel Belden.

strayed
from James Havens from the yard of Silas Church of New London, a brown milch cow.

****

From *The Gazette*, December 6, 1776

alarm of imminent attack by the British
Tuesday last, this town (New London) was alarmed by the appearance of 11 ships from the eastward coming into the Sound, most of which seemed to be men of war, which from their course from time, it was apprehended that they were coming to this port. But they went further up the Sound and in the evening anchored under Long Island shore where they remained until yesterday when being joined by other men of war and transports from New York to the number of near one hundred, they came to sail and anchored near Black Point about 8 miles west of this harbor (New London) where they remained through publication. The appearance e of such a formidable fleet an hour's sail of this place has thrown the inhabitants into great consternation. Our readers, we doubt not, will readily excuse the publication of our paper on a half sheet on the above account.

prisoner exchange
The State of Rhode Island by a committee that came here last week have agreed upon an exchange of prisoners of that State for

a like number in the British fleet which is to take place on the 9th instant here in New London. An exchanger of prisoners in this State is postponed for the present.

parole
Maj. Levi Welles from Colchester, who for some time since has been a prisoner in New York, is out on his parole.

pay and praise
Notice by John Ely that the Company Commanders of each Company of the 3rd Regiment, who were engaged in the late campaign in New York, are desired to meet at the house of Mark Parsons in Lyme and those in New London, Stonington and Groton are desired to meet at the house of Capt. Nathan Douglass of New London to receive the wages due those brave fellows who carried on until they were dismissed with great thanks.

sales of seized hips and cargos
The public are desired to remember that ship *Sally* and her cargo, originally scheduled to be sold on December 4th and the sale deferred because of the alarm that day, has been rescheduled for December 11; per Prosper Wetmore; Marshall.

The public are desired to remember that ship *Clarendon* and her Cargo, has been scheduled for December 17; per Prosper Wetmore; Marshall.

The public are desired to remember that schooner *Mary & Elizabeth* and her Cargo, has been scheduled for December 9; per Prosper Wetmore; Marshall.

wanted
from an American manufacture, hog bristles, well dried and combed for which will be paid in cash by Zabadiel Rogers & Co. in Norwich or Thomas Mumford in Groton.

an active boy between 12 and 15 years of age as an apprentice to the tailor's trade in New London; inquire at Printing Office.

immediately, for cash, by Roswell Saltonstall at the Distilhouse in New London, flax seed, white beans, bees and myrtle wax, small furs, ox and deer horns.

administration of estates
Notice by James Bramin, Executor of the estate of Jonas Brewster of Preston to all creditors of, and debtors to, the estate to come forward and settle accounts.

deserted
Cornelius Dox of the Regiment commanded by Col. John Tyler; an old countryman; about 35 years old; pock broken and has a down look; pretty well set; about five foot six; notice given by Capt. David Sill.

taken up
by Nathaniel Comstock Jr. of New London, a two year old steer;

by John Rogers 2d at New London's Harbor's mouth, a 2 year old red steer;

by William Lynde of Saybrook, two cows from Long Island;.

by William Hempsted of New London, a black cow;

by Joseph Stubbins in New London, a red stag.

runaway
from David Kinsman in Plainfield Windham County, an indented Indian servant man; about 25 years of age; James Simons. He says he sailed out of the *Greenwich* cruiser, Capt. Gardner; he was taken into custody for stealing and escaped from his keepers; he says he follows the sea and was born in Martha Vineyard and sailed out of Nantucket.

stolen
from Samuel Jeffery of Fairfield , a bay colored horse;

by Andrew Maynard of New London, Great Neck, two steers.

lost
Notice by William Webb that he has lost two steers in New London.

thanksgiving
Yesterday was observed as a day of public thanksgiving.

stolen properly recovered
Notice by J. Halsey that Daniel Dunwon, a transient person who has been convicted of theft before Judge Samuel Tracy for stealing, has with him certain items supposed to be stolen that owners may apply to him or to Joseph Waterman Inn holder in New London.

****

From *The Gazette*, December 13, 1776

New London spared, Newport invaded
The fleet of men of war and transports spoken of in our last to be near this harbor came to sail on Tuesday. At 12 o'clock they came abreast of this harbor making a very formidable appearance and for the space of a half hour, it was apprehended that they bound into the harbor, but after that floated out and spent the night on the south shore of Fisher's Island and, the next night, came to Rhode Island since which we have learned that they landed 8000 men at Newport and have taken possession of the town.
It is reported that more than 40 transport have come through Hells Gate[39] a few days ago and bound for this place.

wanted
a journey man printer by Abraham Preston at Elderkin's Bridge in Norwich.

taken up
by Samuel Bradford in New London, North Parish, a white heifer;

by Levi Crosby Hadlyme in East Haddam, a sorrel horse;

George Williams of New London, a two year old heifer.

lost
on the road between New London and Captain Wheeler's Tavern, a knapsack with buttons, shoes, powder horn, powder, bullets and a small bayonet.

real estate for sale
a dwelling house on a half acre in Canterbury, about 14 miles from Norwich on the Great Road between them; inquire of Francis Gillings, Ashford. near Capt. Clark's tavern;

a farm in Hopkinton adjoining the Great Road from Connecticut to Rhode Island, one mile from the Meeting House; 90 acres, well wooded and watered; 3 good orchards and 400 apple trees; good meadow and pasture; large dwelling house, barn and other out buildings; inquire of Henry Tew on premises;

35 acres in Newent parish of Norwich; good house and barn, lying on the public road; convenient for carrying on the clothiers business; also a shop and all utensils in good working order; and a stream of water; inquire of Phineas Knight.

died
Rebecca Church, wife of Silas Church, Jr.

pay up
Ebenezer Backus of Windham wishes all those indebted to him to settle accounts

for sale
cinnamon, cloves, nutmeg, indigo, raisins, women and children's shoes for sale at Printing office
****

From *The Gazette*, December 20, 1776

to be sold
by Hugh Ledlie in Hartford, a number of pieces of choice brocaded and English silk;

choice liver oil to be sold by Jeremiah Clement at Norwich Landing; he also wants two or three apprentices in the nailing blacksmith business;

a sloop 75 tons by William Stewart of New London.

wanted
single worsted and linen yarn at the stocking factory in Norwich by William Russel or Christopher Leffingwell.

farm for sale
At Norwich West Farms, an elegant new dwelling house, very pleasantly situated at the parting of two roads; together with new barn; horse shed and 24 acres; inquire of Nathan Stedman at Norwich West Farms.

taken up
at Gardiner's Island, a clinch work boat -also found 4 sailor hats on beach; apply to Stephen Brooks New London, Great Neck;

by Samuel Belding in New London, a black horse.

strayed
from Matthew Leffingwell of Chelsea in Norwich a 2 year old mare;

from David Jewett, East Haddam, a yellow heifer;

from Joel Spencer of Millington in East Haddam, a red heifer;

from Samuel Bolles of New London, black horse;

administration of estates
Notice by Elias Worthington, John Henry and Asa Daniels, Commissioners, appointed by the Court of Probate of East Haddam to the creditors of the estate of Deacon Thomas of Colchester, to meet at the house of Thomas Custin of Colchester.

deserted

from Capt. Gallup's Company; of the 10th Regiment, Job Bennet, has but one eye; five feet seven inches high; notice by Lt. Thomas Avery.

pay up
William Worthington of Stonington requests those indebted to him to settle accounts.

****

From *The Gazette*, December 27, 1776

ships taken
Captains Goodwin and Howard, from the Connecticut River sailed from this port (New London) for the West Indies and were carried into New York.

administration of estates
Notice to creditors by Solomon Safford, and Elisha Lathrop, Commissioners of the estate of Lt. Samuel Bingham of Norwich, that a meeting will be held at the house of Widow Joanna Perkins;

Oliver Crary has been appointed Administrator of the estate of Capt. John Brewster, late of Preston.

stolen
out of the saddlebags of Samuel M'Clennan at Mr. Tainter's, various articles of clothing

died
very suddenly at Groton, Mrs. Mary Perkins, wife of Elenathan Perkins.

found
in New London, a man's jacket; inquire of the Printer.

a good cash price given
for old brass copper pewter by Richard Collier at his shop near the Meeting House in Norwich; all sorts of copper and brass ware are made, mended and tinned – a few warming pans to be sold.

taken up
by Solomon Dart of New London, a 3 year old heifer;

by Morris Fowler of New London, a young steer;

by David Latimer of New London, two black cows;

by Rustford Rogers in Millington in East Haddam, a black 2 year old heifer.

strayed or stolen
from William Rogers, late of Long Island, a dark brown cow; if found, please return to James Thomson of New London;

from Noble Hinman of New London, a dark colored horse;

from Nathan Scovell of Lebanon, an 8 year old mare; please return to Anderson Martin of Lebanon Village or said Scovell in Colchester;

from Thomas Pelton of Chatham, forty sheep.

wanted
good wages will be given for a good bar keeper or hostler who is honest and able to keep a proper account. Inquire of the Printer

ran away
from Pierpoint Bacon of Colchester, an apprentice boy named Peregrine Dodge, about 16 years of age.

deserted
from the privateer sloop, *Lyon*, commanded by Capt. Timothy Shaler, one Samuel Sith Jr of Worthington, a parish of Middletown; five feet, ten inches tall; dark complexion; has long black hair.

****

END NOTES

1. Runaway servants and deserters were sometimes described as "pock mark'd" or "pox fretten", reflecting how many of the survivors of this disease were permanently scarred by it. An outbreak of small pox was to be feared and efforts, even primitive inoculations, were taken to avoid its spread through the population.

2. Although beyond the scope of this volume, the Susquehanna Purchase and the First and Second Delaware Purchases involve a portion of Connecticut's history rarely studied today.
 The Susquehanna and Delaware companies were among several land companies formed in Eastern Connecticut, especially by the citizens of Colchester and Windham in the early 1750s, for the purpose of developing the Wyoming Valley and Susquehanna territories in Pennsylvania. It was well received and Towns like Winchester, Chester, Salem, Hancock, Bedford, and Warwick, sprung up in Pennsylvania as a result — at least on paper.
 The Town of Thurlow was in the Lackawana Purchase and the town of Westmoreland, which extended from the 41st degree of north latitude to the New York line and from the Delaware River to fifteen miles west of Wyoming, was created in 1774 and annexed to Litchfield County in Connecticut
 Connecticut based its claim to these lands to its charter in 1662 from King Charles II to the territory between the 41st and 42nd degree of north latitude running from Narragansett Bay to the Pacific Ocean. A tract of that land was purchased in 1754 by John Henry Lydius, a Dutch trader, from the Iroquois who owned it by right of conquest of the Susquehannas. Preparations were made for development, when a 1763 massacre in Pennsylvania of settlers by Indians resulted in a proclamation by Connecticut Governor Fitch prohibiting further settlement, until the Indians were pacified. In the meanwhile, Eliphalet Dyer of Windham was sent to England in an unsuccessful attempt to secure confirmation of the land grant.
 It was 1769 before any definite settlement was made. But, almost immediately, the settlers became embroiled in bloody clashes with rival settlers from Pennsylvania, who saws it differently. They claimed the lands by virtue of a grant from Charles II which gave William Penn

the territory between 39 degrees 43 minutes and 43 degrees north latitude, overlapping Connecticut's claim. They argued that the 1754 purchase from the Indians by Connecticut land speculators was a brazen swindle with the help of the Iroquois who sold land they did not own.

After the Revolution, Article 9 of the enacted Articles of Confederation appointed Commissioners to hold hearing and resolve the conflict. On December 30, 1782, it handed down a decision, known as the Trenton Decree, in favor of Pennsylvania. Many thought it a predetermined political decision, not a judicial determination.

3. Lotteries are neither new, nor American born. King James I in 1612, granted the Virginia Colony the right to raise money to help establish settlers in the first permanent English colony at Jamestown. For more than the next century and a half, lotteries– more then two hundred of them, it is said -- played a key part in the financing of roads, libraries, churches, lighthouses, canals, bridges, etc., both private and public ventures. Princeton, Columbia and the University of Pennsylvania had their beginnings financed by lotteries. Lottery tickets, issued by Continental Congress, even helped to finance the Revolutionary War.

4. The Sons of Liberty can be traced to Boston in the summer of 1765 with a group of shopkeepers and artisans. Calling themselves "The Loyal Nine", they vigorously opposed the Stamp Act. As that group grew among the common man, it came to be known as the Sons of Liberty. And grow it did! By the end of that year, the Sons of Liberty existed in every colony. Their initial objective was to force the Crown appointed stamp distributors to resign. but they expanded as did the need to protest, including pressuring merchants who did not comply with the non-importation associations.

5. Referring to the Town or Society's "meeting houses" was common method of giving directions. They were large buildings in the center of a population. New Englanders went for church services there, sitting, suffering the hard wooden benches.. It was used for town meetings as well.

6. A maze of dark caverns and tunnels in East Granby in Simsbury first served as a copper mine. Opened in 1709 and known as Copper Hill, it was America's first chartered copper mine. Then, it became a prison. - New Gate. Connecticut needed somewhere to house prisoners, where escape would be impossible. They attached to the mine an underground room 15 by 12 feet with a new iron gate at the top of it which led to the surface. Imprisoned were burglars, counterfeiters,

robbers and horse thieves, who were forced to perform the hard labor of mining ore. Soon, with the American Revolution, the prison population was increased by British loyalists, captured British soldiers and court-martialed Continental ones. It became notorious in England for the underground conditions of dampness, vermin, insects and darkness.

7. It is difficult to imagine Connecticut as a mining region. Yet, exploration for useful minerals was encouraged by John Winthrop, Jr., first Governor of the colony and exploited for the next 200 years. As mentioned in the endnote above , the first mine was begun at Simsbury.in 1709 and soon there were copper mines all over the Connecticut valley. Chalcocite was the principle ore of the Simsbury Mines, and bornite was the principle ore at the Bristol Mine. Today the "Simsbury Mine and Newgate Prison," near East Granby, is a Connecticut Historic Site and popular tourist attraction.

8. This was the equivalent of saying "a week". Once it was common to record the passage of time by the number of nights rather than days. Se'nnight is an abbreviation of the fuller phrase "seven nights", hence a week. Fourteen nights. were a "fortnight". The latter has survived, especially in Britain, while se'nnight lost out to "a week" both there and in America.

9 In communion" describes the mutually recognized sharing of the same essential doctrines, between a Christian community and other communities or between that community and individuals
An endnote is woefully inadequate to summarize the complicated world of religion in New England in the 1770s. Essential to the concept of being in communion with another, however, was the word "covenant" a pact or agreement. In England there was a King and Parliament; Lords, Dukes, Earls and Squires. Similarly the Anglican Church, as had its predecessor Roman Church, had its Pontiff, Cardinals, Bishops etc. Neither was present in New England, however. There they governed themselves, in town meeting politically and in congregation and societies in the religious sphere. One had a covenant with his God and his fellow church members, an agreement on what they stood for and agreed upon .

10. A 1763 sketch of member of Parliament John Wilkes, friend of liberty and free press, depicted him holding a liberty pole topped with a liberty cap. The *pro* colonial Wilkes was a favorite of Americans, who adopted the symbols to express their own views of political liberty.

Liberty poles with various banners were raised in numerous towns to protest the Stamp Act of 1765. The pole can still be found on for the Great Seal of the United States, the state flag of New York and the state seals of New Jersey, North Carolina, and Arkansas.

11. Edmund Burke served for many years in the British House of Commons. He is mainly remembered for his support of the American colonies in their dispute with the Crown that led to the Revolution.

12. Rubbing, rolling and embracing the body with ashes, salt and camphoronated spirits were the approved method of resuscitating drowning victims. And, in a way, these poor men were drowning victims, in result, if not in cause. In the 1700s, poison gas was called "foul air", "bad air", or the "damps". It was really air without oxygen, sometimes encountered in digging or reworking wells that had not been worked for a long time. In today's parlance, it is carbon monoxide, often referred to as CO. Odorless, colorless, tasteless, and non-irritating, it is formed by the incomplete combustion of particular hydrocarbon fuels, including natural gas. When inhaled, it combines with the body's blood and prevents it from absorbing oxygen.

13. Small pox was not only disease that scarred the survivors for life. In a number of the notices seeking the return of runaways was also described another skin condition of the period, now too a memory only:" "he is much scarified under one of his cheek bones caused by the King's Evil." The disease, with the ominous name, is better known in medical circles as *cervical lymphadenitis* or *scrofula*. Tubercula in nature, it is characterized chiefly by swelling and degeneration of the lymphatic glands, especially around the neck area. It is rare in the United States today because of the elimination of tubercle from the milk and the prevention of mass infections in childhood. Heliotherapy --getting outside in the sun -- was a traditional method of treatment.

14. This report must have ben accompanied with a wink of the eye. The Connecticut colonists were not threatened by either Indians or Canadians, but by the British. The cannons had to be moved from the coast inland, out of reach of the marines from the English men of war.

15. Whalebone technically was not bone, but baleen, a series of stiff keratinous plates found in the moths of certain whales. It is a substance like hair, claws or nails. Whale bone was used to stiffen part of women's stays and dresses like corsets. It was also part of the production of brushes, buggy whips and parasol ribs.

16. Thomas Paine, was an English born philosopher/revolutionist whose writings ,such as his essay *Common Sense,* had steeled most Americans to the realization that the King was not worthy of allegiance, thereby helping to spark the Revolution. As noted in *The Gazette* of March 1, 1776 "Such has been the demand for this pamphlet that eight editions of it has been printed in different colonies in the course of a few weeks only."

The pamphlet advertised in the *Gazette* here, *Crisis,* was written by Paine at night as an enlisted man, serving in Washington's army as it retreated from New York, across New Jersey to Valley Forge at the end of 1776. Published immediately, it gripped the Americans and renewed their spirits: "These are the times that try mens' souls. The summer soldier and the sunshine patriot will, in this crisis, shrink from the service of his country, but he, who stands it now, deserves the love and thanks of man and woman."

General Washington, on the eve of his bold attacks on Trenton and Princeton, had private Paine's *Crisis* read to the troops, leaving no doubt as to the importance of the mission or what was expected of them. The next day -- Christmas, 1776 -- Washington with 2,400 men, crossed the Delaware, attacking the 1,400 man Hessian garrison at Trenton. The plan worked better than could have been hoped. A hundred Hessians were killed, including their commanding officer Colonel Joann Rall; 900 were captured and 400 escaped to tell of the American victory. The Americans had four men wounded:

17. The four thousand American militia involved in the pursuit of the 1700 English regulars uffered 95 casualties, 49 killed and 46 wounded or missing. The English losses were much worse, 264 casualties (some histories indicate 273) total English casualties, of which 65 were killed, 173 wounded and 26 missing

18. This refers to the famous *Yankee Doodle Dandy* ditty. It was written by a British doctor during the French and Indian War to mock the disheveled, disorganized colonials "yankees". "Doodle" mean a fool or simpleton. 'Macaroni' may be translated as "chic" or fancy and had its origins in the London Macaroni Club whose members consisted of young, homosexual men.

The ditty is attributed to Doctor Richard Shuckburgh, a British Army surgeon, who composed the lyrics in 1755 after observing what he thought to be the foolish the appearance of the Connecticut militia, especially that of Colonel Thomas Fitch, Jr., Connecticut Governor Thomas Fitch's son.

19. Lord Pitt, Earl of Chatham, was almost 70 years old, feeble and sometimes disoriented. He was known as the Great Commoner and, for three decades, had been George II's greatest advisor as well as Prime Minister. His successor, George III, while was periodically attracted to Pitt for counsel but, more often than not, he did not care for the advice he received. Pitt opposed Lord North 's repressive and coercive measures against the American colonists.

20. While the exact number of casualties varies among historians, the Americans were estimated at 441 killed and wounded. with the British casualties at 1,150 killed and wounded.

A hidden casualty was the heavy toll on British officers. One-eighth of the British officers in the entire War were killed and one-sixth were wounded on that day.

21. This was Margaret Mansfield, whom Benedict Arnold married in 1767 in Norwich. She had three sons in quick succession until her untimely death some 8 years later. A patriot at first and wounded, Arnold became military commander of Philadelphia and was said to be overly generous to helping himself from the city's coffers. While in Philadelphia, he met and married his second wife, 18 year old Peggy Shippen, daughter of a Loyalist and close friends with John Andre. He was an aide to General Clinton, Commander of the British fores in America. . It was not long before she, Andre and Arnold, now Commander of the key fort of West Point on the Hudson River, concocted a plan to surrender it to the British. Had it been successful, the Revolution might have ended otherwise.

22 Sir James Wallace, as he was to become, captained the *Rose,* then the *Experiment.* He was knighted in 1777 for his service in getting dispatches home to England. In 1779, he was captured by the American ally, the French..

23. His retirement was short lived . The March 29, 1776 issue of *The Gazette (infra)* reported that Thomas Allen was opening a new inn in Jordan on the Post Road, in between New London and Niantic "where every convenience possible for such a place will be erected in order for the accommodation of gentlemen travellers." He also promised "fresh salmon, trout, fish, lobsters etc. lobsters etc.

24 Salt petre is potassium nitrate, essential for making gun powder.

25 a shoat is a young pig, just after weaning.

26 Before wood pulp, cotton and linen rags were the "pulp" needed to make paper.

27. Not a household word today, flax has been an agricultural mainstay since Egyptian times. An annual plant, growing a meter or more high, it has multiple uses from fabrics to dyes, medicines to soap, and paper to fishnet.

28. See endnote 16 *supra*

29. Thomas Gage, of course, was not a well like fellow. As a General, Gage had led the British at the Battles of Lexington and Concord and, in 1775, he replaced Thomas Hutchinson as Governor of Massachusetts.

30. The United Colonies in the beginning especially relied upon privateers. The costs of commissioning privateers was borne by investors and manned by adventurers, both hoping to make profits from enemy merchants captured. Thus motivated by profit as well as patriotism, the ships were given licenses by the Government, called letters of marque and reprisal, to attack the British. They were often successful, causing disruption in British supply lines that necessarily had to stretch thousands of miles from England or the Caribbean all the way to New York City. There were nearly 1,700 of them, carrying almost 15,000 guns. They were successful too, capturing 2,263 enemy ships compared to the Continental Navy's 196

31. War usually results in a shortage of commodities and this in turn results in increases in their price, the well known law of supply and demand at work. In peace times, the ones with the "supply" can in the right situation become millionaires. In a war setting, however, where a common cause comes before profits, they are called war profiteers and disdained.

32. Fortunately for us, the American Revolution was fought predominately on land and not at sea. England's Royal Navy was the greatest naval force known to history, her sailors proven masters of the ocean. In comparison, the newborn America, at the time it declared its Independence, had only 31 ships in the Continental Navy, a number which would increase to 64.

33. The word "mestee", descended from French for "mixed" refers to someone born to parents of different groups as defined by visible physical differences, regarded as racial For example, the related word "*mestizo*" in Spanish a usually describes a person born or descended from the union of a European and a Native American

34. Admiralty law was distinct from the common law in several ways, including some of its phraseology. A "libel" is a claim, a written statement of the plaintiff setting forth his cause of action and the relief he seeks. Here, the crew and owners of the privateers were seeking a piece of the value of the captured prize ship.

35. In Greek mythology, Cerberus was the three-headed dog with a snake's tail that guarded the gates to hell The Ship *Cerberus* was well named. It was the the first British warship to come to North America after the outbreak of hostilities.
George III had adopted a more aggressive strategy and the *Cerberus* and the other warships were ordered to "lay waste, burn and destroy" rebellious seaport towns of New England, New London among them. During the winter of 1775 -1776, the *Cerberus* took up station in the Long Island Sound, often anchoring outside New London harbor and captured many American vessels
Interestingly, it was the *Cerbrus* which was the victim of the first underwater mine. In August 1777, David Bushnell, American patriot later to pioneer the submarine, targeted the *Cerberus* with the explosive device. It was, however, only partially successful.

36. Potash was a cash crop of sorts for colonial farmers. It was refined from the ashes of hardwood trees. The trees themselves were the by products of the farmers clearing their wooded land for crops. The easiest way to clear it was to burn it. Ashes from trees could then be used to make lye, needed to make soap or as potash

37. The Battle of Long Island, also known as the Battle of Brooklyn, fought on August 27, 1776, was the first major battle in the American Revolutionary War following the United States Declaration of Independence. When it was over, the British had captured New York City. Nathan Hale, a patriot spy and, until two years before, a school teacher in New London, was captured and hung.
Most of the battle was concentrated in western Long Island, within about 10 miles of Manhattan. However, the British seized the entire Island, all 110 miles of it to Montauk. The western tip of the Island was but a dozen miles or so, across the Long Island Sound, from New

London. Some families evacuated to Connecticut, taking with them all their possessions including cattle and other stock.

38. The Fire of 1776, as it has come to be known in New York City history, was, like the World Trade Center attack, an intentional act of war. Ironically, the damage on New York City then was inflicted by its own citizens, American patriots. George Washington, unable to withstand the British attack, was forced to abandon the city, allowing the Sons of Liberty to burn it so as to deny the invaders any sustenance.

39. New York harbor, where the British fleet was based, is connected to the Long Island Sound by a strait of often violent water known as Hells Gate.

INDEX TO PERONS

A
ABBE, Shubael - 11/3/75
ABBY, Phineas - 5/5/75
ABRAMS, David - 4/22/74
ACKLEY, Gideon - ½6/76
ADAMS, A. - 11/15/76
ADAMS, David - 1/20/75
ADAMS, Elisha - 10/18/76
ADAMS, Pygan - 1/27/75; 7/12/76
ADAMS, Sam - 2
ALBERTSON, John - 5/6/74
ALDEN, Elizabeth - 6/2/75
ALDEN, Prince - 3/18/74
ALLEN, Capt. Christopher - 5/16/76
ALLEN, Jr, Daniel - 5/13/74
ALLEN, Jason - 8/9/76
ALLEN, Moses - 7/1/74
ALLEN, Thomas 4/29/74; 9/2/74; 10/7/74; 11/18/74; 12/2/74; 4/21/75; 6/23/75; 9/1/75; 11/17/75 3/29/76; note 23
ALSOP, Richard - 4/12/76
ANDROWS, Samuel - 8/23/76
APPLEBY, Jane - 7/19/76
ARNOLD, Col. Benedict - 6/30/75; note 21
ARNOLD, Joseph - 6/28/76
ARNOLD, Mrs. Margaret - 6/30/75; note 21
ARNOLD, Nathan - 4/8/74; 4/22/74
ARNOT, Col, - 4/15/74
ASHCRAFT, , Daniel - 11/8/76
ASHCRAFT, Mrs. Margaret - 7/29/74
ASHLEY, Israel - 7/19/76
ATWELL, Ensign Benj. - 10/18/76
ATWELL, Atwell, Jr. Benjamin - 6/3/74
ATTWOOD, Elijah- 10/14/74
ATWOOD, Joseph - 11/25/74
AUSTIN Jr, ,Daniel - 5/13/74
AVERED, Alvin - 5/6/74
AVERY, David - 12/23/74; 10/18/76
AVERY Jr., Ebenezer - 12/2/74 ; 12/23/74
AVERY 3rd, Ebenezer - 1/6/75
AVERY, Griswold - 10/18/76
AVERY, Jabez - 3/15/76 ; 5/16/76
AVERY, John - 3/4/74; 7/29/74; 3/24/75
AVERY, Jr., John - 6/24/74
AVERY, Joseph - 3/3/75
AVERY, Elder Nathan - 2/24/75
AVERY, P. - 10/18/76
AVERY, Capt. Robert - 4/22/74; 5/5/75; 9/22/75; 10/13/75
AVERY, Thomas - 11/8/76; 12/20/76
AVERY, William - 12/23/74; - 1/20/75; 8/25/75; 6/7/76; 7/19/76
AYERS; John- 3/17/75

B
BABBIT, Benjamin - 4/19/76
BABCOCK, Adam - 3/31/75
BACKER, William - 3/22/76
BACKUS, Andrew, 7/15/74
BACKUS, Benjamin - 4/19/76
BACKUS, Ebenezer -2/4/74; 7/8/74; 2/24/75; 12/13/76
BACKUS, Jr., Ebenezer - 11/17/75

BACKUS, Elijah - 9/2/74; 2/10/75
BACKUS, Nathaniel 1/14/74
BACKUS, Timothy - 9/13/76; 11/15/76
BACON, Pierpont - 1/27/75; 12/27/76'
BACON, Stephen - 3/29/76
BADGER, Edmund - 5/24/76
BADGER, Edward - 1/26/76
BAILEY, Nathan - 3/4/74; 4/8/74
BAKER, , Dr. Joseph - 11/17/75
BAKER, William - 6/28/76
BALDWIN, Caleb - 2/10/75
BALDWIN, Ebenezer- 2/4/74;7/29/74; 10/21/74; 2/10/75; 3/22/76
BALDWIN, Col. - 4/12/76
BALDWIN; Capt. - 7/26/76; 8/2/76
BALEY, Col. - 4/12/76
BALEY, Jared - 5/16/76
BALIE, Jedidiah - 9/29/75
BALY, Ezekiel - 1/6/75
BANNING, William - 6/7/76
BARBER, Elisha - 2/3/75
BARKER, Hannah - 12/16/74
BARKER, Capt. Ignatius - 9/9/74; 12/16/74
BARKER, Joshua - 9/9/74;12/16/74
BARNES, John - 1/6/75
BARREL, David - 7/19/76
BATES, Henry -8/4/75 4/5/76
BATES, Isaac - 7/7/75
BAYH, Jonathan - 7/26/76
BEACH, Miles - 4/21/75
BECKUS, Capt. Andrew - 5/16/76
BECKWITH, Absalom - 3/1/76
BECKWITH, John - 8/9/76

BEEBE[E], Doctor Abner - 2/10/75; 10/27/75
BEEBE[E], Breckway - 10/27/75
BEEBE[E], David - 10/20/75
BEEBE[E], Ebenezer. 1/6/75
BEEBE[E], Jabez - 8/18/75
BEEBE[E], Jonathan - 10/27/75; 4/12/76
BEEBE[E], Russel - 2/24/75; 3/3/75
BEEBE[E], William - 1/6/75; 10/27/75; 12/15/75
BELCHER, Samuel - 3/29/76
BELCHER, Captain William - 6/24/74; 10/28/74
BELDEN, Belden, [see also Belding] Samuel - 10/14/74; 12/20/76; 11/29/76
BELDEN, Miss Sarah - 11/29/76
BELDEN, Maj. Thomas - 4/14/75
BELDING, David - 7/1/74; 4/19/76; 11/1/76
BELDING, John - 3/18/74
BELLAMY, Reuben - 9/1/75
BELTON, David - 11/10/75
BELTON, Capt. Jonas - 7/29/74; 12/2/74; 7/26/76; 8/16/76; 11/22/76
BENEDICT, Abner - 1/20/75
BENEDICT, Rev, Mr. - 6/3/74
BENNET, Henchman - 9/15/75
BENNET, Bennet, James - 5/3/76
BENNET, Job - 12/20/76
BEVINS, Abner - 11/11/74
BICKNELL, Nathan, - 5/24/76
BIDDLE, Captain - 6/28/76; 8/2/76
BIGELOW, Capt. - 8/2/76
BILL, Benjamin - 12/30/74' 1/6/75; 7/22/75; 9/22/75; 6/7/76
BILLINGS, Alpheus - 3/1/76
BILLINGS, Joseph - 3/17/75

BILLINGS, Capt. Roger - 6/14/76
BILLINGS,, Samuel - 10/18/76
BILLINGS, Jun., Ens. Stephen - 9/2/74 ;7/26/76
BILLINGS, Mrs. - 6/14/76
BINGHAM, Elias - 1/6/75
BINGHAM, Ezra - 9/22/75
BINGHAM, John - 9/22/75
BINGHAM, Lt. Samuel - 12/27/76
BISHOP Bishop, Daniel -9/22/75
BISHOP Bishop, Nathaniel - 9/22/75; 6/28/76
BISHOP, Capt. Nicholas - 2/3/75; 3/10/75; 8/9/76
BISSEL, Hezekiah - 12/23/74
BLACK, John - 1/26/76
BLACKLEY, John - 1/21/74
BLAKSLEE, Josiah - 11/25/74
BLANCHEr; Ebenezer - 11/15/76
BLISH, Silvanus - 1/27/75
BLOSSOM; Oliver - 10/11/76
BOIES, James - 2/18/74
BOLLES, Amos - 9/9/74
BOLLES, David - 4/15/74
BOLLES Jr, Enoch- 3/4/74
BOLLES, 6/17/74; 3/17/75; 7/15/74
BOLLES 3rd, John - 12/15/75
BOLLES, Mrs. Meriam - 7/15/74
BOLLES, Samuel - 12/20/76
BOSCAWEN, Mrs. Mary - 3/4/74
BOSCAWEN, Richard- 3/4/74
BOSTER, Capt. Isaac - 4/19/76
BOSTWICK, Capt. Isaac - 9/1/75
BOUTINEAU, Thomas - 5/10/76
BOWEN, Mehitable - 8/23/76
BOWERS, Mary - 11/15/76-
BRADDICK, Mr. - 4/5/76
BRADDICK, Capt. - 6/10/74
BRADFORD, Abigail - 8/16/76

BRADFORD, - James 7/15/74
BRADFORD, Samuel - 12/13/76
BRADFORD, William - 8/16/76
BRADLEY, Abraham - 4/21/75
BRADLEY, Joshua - 11/15/76
BRAINERD,, Benjamin - 12/29/75
BRAINERD, Daniel - 4/15/74; 10/27/75
BRAINERD, David - 10/6/75
BRAINERD, Elijah - 9/16/74
BRAINERD, Col . Hezekiah - 3/17/75; 10/6/75
BRAINERD, Jr., Hezekiah - 9/16/74
BRAINERD, Capt. Jabez - 4/15/74; 9/16/74
BRAINERD, Mary - 3/17/75
BRAINERD, Nathaniel - 7/15/74; 9/16/74; 10/27/75
BRAINERD, Nehemiah - 9/16/74; 10/6/75
BRAINERD, Phineas - 9/16/74; 2/7/76
BRAMIN, James - 12/6/76
BRANCH, Hannah - 4/15/74
BRANCH, Samuel - 4/15/74
BRANCH Jr., Thomas - 5/24/76
BRANFORD, John - 7/7/75
BREED, John - 3/24/75; 5/31/76
BREED, Gershom - 2/4/74
BREED, Mr. - 10/7/74
BREWSTER, Jacob - 2/11/74
BREWSTER, John - 4/22/74;7/15/74; 12/23/74; 10/13/75; 12/27/76
BREWSTER, Jonas - 12/6/76
BRIMMER, John Baker - 4/1/74; 4/8/74; 9/23/74; 1/5/76; 3/15/76
BROCKWAY, Jedidiah - 7/15/74
BROK, Capt Joseph - 4/15/74

BROOKS, Abraham - 10/6/75
BROOKS, Jonathan- 3/31/75; 4/5/76,
BROOKS, Joseph - 9/16/74 4/14/75
BROOKS, Stephen - 12/20/76
BROOKS, Capt. - 5/31/76
BROWN, Abner - 8/19/74
BROWN Amos - 6/21/76
BROWN, Jacob- 11/24/75
BROWN, John - 11/25/74
BROWN, Lt. Samuel - 11/3/75
BROWN,Jr., Samuel - 12/2/74
BROWN, Colonel - 12/2/74
BROWN, Mr. - 4/28/75 ; 8/18/75
BRUCE, Ronald - 10/11/76
BRUSH, Cream - 10/18/76
BUCK, Justus - 2/18/74
BUCKLEY, John- 4/28/75
BUELL, Ensign John - 2/23/76
BUELL, Maj. - 10/18/76
BULKEY, Captain Eliphalet - 2/18/74; 6/3/74
BULKEY, Gershom - 4/1/74; 7/1/74
BULKEY, John - 6/3/74
BULKEY, Peter - ½7/75; 6/7/76
BULKEY, Captain - 6/21/76
BULL, Samuel - 9/2/74
BULL, Mr. - 9/9/74
BULL, Rev. - 9/2/74
BUNTING, William - 6/28/76
BURGES, John - 3/29/76
BURKE, Edmund - note 11
BURNAM, James - 2/11/74
BURNHAM, Asa - 10/28/74
BURNHAM, Ashbell - 10/28/74
BURNHAM, David - 2/18/74
BURNHAM, Joseph - 12/23/74
BURR, Abraham - 10/18/76
BURR, Thaddeus - 5/12/75

BURROWS, John - 10/25/76
BURROWS, Mrs. Mary - 4/22/74
BURROWS, Jr., Samuel - 4/22/74
BURROWS, Silas - 9/9/74; 6/23/75
BURTON, Israel - 2/10/75
BURTON, Miss Marsha - 2/10/75
BURTON, Miss Mary - 2/10/75
BUSHNELL, Aaron - 7/1/74
BUSHNELL Abistai - 6/28/76
BUSHNELL; David, note 35
BUSHNELL E. - 7/19/76
BUSHNELL, Euseebius - 3/3/75
BUSHNELL, Ira - 8/9/76
BUSHNELL, Nathan - 7/1/74
BUSHNELL Jr., Nathan - 5/12/75
BUSHNELL, Deacon Nathaniel - 10/13/75
BUSSEL; James - 11/8/76
BUTLER, Moses - 11/25/74
BUTLER, William - 4/19/76
BUTLER, Col. Zebulon - 9/22/75
BUTLER, Capt. - 7/19/76
BYLEY, Nathan - 2/17/75
BYRNES, Daniel - 2/17/75

C
CALKIN, Simon - 2/4/74
CALKINS, Amos - 10/13/75; 12/22/75
CALKINS Jedidiah - 10/13/75
CALKINS, Pember - 9/20/76
CALKINS; Lt. William - 8/2/76
CAMPBELL, Daniel - 5/3/76
CAREY, Eleazer - 5/24/76
CARPENTEr, Ann - 7/19/76; 11/15/76
CARTER, John - 2/23/76
CARVER, Nathan 12/30/74
CARY, Mrs. Elecer - 12/2/74
CARY, Dr. John - 12/23/74;

7/26/76
CARY, Thomas - 8/11/75
CASE, Joseph - 3/22/76
CASE Manuel - 6/21/76
CASE, Ruth - 3/22/76
CESEY, Ebenezer - 2/17/75
CHACE, Capt. William - 8/9/76
CHAMPION, Maj. Henry -4/1/74; 4/15/74; 8/12/74 ;1/6/75; ½7/75
CHAMPLIN, Asa - 10/11/76
CHAMPLIN John - 1/14/74; 2/25/74
CHAMPLIN, Samuel - 7/15/74; 4/12/76
CHAMPLIN, William - 7/8/74
CHANCY, Sarah - 11/15/76
CHANDLER, Charles C. - 7/8/74
CHANDLER, Daniel - 12/22/75
CHAPEL, Guy- 3/25/74
CHAPIN, Dr. Benjamin - 11/15/76
CHAPMAN, Abram - 11/15/76
CHAPMAN Alpheus - 11/15/76
CHAPMAN Edward - 1/26/76; 2/9/76
CHAPMAN George - 4/19/76
CHAPMAN Jabez - 3/18/74; 4/15/74; 2/10/75; 10/27/75; 8/2/76; 11/22/76
CHAPMAN Jr. Jabez - 4/15/74
CHAPMAN Maj. James - 9/27/76
CHAPMAN, Jr., James - 2/4/74
CHAPMAN John - 4/5/76
CHAPMAN, Lemuel - 12/22/75
CHAPMAN, Nathan - 6/2/75
CHAPMAN Richard - 10/18/76
CHAPMAN, Samuel- 3/25/74
CHAPMAN Uria - 7/29/74
CHAPMAN, Captain - 8/11/75
CHAPPEL Comfort - 9/9/74
CHAPPEL; Joshua - 4/22/74
CHAPPEL, Mrs. Sarah - 2/25/74

CHAPPEL, Captain Stephen - 2/25/74
CHARLES II, King - 6/10/74; note 2
CHASE, Consider - 11/8/76
CHATFIELD, John - 7/ 22/ 74
CHATHAM, Earl of - note 19
CHAUNCEY, Isaac - 7/19/76
CHENENY, Abiel - 11/15/76
CHESEBROUGH, Colonel Amos - 7/29/74; 10/14/74; 11/11/74
CHESEBROUGH, Charles - 4/12/76; 5/24/76
CHESEBROUGH, Joseph - 3/18/74; 12/23/74
CHESEBROUGH, Nathan - 1/27/75
CHESEBROUGH, Nathaniel Peleg - 1/27/75
CHESEBROUGH, Robert - 1/27/75
CHESEBROUGH, Samuel - 10/14/74; 11/11/74
CHESTER, Capt. John - 4/22/74
CHESTER, Mrs. Mary - 4/22/74
CHEW, Capt. Samuel - 11/15/76
CHILD, Capt. Elisha - 7/8/74; 5/16/76
CHILD, Nathaniel - 7/8/74
CHRISTOPHERS, Christopher - 10/27/75; 3/1/76; 5/16/76
CHRISTOPHERS, Richard - 2/9/76; 8/2/76
CHURCH, Rebecca - 12/13/76
CHURCH Silas - 3/10/75;4/5/76; 7/19/76; 10/18/76; 11/29/76
CHURCH, Jr., Silas - 8/23/76; 10/11/76; 12/13/76
CHURCH, Dr. - 12/8/75
CHURCH, Mr. - 6/30/75
CLARK, Ashel - 2/24/75

CLARK, Benjamin - 3/29/76; 5/31/76; 10/18/76
CLARK Charles - 3/22/76
CLARK Daniel - 8/9/76
CLARK Darius - 8/9/76
CLARK, Elihu - 3/22/76
CLARK, Ezra - 3/22/76
CLARK, Francis - 9/13/76
CLARK Joel - 7/7/75
CLARK, John [see also Clarke] - 12/30/74; 10/18/76
CLARK, Deacon Joseph - 9/13/76
CLARK, Perry- 7/15/74
CLARK, Roger - 8/9/76
CLARK, Samuel - 2/24/75
CLARK, Timothy - 1/5/76
CLARK, Ensign Waters - 5/16/76
CLARK, William - 7/19/76; 11/15/76
CLARK, Capt. - 12/13/76
CLARKE, John - 4/22/74; John - 1/20/75
CLARKE, Captain - 9/6/76
CLAYTON, William - 1/26/76
CLEMENT, Jeremiah - 6/17/74; 12/8/75; 6/28/76; 12/20/76
CLEVELAND, Aaron - 10/28/74; 5/31/76
CLEVELAND, Jabez - 7/5/76
CLEVELAND, James - 5/10/76
CLINTON, Gen. Henry note 21
CLOES - 2/7/76;
COCKRAN; Capt. John 12/30/74
COGGIN, John - 11/15/76; 11/29/76
COGWELl, James - 4/14/75
COIT, Benjamin - 6/24/74
COIT, Daniel - 10/14/74
COIT, Isaac - 7/15/74; 5/16/76
COIT, John - 7/28/75

COIT, Joseph - 11/4/74
COIT, Mrs. Mehetabel - 3/11/74
COIT, Capt. Nathaniel, - 3/11/74
COIT, Capt. Oliver - 8/19/74; 11/8/76 - 11/8/76
COIT, Mrs. Parthenia - 1/21/74
COIT, Col. Samuel - 6/24/74
COIT, Mrs. Sarah - 11/17/75
COIT, Thomas - 5/13/74; 10/28/74
COIT, Wheeler - 3/11/74
COIT, William - 10/14/74; 11/18/74; 5/5/75; 11/17/75; 5/31/76; 8/23/76; 10/11/76
COIT, Captain - 6/30/75
COLEMEN, Edward S. - 1/26/76
COLES; John - 3/29/76
COLFAX, Widow - 7/14/75
COLLIER, Richard - 12/27/76
COLLINS, Benjamin - 12/30/74
COLLINS, Zerubbabel - 9/15/75
COLMAN, Noah 12/30/74
COLT, Harris - 9/9/74
COLUMBUS, Christopher - 2/25/74
COLYER, Capt. - 5/3/76
COMPSON, Mr. - 4/19/76
COMSTOCK, Abner - 1/6/75
COMSTOCK, Elisha - 7/19/76
COMSTOCK, John - 3/18/74
COMSTOCK,Jr., Nathaniel - 12/6/76
CONANT , Caleb 10/6/75
CONANT , Josiah - 12/16/74;10/6/75
CONANT , Roger - 10/6/75
CONANT , Ruth Conant - 10/6/75
CONANT, Shubael - 2/18/74; 1/6/75;10/6/75; 1/26/76
CONANT, Jr., Shubael - 1/26/76

CONE, Martin - 9/13/76
CONE, Nathaniel - 1/6/75
CONKLIN, John - 1/26/76
CONKLIN, Mr. - 1/1375
COOK, Elias - 7/15/74
COOK, William - 11/15/76; 11/29/76
COOKE, Thaddeus- 3/25/74
COOPER, William 7/15/74
COPP, J. - 11/22/76
COPP, Widow Sarah - 11/15/76
CORLIS, William- 4/5/76
CORTON, Collins - 11/22/76
COX, William - 9/13/76
CRAMPTON, John - 1/26/76
CRANE, Elisha - 2/10/75
CRANE, Maj. - 4/12/76
CRARY, Ezra - 5/16/76
CRARY, Oliver - 12/27/76
CRARY, Peter - 11/1/76
CRARY, Jun, Peter - 10/6/75
CRAWFORD, William- 3/4/74
CRAWFORD, William Johnson - 5/6/74
CROCKER, Constant - 7/8/74
CROCKER, Capt. Freeman - 3/29/76
CROCKER, James - 9/15/75
CROCKER, Lucretia - 9/20/76
CROCKER, Mary - 11/18/74
CROCKER, Mrs. Sarah - 6/7/76
CRONE, Jonah - 7/19/76
CROSBY, Levi - 12/13/76
CROSBY Capt. Stephen - 5/16/76
CROWE, Benjamin - 1/21/74
CUDGO - 9/8/75
CUISH, Jacob - 2/23/76; 4/5/76
CUISH, Mary - 2/23/76
CUMMINGS, Miriam - 10/14/74
CUMMINGS, William - 10/14/74
CURTIS, John - 7/15/74

CURTIS, Jonathan - 1/20/75
CUSTIN, Thomas - 12/20/76
CYRUS - 6/7/76

D
DALEY, Capt. John - 6/3/74
DANE, Lieut. - 6/30/75
DANSTABLE - 10/28/74
DARBY, Nathaniel - 3/15/76
DARBY, Mrs. - 3/15/76
DARE, Mrs. Mary - 6/30/75
DARE, Thomas - 6/30/75
DARROW, Christopher - 8/2/76
DARROW, Jr., Christopher - 5/24/76
DAVENPORT; Abraham - 5/16/76
DAVIS, Ebenezer - 12/2/74
DAVIS, Capt. - 4/15/74
DAY, Lieutenant David - 1/27/75; 9/22/75
DAY, Noah - 4/1/74
DEANE, John - 4/15/74; 5/16/76
DEANE, Silas - 7/15/74; 8/12/74; 8/26/74; 11/4/74; 11/18/74; 4/14/75
DECALPH, Charles - 7/7/75
DENISON, Benadam - 3/29/76
DENISON, 4th, George - 5/10/76
DENISON, Capt Jesse ????- 3/4/74
DENISON, Capt John - 4/22/74
DENISON, IV, John -1/7/74; 5/26/75
DENISON, 5th, John - 10/20/75
DENISON, II, Joseph - 5/26/75
DENNIS, Ebenezer - 10/14/74
DENNYS, Thomas - 12/29/75
DESHON, Daniel - 1/1375
DESHON,, J - 12/29/75.
DESHON, John - 11/18/74; 5/16/76

DESHON, Richard - 9/9/74; 8/2/76
DESHON, Mrs. Ruth - 1/1375
DEVOTION, Ebenezer - 1/14/74; 6/10/74; 12/23/74; 1/27/75; 3/24/75; 4/14/75
DEVOTION, Miss Elizabeth - 3/24/75
DEVOTION, Jonathan - 6/10/74
DEWITT, Henry - 5/31/76
DICK - 9/13/76; 3/29/76; 5/3/76
DICKERSON, Nehemiah - 9/16/74
DICKINSON; Capt. Richard 12/30/74
DIMOCK, Mrs Joanna - 10/6/75
DIMOCK, Shubael - 10/6/75
DIXON, Edward - 11/17/75
DIXON, Molly - 7/19/76
DODGE, Jordan - 7/5/76
DOLBEARE - Hannah - 1/26/76
DOLBEARE, John - 1/21/74
DOOLITTLE, Isaac - 8/5/74
DOUGLAS[S] Ebenezer - 10/14/74
DOUGLAS[S] George - 8/9/76
DOUGLAS[S] James - 12/29/75
DOUGLAS[S] John - 7/15/74; 7/7/75
DOUGLAS[S] Jonathan - 7/15/74; 7/21/75
DOUGLAS[S], Captain Nathan - 3/4/74; 6/24/74; 7/8/74; 8/19/74; 3/10/75; 3/17/75; 3/24/75; 5/10/76; 8/9/76; 8/16/76
DOUGLAS[S], William- 2/3/75; 3/10/75
DOUGLASSs Jr Robert, - 1/21/74; 8/26/74
DOUGLASS, Daniel - 2/4/74; 10/28/74

DOWNES, Dr Joshua - 9/20/76
DRONANCE, Rev Samuel - 12/22/75
DUMAR, Philip - 12/2/74
DUNK, Samuel - 9/29/75
DUNLAP, Joshua - 7/15/74; 5/16/76
DUNLAP, Robert - 5/31/76
DURFEE[y] ,Thomas- 2/3/75; 8/9/76
DURKEE,,Lt. Colonel John - 1/19/76
DURKEES, Col. - 4/12/76.
DURKERS, Joseph - 12/23/74
DURLY, Thomas - 3/10/75
DURSEY, Thomas - 10/13/75
DYAR, John - 10/13/75
DYER, Benjamin - 12/30/74
DYER, Eliphalet - 7/15/74; 8/12/74; 8/26/74; 11/4/74; 11/18/74; 5/16/76; note 2

E
EASTON, Capt. Job - 4/22/74
EATON, Capt. Joseph 7/15/74
EATON, Capt. - 5/24/76
ECCLESTON, Ichabod - 10/11/76
EDGECOMB, Jesse - 7/22/74
EDGERTON, John - 2/4/74
EDWARDS Jr., C. - 12/1/75
EDWARDS, Thomas Gage - 4/19/76
EDWARDS, Thomas - 4/19/76
EDWARDS, Thomas, Mrs. - 4/19/76
EELLS, Edward - 4/22/74; 10/18/76
ELDERKIN, Maj. Jedidiah - 2/4/74; 4/15/74; 4/14/75; 5/16/76
ELDERKIN, John - 12/23/74 ;2/16/76; 7/26/76; 9/27/76

ELDERKIN, Joshua - 4/22/74; 12/23/74; 3/22/76
ELDERKIN, Luther - 7/1/74
ELDERKIN, Capt. Vincent - 9/20/76
ELDRIDGE, Charles - 8/19/74; 5/5/75
ELDRIDGE, Jr, Charles - 1/6/75
ELDRIDGE,,George - 8/18/75
ELDRIDGE, James - 1/20/75
ELIOT, Aaron - 2/10/75; - 6/7/76
ELIOT, George - 2/10/75
ELIOTT, Mr. - 8/4/75; 4/5/76
ELLSWORTH, Jr., Giles - 7/21/75
ELLSWORTH,, John - 7/15/74
ELLSWORTH, Oliver - 11/17/75
ELY, Elisha - 2/4/74; 10/21/74; 6/9/75
ELY, John - 2/4/74; 10/21/74; 7/5/76; 12/6/76; 12/30/74
ELY, Simon - 6/17/74
ELY, Captain - 8/11/75
ENSWORTH, T. - 11/15/76
ESTABROOK, Rev. Hobart - 7/19/76
ESTABROOK, Mrs. Jervina - 7/19/76
EVINS, John - 8/30/76

F
FAIRFIELD, Eleanor - 7/26/76; 8/23/76
FAIRFIELD, William - 7/26/76; 8/23/76
FANNING, David - 1/20/75
FANNING, William - 6/28/76
FARGO, William - 3/1/76; 11/15/76
FARNHAM, Jun., Joseph - 7/12/76
FIELD, Samuel - 12/30/74; 10/18/76

FIS, Sarah - 5/10/76
FISH, Capt. Daniel - 4/12/76; 5/24/76; 10/18/76
FITCH, Jabez - 9/13/76
FITCH, John - 7/19/76
FITCH, Joseph - 7/19/76
FITCH Governor Thomas - notes 2, 18
FITCH, Jr. Col. Thomas - note 18
FLINT, Luke - 7/5/76
FOOT, Daniel - 3/22/76
FORD, Nathaniel - 3/17/75
FORDHAM, Capt. Daniel- 9/15/75
FOSDICK, Widow Grace - 8/30/76
FOSDICK, Dr. Thomas - 7/22/74; 4/19/76
FOSTER, John -7/15/74; 12/2/74; 2/24/75
FOSTER, Jr., John - 9/15/75
FOSTER, Jonathan - 11/15/76
FOWLER Dijah - 3/10/75
FOWLER, Esther - 4/5/76
FOWLER Jacob - 11/15/76-
FOWLER, John - 4/8/74
FOWLER, Mrs. Mary - 4/8/74
FOWLER, Morris - 9/9/74; 11/17/75; 12/27/76
FOX Ezekiel - 7/1/74; 2/3/75; 3/10/75; 6/28/76
FOX, Mary - 8/23/76
FOX Stephen - 7/21/75
FOX, Thomas - 8/23/76
FOX, Mrs. - 6/28/76
FRANKLIN, Dr. Benjamin - 11/3/75
FREEMAN, Edmund - 2/25/74; 11/11/74; 10/18/76
FREEMAN, Edward - 12/16/74
FREEMAN, Halfuld. - 11/25/74

FREEMAN, Nathaniel - 11/25/74
FRENCH, William - 1/20/75
FRIEND, John - 8/25/75
FRINK, Mrs. Joanna - 5/20/74
FRINK, Nathan - 5/16/76; 10/18/76
FULLER, Thomas - 2/17/75
FULLER, Timothy - 5/16/76

G

GAGE, General Thomas - 6/9/75; 10/27/75; note 29
GAGER, Simon - 3/18/74
GALE, Joseph - 5/24/76
GALES, Doctor Samuel - 2/10/75; 10/18/76
GALES, Benjamin 4/29/74
GALLOP, Capt. Benadam - 12/23/74; 4/26/76; 5/16/76
GALLUP, Elisha - 1/21/74
GALLUP, Joseph - 1/26/76
GALLUP, Nathan - 4/14/75; 8/16/76; 11/22/76
GALLUP, William - 9/23/74
GALLUP, Capt. - 12/20/76
GARDINER, Mrs Abigail - 3/31/75
GARDINER, Abraham [see also Gardner], - 7/22/74; 12/30/74;
GARDINER,, David [see also Gardner]- 9/2/74; 9/16/74;12/30/74; 1/26/76; 3/22/76
GARDINER, Jr. David - 12/16/74
GARDINER, John - 7/22/74; 3/29/76
GARDINER, Jonathan - 3/18/74
GARDINER, Samuel - 3/31/75
GARDNER, Abraham [see also Gardiner]- 11/15/76
GARDNER, Benajah - 12/8/75
GARDNER, Benjamin - 10/25/76

GARDNER, Caleb - 6/21/76
GARDNER, David [see also Gardiner]- 10/25/76
GARDNER, Thomas - 12/8/75
GARDNER, Capt. - 12/6/76
GATES, John - 8/25/75; 7/26/76; 10/4/76
GATES Jr., Joseph - 1/5/76
GATES, Joshua Gates - 2/25/74
GATES, Liddy - 2/25/74
GATES Noadiah - 3/31/75
GATT, Thomas - 11/15/76
GATTES, Thomas - 8/11/75
GAYLORD, Lucy - 2/17/75
GEER, Allen - 2/10/75
GEER, Amos - 12/23/74; 8/16/76; 11/22/76
GEER, Catherine - 5/10/76
GEER, John - 4/1/74
GEER, Jonas - 2/10/75
GEER, Samuel - 5/10/76
GELSTON, John - 12/8/75
GEORGE II'. King note 19
GEORGE III, King -1,2;; 7/1/74; 11/11/74; 7/12/76; notes 19, 35
GEORGE, Samuel - 11/8/76
GIBSON, Roger - 7/8/74; 8/19/74; 8/25/75
GILBERT, Giles - 1/26/76
GILDERSLEEVE,- Obadiah - 11/15/76
GILLINGS, Francis - 12/13/76
GIRAND, Monsieur - 11/15/76
GLAD, Danielle - 9/23/74
GLEESON, Elisha - 2/4/74
GODDARD, William - 5/20/74; 9/20/76
GOLDEN, Cadwalader - 11/8/76
GOODFIELD, Nathan - 11/24/75
GOODRICH, Col. Elizur - 7/8/74
GOODWIN, Jonathan - 2/24/75
GOODWIN, Captain - 12/27/76

GOOLD, James - 1/6/75
GORDON, Capt. John - 5/16/76
GORTON, John - 8/4/75
GORTON, William- 12/1/75
GOSNER,Christian - 11/15/76
GOTTEN, Nabby - 1/26/76
GRAVE, Samuel - 1/20/75
GRAVES, Joseph - 3/29/76
GRAY, Samuel- 2/4/74; 5/13/74; 7/1/74; 12/23/74; 1/27/75 4/26/76
GRAY, Simon - 1/6/75; 9/22/75
GREEN, Capt. Benjamin - 1/1375; 3/17/75
GREEN, Elizabeth - 3/17/75; 4/28/75
GREEN, James -6/17/74; 3/17/75; 4/28/75
GREEN, Captain Samuel, - 1
GREEN, Timothy E.- 1; 4/8/74; 7/1/74; 7/22/74; 9/9/74; 3/31/75;8/18/75; 10/27/75; 4/19/76; 6/28/76; 7/5/76; 8/16/76; 10/18/76; 12/27/76
GREEN, William - 8/19/74
GREEN, Widow - 9/22/75
GREENE, Captain Samuel - 5/12/75
GREENHILL; Joseph - 10/14/74; 11/25/74
GRENELL, Thomas - 1/26/76
GRENELL, Jr., Thomas - 7/19/76
GRIFFING, Lemuel - 12/29/75
GRIFFING, Samuel - 1/26/76
GRIGGS, Abigail - 8/23/76
GRIGGS, Ephraim - 8/23/76
GRIGGS, Hannah - 8/23/76
GRIGGS, Sarah - 8/23/76
GRIGGS, Stephen - 8/23/76
GRINER, David - 11/25/74
GRISWOLD, George - 1/6/75
GRISWOLD, Joseph - 2/18/74; 2/17/75
GRISWOLD, Matthew - 5/16/76
GROVER, Thomas - 8/11/75
GUSTIN, Thomas - 12/8/75
GUSTIN, Deacon Thomas - 12/8/75

H

HAIDEN, Noah - 5/16/76
HAIR, David - 4/5/76
HAKES, Jonathan - 7/19/76
HALDIMAN, General- 4/28/75
HALE, John - 3/31/75; 5/5/75
HALE, Josiah - 7/15/74
HALE, Nathan - note 37
HALL, Abijah - 12/23/74
HALL, Ebenezer 5/12/75
HALL, Ezra - 6/28/76
HALL, Jonathan - 8/19/74
HALL, Street - 7/7/75
HALL 2d, Thomas - 7/12/76
HALLAM, Jr., Amos - 11/15/76
HALLAM, Edward - 3/11/74; 1/1375; 11/1/76
HALLAM, John - 1/21/74; 4/26/76
HALLAM, Sarah - 12/16/74; 1/20/75
HALLAM, Mr. - 6/30/75
HALLEY, Capt. Jeremiah - 5/16/76
HALRANt, Mr. - 1/20/75
HALSEY, J. - 12/6/76
HALSEY, Jeremiah - 10/20/75
HALSEY, Silas - 7/15/74
HALSEY Jr., Silas - 3/10/75; 12/8/75
HAMBLIN, Ebenezer - 4/1/74
HAMLIN, Jabez - 7/15/74; 5/16/76
HAMMOND, Elisha - 5/5/75
HAMMOND, Rev. Noah - 5/5/75

HANCOCK, Ann - 4/7/75
HANCOCK, John - 10/27/75; 7/12/76
HANCOX, Edward - 3/18/74
HANMORE, John - 4/7/75
HARDING, Capt. Seth - 5/24/76; 5/31/76; 6/21/76; 10/4/76; 10/18/76
HARLAND, Thomas - 2/25/74; 11/25/74
HARRIS, Harris, David - 8/30/76
HARRIS, Mrs. Hannah - 8/23/76
HARRIS, Capt James - 8/23/76
HARRIS, Captain Jeremiah- 12/9/74
HARRIS, 3rd, John - 7/28/75
HARRIS, Captain Peter - 3/3/75; 8/23/76
HARRIS, Thomas - 2/3/75; 3/10/75; 5/31/76; 10/18/76
HARRIS, William, - 7/21/75; 1/12/76; 11/15/76
HARRY - 2/7/76
HART, Rev. M. T. - 3/24/75
HART Jr., William - 3/11/74
HART, Capt. - 3/29/76
HARTSHORN, Beriah - 6/28/76
HARVEY, Elisha - 5/10/76
HARVEY, John - 5/10/76
HASSARD, Samuel - 9/15/75
HASSARD, Jr.; Lt. Samuel - 8/2/76
HATCH; Zepheniah - 10/7/74
HAUGHTON, James - 2/11/74; 2/3/75; 3/10/75
HAUGHTON, inn keeper - 3/18/74
HAVENS, James - 11/22/76; 11/29/76
HAVENS, Obediah - 10/4/76; 11/22/76
HAWKINS, Lavina - 5/19/75

HAWLEY, Aaron - 9/15/75
HAYDEN, Clement - 7/19/76
HAYDEN, Capt. Uriah 12/30/74
HAZELTON, Charles - 9/16/74
HAZELTON, James - 9/16/74
HEATH, John - 1/26/76
HEBARD, James - 11/4/74
HEBARD, Nathaniel - 5/24/76; 11/8/76; 11/15/76
HEBARD, Paul -10/28/74 5/24/76
HEBARD, Capt. Zebulon - 12/23/74
HEDGES, David - 7/15/74
HEMPSTED John - 6/9/75;7/19/76; 9/20/76; 10/18/76
HEMPSTED Joshua - 3/29/76
HEMPSTED Jr., Joshua - 3/17/75
HEMPSTED Nathaniel - 5/10/76
HEMPSTED, Robert - 3/17/75
HEMPSTED Stephen - 3/3/75; 5/5/75
HEMPSTED, Thomas - 3/3/75; - 5/5/75
HEMPSTED, William - 3/3/75; 5/5/75; 12/6/76
HEMPSTED, W. - 7/19/76
HENDERSON, William - 11/15/76
HENRY, John - 12/20/76
HENSHAW, Benjamin - 5/3/76; 5/10/76
HERN, Elizabeth - 1/26/76
HERRICK, Henry - 7/15/74
HERRICK, John - 5/16/76
HERRICK, Robert -9/22/75; 9/6/76
HERROD, Stephen - 1/20/75
HERTTELL, John - 1/12/76
HEWIT, Mary - 12/1/75
HEWIT, Nathaniel - 1/20/75;

3/31/75
HEWIT, Mrs. Rebecca - 3/31/75
HEWIT, Capt. Richard - 10/11/76
HIBBARD, Paul - 1/27/75
HIGBE, Zacccheus - 3/29/76
HIGGINS, Cornelius - 9/16/74
HILL, Benjamin - 11/18/74
HILL Charles - 3/31/75
HILL, Henry - 4/5/76
HILL John - 3/29/76; 10/18/76
HILL, Samuel - 1/14/74
HILLARD, Benomi - 2/10/75
HILLARD, John - 1/21/74; 1/20/75
HILLARD, Lt. Joseph - 10/11/76
HILLARD, Lois - 10/11/76
HILLHOUSE, William - 4/15/74; 9/2/74; 2/3/75; 3/10/75; 4/14/75; 6/9/75; 5/16/76; 10/18/76
HINCKLEY, Charles - 3/10/75; 1/19/76
HILLARD, Capt. Elisha - 11/15/76
HILLARD, Noble - 10/25/76; 11/15/76; 12/27/76
HINMAN, Captain - 6/28/76
HITCHCOCK, Col. - 4/12/76
HOAR, Capt. - 8/2/76
HODGES, Abraham - 2/7/76
HODGES, Stephen 7/22/74
HODGSON, Col.- 4/28/75
HOLBROOK, John - 6/2/75
HOLDEN, . Phineas - 11/22/76
HOLLIDAY, Robert - 4/5/76
HOLLISTER, Elisha - 7/15/74
HOLMES, Bulah - 8/23/76
HOLMES, Christopher - 7/15/74
HOLMES, Mary - 8/23/76
HOLMES, Seth -Wymund - 1/7/74

HOLMES, William - 8/23/76
HOLT, Daniel - 11/22/76
HOLT Ebenezer - 1/1375
HOLT, Lt. James - 3/1/76
HOLT, Mrs. Jennaham - 1/1375
HOLT John - 8/2/76
HOLT, Mrs. Sarah - 8/2/76
HOLT William - 6/9/75
HOLT, Zabadiah - 5/10/76
HOLT Mr. - 1/21/74
HOLT, Mrs. - 6/9/75
HOMES; John - 8/2/76
HOPKINS, Alex - 11/15/76
HUNTINGTON, Commodore- 4/12/76
HORTON, Mr. - 8/2/76
HOSMER, Martha - 11/1/76
HOSMER, Titus - 7/15/74; 11/18/74; 11/3/75
HOUGH, David - 9/2/74; 2/10/75
HOUGHTON, James - 8/9/76
HOVEY, Ebenezer - 7/1/74; 10/14/74; 12/22/75
HOWARD, John - 12/23/74; 7/26/76
HOWARD, Captain - 12/27/76
HOWE, Rev. Joseph - 9/1/75
HOWE, Nehemiah - 9/30/74
HOWE, Dr. Samuel - 10/6/75
HOWE ,Timingham 4/12/76
HOWE, General - 10/18/76
HOWELL, Elisha- 7/15/74
HOWELL, Reil - 11/1/76
HOWELL, William - 1/7/74
HOWLAND, Mr. - 10/7/74
HU, John - 7/15/74
HUBBARD, Isaac - 1/21/74
HUBBARD, Jeremiah - 9/16/74
HUBBARD, Col. Leveret - 4/8/74

HUBBARD, Russell - 4/15/74; 4/21/75

HUBBARD, Timothy - 9/20/76
HUBBARD, William -6/10/74; 3/3/75; 10/11/76
HUBBARD, Wyllys - 4/8/74
HUDSON, John - 11/1/76
HUGHES, John - 4/19/76
HULBERT, Capt. - 12/1/75
HULL, Samuel Dyer - 3/11/74
HUMPHREY, Daniel - 4/8/74; 5/6/74
HUMPHREY, Daniel Collyer - 5/6/74
HUNT, Daniel - 1/26/76
HUNT, Sr, John - 3/8/76
HUNT, Jr. John - 3/8/76
HUNTER, John - 10/14/74
HUNTINGTON, Andrew - 8/16/76
HUNTINGTON, Benjamin - 4/15/74; 6/10/74; 9/2/74; 4/14/75; 5/16/76; 10/18/76
HUNTINGTON, Mrs. Doratha- 3/4/74
HUNTINGTON, Eliphalet - 10/25/76
HUNTINGTON, Mrs. Faith - 12/8/75
HUNTINGTON, Capt Hezekiah - 3/4/74; 12/23/74
HUNTINGTON, Jabez - 6/10/74;5/16/76; 10/18/76
HUNTINGTON, Jedidiah - 6/10/74; 1/1375; 7/7/75; 12/8/75; 4/19/76; 10/25/76
HUNTINGTON, Jonathan - 1/14/74; 6/10/74
HUNTINGTON, Josiah - 2/7/76
HUNTINGTON, Nehimia 1/14/74
HUNTINGTON, Samuel - 4/14/75; 11/3/75; 5/16/76
HUNTINGTON, Theophilus - 10/21/74
HUNTINGTON, Thomas - 7/29/74
HUNTINGTON, Uriah - 10/21/74
HUNTINGTON, Rev. Mr. - 3/24/75
HUNTINGTON, Col. - 8/18/75; 4/19/76; - 9/6/76
HURLBOT, Capt. Joseph - 8/30/76
HURLBOT,t, Nancy - 8/30/76
HURLBUT, Elisha - 12/2/74
HURLBUT, John - 12/23/74; 9/29/75; 10/18/76
HURLBUT,, Joseph - 12/16/74; 3/3/75; 3/10/75; 1/5/76; 7/19/76; 9/20/76; 10/18/76
HURLBUT, Jr., Joseph - 11/4/74
HURLBUT, Mrs. Mary - 11/4/74; 1/5/76
HUTCHINSON, Governor Thomas- 7/15/74; 12/2/74; note 29
HYDE, Daniel - 5/10/76; 5/24/76
HYDE, Jr,[Hide] Elijah - 9/9/74; 12/16/74; 12/30/74
HYDE, Jr., [Hide] Samuel - 6/2/75; 12/30/74
HYDE, Capt. Walter Hyde - 5/10/76
HYDE, Lieut. - 6/30/75

I
IDE; Abigail - 5/27/74
INGERSOL, David - 7/29/74
INGERSOLL, Mr. 4/29/74.
ISBAIN Jr., Jacob - 4/1/74
ISHAM Jr., Joseph - 8/12/74
ISRAEL - 3/25/74
IVES, John - 7/8/74
IRISH, Elias - 5/31/76

J
JACK - 9/15/75; 7/12/76

JACKSON, William- 10/18/76
JACOBS, Dufty - 12/23/74
JACOBS, Katurah - 12/23/74,
JACQUIES, Jonathan - 8/11/75
JAMES I, King -note 3
JEFF - 1/26/76
JEFFREY, Charles - 7/15/74
JEFFREY, Joseph - 11/15/76
JEFFERY, Samuel - 12/6/76
JENNINGS, Anne - 7/15/74
JENNINGS, Daniel - 7/15/74
JEROM, Benjamin - 12/15/75
JEWET, Eleazar- 3/4/74
JEWETT, Rev. David -7/8/74 ; 4/14/75; 10/13/75; 12/20/76
JEWETT, Gibbons - 7/15/74; 4/12/76
JEWETT, Capt. Joseph - 4/19/76; 6/14/76
JOHNSON, Rev. Jacob - 9/22/75
JOHNSON, Joseph - 5/20/74
JOHNSON, Miss Lydia - 9/22/75
JOHNSON, Rebecca - 1/20/75
JOHNSON, William Samuel - 7/15/74
JOHNSON, Steven - 9/30/74
JOHNSON Jr.,Stephen - 5/20/74
JOHNSON, Sr, Thomas - 8/18/75
JOHNSON, Jr. Thomas - 8/18/75
JONES, Abel - 6/28/76
JONES, Abijah - 3/4/74; 11/18/74; 6/9/75; 8/25/75
JONES, Capt. Jabez - 6/9/75
JONES, James - 7/26/76
JONES, Obidiah - 7/15/74
JONES, Samuel - 6/17/74
JONES, Seth - 5/20/74; 7/22/74
JONES, Thomas - 1/20/75; 6/16/75; 7/14/75; 7/19/76; 11/22/76
JONES, Capt. - 5/31/76
JONES, Mr. - 4/19/76

JORDAN - 10/13/75

K
KANE, Jonathan - 6/14/76
KATE - 4/29/74
KEEN, Charles - 9/15/75
KEENY, Hannah - 4/5/76
KEITH, John - 3/17/75
KELLY, James - 10/25/76
KELLY, Shaddrick - 4/5/76-
KELSEY, Mr.- 11/18/74
KENEDY, Dennis - 1/20/75
KENNEDY, Capt. Thomas - 11/15/76
KEYES, John - 9/30/74
KILLEY, Capt. Christopher - 3/18/74
KIMBERLEY, Thomas - 7/15/74
KINGSBURY, Lieut. Asa - 9/15/75; 4/19/76
KINGSBURY, Ebenezer - 10/18/76
KINGSBURY, Ephraim - 10/11/76
KINGSBURY, Elisha - 5/16/76
KINGSBURY, Dr. Obidiah - 2/4/74; 4/19/76; 6/7/76; 10/11/76
KINGSBURY, Sarah - 10/11/76
KINSMAN, David - 12/6/76
KINSMAN, Capt. Jeremiah - 10/13/75
KINSMAN, Robert 7/15/74
KNAP, Benjamin - 9/2/74
KNEELAND, John - 2/17/75
KNIGHT, Mrs. Abigail - 7/22/74
KNIGHT, Caleb - 11/17/75
KNIGHT, Jonathan - 7/22/74
KNIGHT, Joseph - 3/11/74; 7/1/74; 12/2/74; 2/29/75; 11/17/75
KNIGHT, Phineas - 12/13/76

KNOT, Capt. William - 11/15/76
KNOWLTON, Capt. - 6/30/75
KUFMAN, Jeremiah - 3/15/76
KYES, Capt. John - 2/23/76

L

LADD, Henry - 9/9/74
LAMB, David - 6/28/76
LAMB, Lemeuel - 12/8/75
LAMSON, William - 3/18/74
LANE, Hezekiah - 5/16/76; 10/18/76
LASELLS, Capt. John - 5/24/76
LATHAM, Mr. - 9/20/76
LATHROP, Azariah - 2/4/74;- 3/11/74; 6/3/74; 3/29/76; 11/1/76
LATHROP, Captain Elisha - 1/28/74; 9/22/75; 5/31/76; 12/27/76
LATHROP, 3d , Elisha - 6/23/75; 10/13/75
LATHROP, Jabez - 2/4/74
LATHROP, Joshua - 5/6/74; 10/14/74
LATHROP, Rufus - 5/6/74; 10/18/76
LATHROP, Samuel - 1/28/74
LATHROP, Thomas - 5/27/74
LATHROP, William - 2/4/74
LATHROP, Zachariah - 9/2/74
LATHROP, Mrs - 1/28/74
LATIMER, Daniel - 3/15/76;
LATIMER, David - 12/27/76
LATIMER, Mrs. Elizabeth - 9/6/76
LATIMER, Henry - 3/1/76
LATIMER, Capt. Jonathan - 6/16/75; 12/22/75; 3/15/76; - 6/28/76
LATIMER, Jr., Jonathan - 7/7/75; 10/20/75

LATIMER, Samuel - 5/27/74 , 7/1/74; 8/18/75; - 9/6/76
LATIMER, Latimer Jr, Samuel - 5/27/74
LAW, Richard - 3/18/74; 4/15/74; 7/1/74; 7/15/74; 9/2/74; 2/3/75 ;3/10/75; 3/24/75; 4/14/75; 4/21/75; 10/11/76; 5/16/76; 6/14/76; 10/18/76; 11/1/76; 11/15/76
LAWRENCE, Joseph - 5/16/76
LAY, Ann - 4/5/76
LAY, Elisha - 6/16/75
LAY, John - 10/18/76
LAY II, John - 9/2/74
LAY, Jonathan, 12/30/74
LEACH, Joseph - 1/21/74
LEACH, Mananssa - 6/28/76
LEAMING, Rev. Mr. - 4/19/76
LEARNED,, Simon - 10/18/76
LEARNED, Col. - 4/19/76
LEAVINGS, Benjamin - 10/18/76
LEDLIE, Hugh - 3/3/75; 3/8/76; 12/20/76
LEDYARD, Ebenezer - 12/23/74; - 6/9/75; 7/19/76
LEDYARD, John - 1/26/76
LEDYARD, Capt. William - 5/16/76; 7/19/76; 10/18/76
LEE, Benjamin - 3/11/74
LEE, Joseph - 1/26/76
LEE, Levi - 8/11/75
LEE, Robert - 8/5/74
LEE, Thomas - 4/19/76
LEECH, Amos - 1/27/75
LEECH, Joseph - 1/27/75
LEFFINGWELL, Benajab - 5/5/75
LEFFINGWELL, Christopher - 2/18/74; 2/25/74; 6/10/74; 6/17/74; 7/29/74; 2/24/75; 9/22/75; 12/1/75; 13/15/76 ;7/19/76; 8/16/76; 9/6/76;

10/25/76; 11/8/76; 11/22/76; 12/20/76
LEFFINGWELL, Daniel - 10/14/74
LEFFINGWELL Hez. - 2/24/75; 3/3/75
LEFFINGWELL, Captain John - 6/24/74
LEFFINGWELL, Matthew - 12/20/76l
LEFFINGWELL Samuel - 10/14/74
LEMON - 5/6/74;7/8/74
LEONARD, Rev. Mr. - 5/5/75
LERAY, John - 8/2/76
LESTER, David - 3/1/76; 6/7/76; 7/19/76; 8/16/76; 11/ 22/76
LESTER, Elipalet - 3/10/75; 11/15/76
LESTER, Jonathan - 8/19/74; - 5/5/75
LESTER, Timothy - 1/28/74; 3/29/76
LESTER, Thomas - 7/19/76
LESTER, Mrs. - 3/29/76
LEWIS, Dr.- 9/1/75
LEWIS, Mr. - 11/29/76
LINE, William - 1/28/74
LINKEN, Nathaniel - 6/21/76
LITTLE, Col. - 4/12/76
LITTLE, Gamaliel - 9/22/75; 10/13/75
LONGFEFFIS, Nicholas - 8/2/76
LONGWORTHY, Sanford - 5/3/76
LOOMIS, Ebenezer - 10/25/76
LORD, Ebenezer - 2/4/74
LORD, Dr. Elisha - 2/4/74
LORD, Sr., John - 6/7/76
LORD, John - 1/12/76
LORD, Jr., John - 6/7/76
LORD, Martin - 2/10/75

LORD, Nathan - 8/19/74
LORD, Samuel - 5/31/76
LORD, Solomon - 5/24/76
LOTHROP, Captain Cyprian - 3/18/74
LOTHROP, Rufus - 5/16/76
LOUDON, Samuel - 10/25/76
LOVELAND, Capt. John - 7/26/76
LOVELAND, Susanna - 7/26/76
LOVETT, Josephus - 1/14/74
LOYDE, James - 4/12/76
LUCE, James - 12/23/74; 9/15/75;
LUCE, Captain - 1/6/75
LUNT, Captain - 6/30 75
LYDIUS, John Henry - note 2
LYMAN, Elijah - 4/22/74
LYNDE, William - 12/6/76
LYON, Amos - 1/26/76
LYON, Humphrey - 4/15/74; 7/15/74; 4/12/76

M
M'CLENNAN, Samuel - 10/18/76; 12/27/76
M'NEIL, Alexander - 3/29/76
MACEY, Latham. - 12/9/74
MAHER, Joseph - 2/3/75
MAIN, Amos - 4/19/76
MAIN, David - 12/30/74
MAIN, Stephen - 4/19/76
MAINS, Joseph - 6/28/76
MAN, Elisha - 3/1/76
MANSFIELD, Deacon Jonathan - 1/20/75; 9/20/76
MANSFIELD, Margaret - note 21
MANSFIELD, Samuel - 7/7/75
MANSFIELD, Capt. Stephen - 7/29/74
MANWARING, David - 3/10/75; 3/11/74; 11/25/74

MANWARING, Thomas - 11/17/75
MANWARING, William - 12/22/75
MARSH, Peletiah, 12/30/74
MARSHALL Jun, Elijah - 10/14/74
MARSHALL, Mary - 9/15/75
MARTIN Martin, Anderson - 12/27/76
MARTIN, Rev. Ebenezer - 2/25/74; 12/16/74
MARTIN, Jonathan - 8/18/75
MARTIN, Lawrence - 7/19/76
MARVIN, Reynold - 4/21/75
MASON, Capt. Jeremiah - 3/10/75; 5/16/76
MASON, Samuel - 1/20/75
MATHER, Joseph - 1/6/75
MATHER Jr., Samuel - 7/15/74
MATTHER, Eleazer 4/29/74.
MAYER, Nathaniel - 1/7/74
MAYNARD, Andrew - 12/6/76
MCCLENNAN, Samuel - 7/8/74
MCCLURY, Robert - 11/15/76
McColl, Mr.- 8/19/74
MCCURDY, John - 4/7/75; 4/14/75
MCDONALD, John - 8/4/75
MCFEE, Matthew - 11/15/76
McGibbin, Capt. - 9/8/75
MCKEE, John - 3/3/75
MCKENZIE, Alex. - 11/15/76
MCMASTER, Hugh - 8/25/75
MCNEIL, Mrs. - 11/15/76
MECOY, Daniel - 1/20/75
MEEGS, Captain Benjamin- 12/9/74
MERRELL, Alexander - 4/14/75
MERRIL, Abel - 5/16/76
METCALF, Elijah - 6/17/74
MILLER, Lady Ann - 6/7/76

MILLER, Burnet - 7/ 22/ 74
MILLER, Eleazer - 7/ 22/ 74
MILLER, Elisha - 5/6/74
MILLER, Jeremiah Miller - 6/7/76
MILLS, Mrs. Elizabeth - 8/5/74
MILLS, Rev. Gideon Mills - 8/5/74
MINARD, Jonathan - 10/11/76
MINER, Charles - 5/20/74
MINER, Ephraim - 9/1/75; 8/30/76
MINER, Nathaniel - 4/15/74; 4/14/75; 5/26/75; 1/26/76; 4/5/76; 11/15/76
MINER, Stephen - 2/17/75
MINER, Turner - 12/1/75
MIX, Zebediah - 11/15/76
MOBS; Parce - 4/19/76
MOFATT, Edward - 3/29/76
MONRO, Thomas - 1/21/74
MOORY, Joseph - 8/2/76
MORGAN, Ensign Benjamin- 4/28/75
MORGAN, Samuel - 7/26/76
MORGAN, Captain William - 1/14/74; 4/15/74; 12/23/74
MORRELLS, Messrs.- 9/1/75
MORRIS, Col. - 7/26/76
MORSE, Jedidiah - 7/8/74
MORSE, Parker - 4/22/76
MORSEE, Moses - 4/21/75
MORSS, Moses - 1/21/74
MORTIMER, Philip - 3/17/75
MOSELY, Capt. Ebenezer - 10/18/76
MOSELY, Isaac - 7/15/74
MOSELY, Dr. Thomas - 1/5/76
MOTT, Mrs. Abigail - 8/16/76
MOTT, Edward - 4/15/74
MOTT, Samuel - 6/24/74; 8/16/76

MOTT, Col. - 8/2/76; 9/20/76
MULFORD, David - 7/22/74; 12/30/74
MUMFORD, Benjamin - 8/18/75
MUMFORD, Captain George - 10/13/75
MUMFORD, Hannah - 10/13/75
MUMFORD, James - 1/14/74; 4/15/74
MUMFORD, John - 12/2/74
MUMFORD, R. - 3/22/76
MUMFORD, Robinson - 1/14/74; 4/29/74; 7/19/76; 9/13/76; 10/18/76; 11/1/76
MUMFORD, Sarah - 1/14/74
MUMFORD, Thomas - 1/14/74; 4/15/74; 9/2/74; 12/23/74; 3/3/75; 4/14/75; 5/26/75; 7/21/75; 11/3/75; 9/13/76; 9/20/76; 10/18/76; 11/8/76; 12/6/76
MUNRO, Bennet - 6/14/76
MUNRO; Capt. James - 10/11/76

N
NASH, Jonathan - 2/4/74
NEVINS, David - 2/18/74
NEWBURY, Daniel - 11/15/76
NEWPORT - 5/10/76
NEWTON, Mark - 5/10/76; 11/15/76
NICKELSON, Thomas - 10/18/76
NICKOLSON, James B. - ½1/74
NILES, Lathrop - 4/22/74
NILES, Capt. Robert - 9/13/76; 10/11/76
NILES, Stephen - 5/20/74
NILES, Capt - 5/31/76; 6/21/76
NIXON, Col. - 4/12/76; 7/19/76
NOBLES, Jonathan - 4/5/76
NORTH, Lord - note 19
NOULTON, William - 3/4/74

NOYES, William - 4/15/74; 1/26/76

O
OCCOM, Samson - 4/8/74
OLDS, Daniel - 7/7/75
OLDS, Robert - 7/7/75
OLMSTED, Ichabod - 7/15/74
OSBORNE, Osborne, Mrs. Hannah - 12/2/74
OSBORNE, Deacon - 12/2/74
OSBORNE, Mr. - 5/5/75
OWEN, John - 6/3/74; 7/1/74; 9/9/74
OCCUM, Mary - 4/5/76
ORCUTt, Lt. Solomon - 4/19/76
OSGOOD, John Fisk - 3/15/76
OSGOOD, Mrs. Lucy - 3/15/76
ORMSBEE, Joseph - 8/23/76
OTNEY, Joseph - 7/19/76; 11/15/76

P
PACKER, Joseph - 9/9/74; 12/23/74; 10/18/76; 10/25/76;
PACKWOOD, Capt. Joseph - 8/2/76; 11/15/76
PADDOCK, Zechariah - 5/16/76
PAG, Abraham - 4/22/74
PAGE, Jeremiah - 4/5/76; 7/19/76
PAIN, David - 5/16/76; 10/18/76
PAIN, Joshua - 8/11/75
PAINE, Benjamin - 11/15/76
PAINE, Elisha - 4/15/74
PAINE, Thomas - note 16.
PALMER, Amos - 5/24/76
PALMER Captain Andrew - 3/18/74; 12/23/74; 4/5/76
PALMER, Benj. - 4/22/74
PALMER, David - 11/8/76

PALMER, Denison- 4/28/75
PALMER, Elijah - 4/12/76
PALMER, Gershom - 5/3/76
PALMER, James - 4/12/76
PALMER, Jonah - 7/26/76
PALMER, John - 4/19/76
PALMER, Jr., Joseph - 4/26/76
PALMER, Joseph -1/14/74; 5/3/76
PALMER, Mary - 6/28/76
PALMER, Capt. Nathan - 11/15/76
PALMER Jr., Nathan - 3/18/74
PALMER, William - 6/28/76
PALMES, Captain Edward - 6/3/74; 9/9/74; 10/14/74; 4/21/75; 11/3/75 6/7/76; 7/19/76; 8/23/76; 10/18/76
PARENT, Nathan - 9/1/75
PARK, Hannah S. - 8/4/75
PARK, Thomas - 1/26/76
PARKER, Deacon Samuel - 2/23/76
PARMELE, Samuel - 2/18/74
PARSONS, John - 11/1/76
PARSONS, Rev. Jonathan - 8/2/76
PARSONS, Mark - 12/6/76
PARSONS, Marshfield - 7/15/74; 1/6/75; 4/14/75; 5/16/76; 10/18/76
PARSONS, Maj. Samuel Holden - 4/15/74; 7/1/74; 10/14/74; 11/25/74; 8/11/75
PARSONS, Rev. Mr. - 7/19/76
PARSONS, Col. - 6/28/76
PATTEN, Nathaniel - 4/7/75; 2/9/76
PATTERSON, Miss Ruth - 7/8/74
PEABODY, Samuel - 5/5/75
PEASE, Jesse - 9/15/75
PECK, Elias - 8/25/75; 9/20/76

PELLETREAU, Elias - 7/15/74; 8/9/76
PELTON, Thomas - 12/27/76
PEMBERTON, Patrick Grant - 1/19/76
PENNIMAN, John - 3/1/76
PERIT, Anthony Perit, - 4/15/74
PERIT, Mrs. Mary - 4/15/74
PERIT, Capt. Peter - 3/29/76
PERKINS, Andrew - 7/29/74
PERKINS, Elenathan - 12/27/76
PERKINS, Elisha - 4/22/74; 7/15/74; 10/18/76
PERKINS, Hezekiah - 10/7/74
PERKINS, Isaac - 4/1/74
PERKINS, Capt. Jabez - 4/1/74; 1/26/76; 6/28/76
PERKINS, Jacob - 4/19/76
PERKINS, James - 5/13/74; 12/15/75
PERKINS, Widow Joanna - 12/27/76
PERKINS, John - 11/8/76
PERKINS, Joseph 4/29/74; 5/12/75
PERKINS, Luke - 5/13/74
PERKINS, Mrs. Mary - 12/27/76
PERKINS, Capt. Solomon - 12/23/74; 6/9/75
PERKINS, Dr. - 7/19/76
PERRIN, Capt. Timothy - 10/18/76
PETER - 3/15/76
PEVE; Ichabod - 7/12/76
PHELPES, Elijah- 3/25/74
PHELPS, Major Charles - 1/7/74; 9/2/74;1/6/75; 4/14/75; 7/7/75; 2/9/76; 7/7/75; 5/16/76
PHELPS, Silas - 1/6/75; 9/22/75
PHELPS, William - 4/5/76
PHILIPS, Elijah - 5/27/74
PHILIPS, Mrs. Margarette -

POMP - 12/2/74
PHILIPS, William - 3/8/76
PIERSON, - Lemeul - 11/15/76
PINNCO, James 12/30/74
PITKIN, Col. John - 4/14/75
PITKIN, William - 11/17/75; 5/16/76
PITT, Benjamin - 4/15/74
PITT, William - 6/9/75
PITT, Lord - note 19
PLATT, Obidiah - 5/12/75
PLUMB, Samuel - 3/11/74
PLUMBE, Mrs. Esther - 4/19/76
PLUMBE, John - 11/17/75
PLUMBE, Mr. Nathaniel - 4/19/76
PLUMMER, Ebenezer - 4/15/74; 7/15/74
POAT, John - 7/29/74
POLLARD, Jeremiah - 9/20/76
POMEROY, Eleazer - 9/15/75
POMEROY, Noah - 1/27/75
POMP - 12/2/74
POND, Peter - 3/15/76
POND, Captain - 9/6/76
POOR, Col. - 4/12/76
PORTER, Nathaniel - 1/14/74; 6/2/75
PORTER, Mrs. Sarah - 4/14/75
PORTER, Mr. - 4/14/75
POST; John - 2/4/74; 10/21/74
POTTER, Abigail - 7/8/74; 12/30/74; 11/15/76
POTTER, William - 7/8/74; 8/19/74; 12/30/74
POWERS, Ichabod - 7/19/76
POWERS, Joshua - 3/17/75; 3/22/76
PRATT, David Beebe - 8/11/75
PRENTICE, Joshua - 10/18/76
PRENTICE, Capt. - 8/11/75
PRENTICE, Samuel -9/2/74; 7/7/75
PRENTIS, 2d, John - 3/1/76
PRENTIS, Jonathan- 3/4/74
PRENTIS, Capt. Joseph- 3/4/74
PRESCOTT, Col. - 4/12/76
PRESTON, Abraham - 12/13/76
PRESTON, John - 5/31/76
PRIDE, Joseph - 3/11/74
PRINCE, Benjamin - 1/26/76
PRINCE, Mrs. Mary - 7/8/74
PRINCE, William - 7/8/74
PRITKIN, Richard - 6/21/76
PROCTOR, John - 6/9/75
PROCTOR, Miss Polly - 6/9/75
PRUDDIN, Mrs. Esther - 10/27/75
PRUDDIN,, Rev. 10/27/75
PUNDERSON, Ebenezer - 4/21/75
PUTNAM, Israel - 6/10/74
PYGAN, Hannah - 2/3/75

Q
QUIRK, William - 6/28/76

R
RALL, Col. Joann, note 16
RAMSDEL, Mr..- 3/4/74
RANDAL, Joshua - 1/20/75; 4/28/75; 5/10/76
RANDALL, Amos - 8/16/76
RANNEY, Abijah - 12/2/74
RANSOM, Bliss - 4/5/76
RANSOM, Elias - 2/4/74
RANSOM, James - 1/27/75
RANSOM, Robert- 4/28/75
RATCHFORD, Thomas - 5/27/74; 3/31/75
RATHBUN, Abel - 1/21/74
RATHBUN, Joshua - 4/22/74
RATHBUN, Joshua the third, - 1/7/74
RATHBURN, Job - 5/6/74

RAWSON, Benjamin - 3/15/76
RAWSON David - 4/19/76
RAWSON, Dr. Eliot - 11/22/76; 3/15/76
RAWSON, Rev. Mr. 7/1/74
RAYMOND, Joshua -
RAYMOND, Christopher - 12/2/74
RAYMOND, John - 12/22/75
RAYMOND, Joshua - 11/18/74; 8/9/76
RAYNOLDS, Reverend Peter- 3/4/74
RAYNOLDS, Samuel- 3/4/74
READ,[see also Reed] Joseph - 6/3/74
READ, Read, Col. - 4/12/76
READ, Read, Samuel - 3/29/76
REED, Joseph - 11/8/76
REYNOLD, Mrs. Elizabeth - 12/23/74
REYNOLD, Rev Peter - 12/23/74
RICHARDS, Jr., David - 9/8/75
RICHARDS, Capt. Guy - 7/1/74 2/3/75; 3/10/75; 4/21/75
RICHARDS, Jabez - 12/22/75
RICHARDS, Jeremiah - 6/16/75
RICHARDS, John - 1/21/74
RICHARDSON, Elezer - 9/15/75
RICHMOND, Col. - 10/18/76
RIEVE, Rev Ezra Rieve - 11/17/75
RIEVE, Mrs. Mary - 11/17/75
RILEY, Captain Levi - 2/25/74
RIPLEY, Elijah - 3/31/75; 5/5/75
ROACH, Thomas - 8/11/75
ROBBINS, Edward - 2/18/74
ROBBINS, Joseph - 9/9/74
ROBERTS, Eliphalet - 4/22/74
ROBERTS, John- 3/4/74
ROBERTSON, Archibald - 1/26/76; 8/16/76

ROBERTSON, Daniel - 2/4/74
ROBERTSON, Patrick - 12/15/75; 1/26/76; 7/19/76; 10/18/76
ROBINS, John - 2/17/75
ROBINSON, Dr. Ebenezer 7/15/74
ROBINSON, Edward - 3/11/74; 8/26/74
ROBINSON, Experience - 2/11/74 ;12/22/75
ROBINSON, J. - 2/24/75; 3/10/75; 6/2/75; 1/20/75
ROBINSON, James -12/22/75 2/7/76
ROBINSON, John - 9/27/76
ROBINSON, Joseph - 2/23/76
ROBINSON, Rebecca - 2/23/76
ROBINSON, William 7/15/74
ROBINSON, Captain - 1/28/74
ROGERS, Charity - 7/28/75
ROGERS, David - 5/26/75; 11/1/76
ROGERS, Elizabeth - 11/18/74
ROGERS, James - 1/1375; 6/7/76
ROGERS, John - 3/10/75
ROGERS, 2d, John - 12/6/76
ROGERS, Miss Lucy - 1/28/74
ROGERS, Nathaniel - 11/4/74; 1/20/75; 1/26/76; 11/22/76
ROGERS, Rustford - 12/27/76
ROGERS, Dr. Theophilus - 6/10/74
ROGERS, Thomas - 9/22/75
ROGERS, William - 10/11/76; 12/27/76
ROGERS, Zabadiel - 10/4/76 ;12/6/76
ROGERS, Uriah - 2/4/74; 7/15/74
ROGERS, ROGERS, Captain - 9/6/76

ROLLAND, William - 5/3/76
ROOT, Ephraim - 3/31/75; 5/5/75; 5/16/76
ROSSETER, Mrs Abigail - 9/13/76
ROSSETER, Elnath - 3/18/74
ROSSETER, Rev. - 9/13/76
ROWLEE, Capt. - 8/18/75
ROWLEY, Joseph, - 12/9/74
ROWLEY, Capt. - 8/2/76
RUDE, Zephaniah- 4/28/75; 4/19/76
RUSSEL, Hezekiah - 7/8/74
RUSSEL, John - 11/15/76; 11/29/76
RUSSEL, William - 11/22/76; 12/20/76
RUSSELL, Captain Giles - 10/14/74; 10/28/74; 11/11/74; 10/11/76

S
SAFFORD, David - 5/10/76
SAFFORD, Solomon - 12/27/76
SAGE, Capt. Comfort - 1/1375
SAGE, Captain Giles - 2/25/74
SAGE, Miss Polly - 1/1375
SAGE, Rev. Mr.- 7/22/74
SALTER, John - 11/11/74
SALTER, Rev. Richard - 10/6/75
SALTMARSH, John - 3/15/76; 5/16/76
SALTONSTALL, Dudley - 2/11/74; 12/8/75
SALTONSTALL, G. - 2/3/75; 6/23/75; 11/17/75
SALTONSTALL, Gilbert - 9/20/76
SALTONSTALL, Hon. Gurdun - 7/1/74; 9/16/74; 10/27/75; 9/20/76; 11/1/76
SALTONSTALL, Mrs. Rebecca - 11/1/76
SALTONSTALL, Roswell - 12/23/74; 7/19/76; 12/6/76
SALTONSTALL, Winthrop - 5/16/76; 10/11/76; 10/18/76; 11/15/76
SAMBO - 12/2/74
SAMSON - 7/1/74
SANFORD, Benjamin - 4/15/74
SANFORD, Miss Hannah - 9/6/76
SANFORD, John - 7/19/76
SANFORD, Kingsbury - 12/23/74
SANFORD, Thomas - 9/6/76
SCARMAN, Neal - 7/29/74
SCOTT, John - 10/7/74; 2/23/76
SCOVEL Scovel, Elisha - 12/2/74; 1/20/75
SCOVEL, Nathan - 1/26/76
SEAMAN, Silvanus - 6/7/76
SEARS, Hezekiah - 2/18/74; 2/17/75
SEDGWICK, Theodore - 2/4/74
SELDEN, Ezra - 9/2/74 ;1/6/75; 4/14/75; 3/29/76
SELDEN, Joseph - 9/16/74
SELDEN, Col. Samuel -5/16/76; 8/2/76 9/13/76; 9/27/76
SEYMOUR, Moses - 4/21/75
SEYMOUR, Thomas - 11/17/75
SHACKMAPLE, Bet - 8/18/75
SHACKMAPLE, Capt John - 6/7/76
SHACKMAPLE, Mrs. Phoebe - 6/7/76
SHACKMAPLE, Mr. - 7/19/76
SHALER, Capt. Timothy - 12/27/76
SHAND, Captain - 12/30/74
SHAPELY, Adam - 3/11/74
SHAPELY, Joanne - 8/23/76
SHAPELY, Thomas - 8/23/76
SHAW, Nathaniel - 2/3/75 ; 6/9/75

SHAW Jr., Nathaniel - 4/15/74; 7/1/74; 2/3/75 ;3/3/75; 3/10/75; 8/9/76;- 10/18/76 1
SHAYLE, Nathaniel - 9/2/74
SHEFFIELD, George - 9/13/76
SHEFFIELD, James - 9/13/76
SHEFFIELD, Robert - 11/15/76
SHELBY, Jeremiah - 5/16/76
SHEFFIELD, Elisha - 5/16/76
SHELDEN, Col. - 11/1/76
SHEPERD, Abraham 7/15/74
SHERIFF, Mrs. Elizabeth - 6/14/76
SHERIFF, Maj. - 6/14/76
SHERMAN, James - 8/19/74; 12/15/75
SHERMAN, Roger - 8/12/74; 8/26/74; 11/4/74; 11/18/74; 11/3/75; 5/16/76
SHERMAN, Samuel - 9/13/76
SHERMAN, William - 9/13/76
SHERRY, Roger - 12/2/74
SHIPMAN, Captain Edward - 2/18/74; 12/30/74
SHIPMAN, Capt. Samuel - 5/16/76
SHIPPEN, Peggy - note 21
SHOLES, John - 7/26/76
SHUCKBURGH, Dr. Richard, note 18
SILL, Capt. David - 12/6/76
SILLIMAN, Hon Ebenezer - 10/27/75
SILLIMAN, Mrs. Martha - 8/12/74
SILLIMAN, Selleck - 8/12/74
SIMMONDS, Capt. - 8/2/76
SIMONS Jacob - 3/18/74; 7/15/74; 10/28/74; 1/27/75; 2/17/75; 10/13/75
SIMONS, James - 12/6/76
SIMPSON, Capt. John - 2/16/76

SISTAR, Gabriel - 4/5/76
SITH Jr ,Samuel - 12/27/76
SKINNER, John - 8/4/75
SKINNER, William - 5/16/76
SLATE, Ezekiel - 7/5/76
SLATE, Miss Mary - 7/5/76
SLUMAN, Joseph - 8/16/76
SMEDLEY, Samuel - 7/19/76
SMITH, Abiezer - 5/31/76
SMITH, Abner - 9/16/74
SMITH, Charles - -9/16/74; 2/9/76; 6/14/76; 9/27/76
SMITH, David - 2/18/74; 2/17/75
SMITH, Capt. Elijah - 1/27/75; 3/22/76; 6/14/76
SMITH, Mrs. Elizabeth - 7/5/76
SMITH, Esther - 6/14/76
SMITH, Ezra - 5/16/76; 5/31/76
SMITH, Gilbert - 6/23/75
SMITH, Smith, Jr., Jabez - 6/23/75
SMITH, James - 9/9/74
SMITH, Jonathan - 6/3/74
SMITH, Joseph - 2/4/74; 4/29/74; 9/16/74; 4/14/75; 5/3/76
SMITH, Josiah - 2/4/74
SMITH, Lucretia - 8/23/76
SMITH, Nathan - 12/15/75; 7/5/76; 11/8/76
SMITH, Lt. Nehamiah - 9/20/76
SMITH, Noah - 2/23/76;
SMITH, Oliver - ½6/76; 7/19/76
SMITH, Peter - 7/12/76
SMITH, Mrs. Sarah - 6/3/76
SMITH, Simon - 2/25/74; 3/17/75; 6/23/75 -
SMITH, Thankful 4/29/74
SMITH, Uriah - 5/5/75
SMITH, Waitstill - 2/18/74
SMITH, William - 6/28/76
SMITH, 2d, William - 6/16/75

SMITH, Capt. - 11/8/76
SNEID, Capt. Edward - 6/14/76
SNEYD; Lt. Edward - 11/15/76; 11/29/76
SOLOMON, Isaac - 9/2/74
SOMMERS, Lord - 7/1/74
SOUTHMAYD, Mrs. Elizabeth - 7/1/74
SOUTHMAYD, William - 7/1/74
SOUTHWARD, Constant - 11/11/74; 10/18/76
SOUTHWARD, Gideon - 11/1/76
SOUTHWICK, Solomon - 7/1/74
SOUTHWORTH, Beriah - 6/2/75
SPAIN, KING OF - 2/25/74;
SPALDING, Curtis - 7/15/74
SPAULDING, Asa - 9/6/76
SPENCER, Joel - 12/20/76
SPENCER, John - 1/28/74
SPENCER, Joseph - 7/15/74; 5/16/76
SPENCER, Peter - 6/7/76
SPENCER, Ruth - 1/28/74
SPICER, Oliver - 9/20/76
SPINGER, Mr. - 3/22/76
SPOONER, J. P. -7/29/74; 3/1/76
SPOONER, Judah P. - 5/24/76; 8/16/76
SPOONER, Mr. - 6/17/74
SQUIRE, David - 10/14/74
STACK, Amos - 9/13/76
STACK, Samuel - 9/13/76
STACK, William - 9/13/76
STANDON, Capt Theo. - 11/15/76
STANTON, Joshua - 11/22/76
STANTON, Phineas - 4/5/76
STARR, Amariah - 10/14/74
STARR, Cornelius - 10/14/74
STARR, Capt. Daniel - 2/25/74; 11/15/76; 11/29/76
STARR, Elihu - 9/2/74

STARR, Mrs. Elizabeth - 11/29/76
STARR, Jr., Jonathan - 3/10/75
STARR, Joseph - 7/29/74
STARR, Joshua - 8/23/76
STARR, Jr. Joshua -3/10/75; 2/7/76
STARR, Mrs. Sarah - 3/10/75
STARR, Captain - 11/18/74
STEDMAN, James - 3/18/74 ;7/15/74; 10/13/75
STEDMAN, Nathan - 3/29/76; 12/20/76
STEDMAN, Deacon Thomas - 3/18/74
STEEL, Richard - 11/4/74
STEEL, Mr.- 4/15/74
STERRY, Roger - 11/24/75
STEVENS, Aaron - 2/10/75
STEVENS, Isaac - 11/15/76
STEVENS, John - 9/30/74
STEWART, W. - 2/11/74
STEWART, William -4/21/75; 8/18/75; 9/15/75; 10/13/75; 3/8/76; 4/5/76; 7/5/76; 11/15/76; 12/20/76
STOCKER, John - 9/2/74
STOCKWELL, Eleaser, - 7/19/76
STODARD, Mortimer - 2/7/76
STODDARD, Ralph - 8/16/76; 11/22/76
STODDARD, Thomas - 1/26/76
STODDARD, Rev. Venerable - 3/15/76
STORRS, Amariah - 2/18/74
STORRS, Rev John - 10/6/75
STORRS, Major Joseph - 11/11/74
STORRS, Judah - 7/5/76
STORRS, Mrs. Eunice - 10/6/75
STORRS, Capt. Experience - 11/11/74; 5/16/76

STORRS, Rev John - 10/6/75
STRAING, Jack - 7/19/76
STRICKLAND 2d, Peter - 3/1/76
STRONG, Ens. Asa - 9/13/76
STRONG, Ebenezer - 1/27/75
STRONG, Jedidiah - 7/8/74
STUART, John - 4/7/75
STUBBINS, Joseph - 12/6/76
STURGIS, Jonathan - 11/18/74
SULLIVAN, Elizabeth - 11/15/76
SUMNER, George - 7/15/74
SUMNER, Captain - 4/19/76
SUMNERS, Capt. Benjamin - 5/16/76
SWAN, SWAIN, Captain Peleg - 10/14/74
SWAN, Joshua - 6/21/76
SWAN, Capt. Robert - 10/11/76
SWEETLAND, Joel - 5/3/76
SWIFT, John - 12/9/74
SWIFT, Col. - 8/2/76
SY - 3/22/76; 6/7/76
SYDNEY - 7/19/76
SYMONDS, Capt. - 11/8/76

T
TABER, Capt. Jeremiah - 2/3/75
TABOR, Jeremiah - 3/10/75
TABOR, Job - 5/6/74
TABOR, Samuel - 5/6/74
TAINTER, Mr. - 12/27/76
TALCOTT, Elizur - 7/15/74
TALCOTT, Matthew - 3/11/74
TANNER, Mrs. Mary - 3/29/76
TANNERS, John - 3/29/76
TARBOX, Solomon- 3/3/75,
TAYLOR, Edward -12/23/74; 12/22/75
TAYLOR, James - 11/1/76
TAYLOR, Samuel -
TAYLOR, Samuel - 12/23/74 5/16/76

TAYLOR, Susanna - 8/4/75
TERRETT, William - 10/20/75
TERRY, Ephraim - 9/2/74
TERRY, Jr., Ephraim - 8/26/74
TEW, Henry - 12/13/76
THATCHER, Oxenbridge - 2/18/74
THATCHER, Mr. - 8/4/75; 4/5/76
THAYER, John - 8/18/75
THOMAS, Deacon - 12/20/76
THOMAS, James - 1/6/75; 9/22/75
THOMAS, Seth Cote, - 1/20/75
THOMISON, Matthew - 8/30/76
THOMPSON, Charles - 7/12/76
THOMPSON Jr. David - 4/14/75
THOMPSON, James - 1/26/76; 12/27/76
TIFFANY, Timothy - 1/21/74
TILESTON, John - 5/10/76
TILESTON, Thomas - 7/21/75
TILESTON , Mrs. - 5/10/76
TILEY, James - 9/6/76
TILLAGE, Richard - 11/8/76
TIM - 5/6/74
TINKER, Edward - 11/15/76
TINKER, Silvanus - 7/15/74
TINKER, Stephen - 1/26/76; 4/5/76
TOPPING, David - 7/15/74
TOPPING Jun., Thomas - 12/1/75
TOWNSEND, Nathaniel - 5/24/76
TOZER, Samuel - 1/20/75; 11/1/76
TRACY, Elisha - 2/18/74; 4/29/74; 2/17/75; 1/5/76;
TRACY, Isaac - 2/18/74; 4/15/74; 9/2/74; 2/17/75
TRACY, Judge Samuel - 5/6/74; 12/6/76
TRACY, Simon - 9/22/75
TRAPP, Thomas - 3/11/74

TREAT, Thomas - 12/1/75
TROOP, Daniel - 5/10/76
TROTT, Jonathan - 12/30/74
TRUMBULL, Jonathan - 12/30/74; 5/16/76
TRUMBULL Jr., Jonathan - 4/14/75
TRUMBULL, Gov. Joseph - 1/1375;12/8/75
TRUMBULL, Capt. Joseph - 6/10/74; 8/12/74
TRYON, Noah - 3/31/75
TUBBS, John Miller - 5/3/76
TURNER, Pain - 10/20/75
TUTHILL, Jonathan - 11/1/76
TUTHILL, Rufus - 10/11/76;
TYLER, Daniel - 7/1/74; 5/10/76
TYLER, James - 5/10/76
TYLER, John - 1/14/74; 6/24/74; 12/6/76
TYLER, Jr., Joseph - 8/18/75
TYLER, Moses - 8/19/74
TYLER, Capt. - 4/19/76

U

UNCAS, Abimelect - 9/22/75
UNCAS II, Benjamin - 2/18/74
UNCAS, Mary - 2/18/74
UNDERWOOD, Ann - 4/15/74

V

VERNON, Col. - 4/12/76
VIETS, John - 5/6/74
VILBY, John - 1/20/75

W

WADSWORTH, Col James - 4/14/75
WAIT, Joseph - 10/11/76
WAIT, Marvin - 3/4/74; 3/11/74; 8/26/74; 1/1375; 3/17/75; 5/5/75; 10/13/75; 4/12/76;
5/16/76; 8/23/76; 9/13/76; 10/11/76; 10/18/76; 11/15/76
WAIT, Jr., Richard - 1/6/75
WALES, Capt. Elisha - 10/18/76
WALES, Nathan - 4/15/74
WALES Jr., Nathaniel - 2/4/74; 4/15/74; 7/1/74; 12/23/74
WALEY, Miss Fanny - 2/3/75
WALKER, Silas - 7/19/76
WALKER, Thomas - 5/10/76
WALLACE, Capt. James - 2/23/76; 4/12/76; 8/18/75; 9/1/75; 9/8/75; 10/6/75; note 22
WALLACE, Captain John - 6/14/76
WALLACE, Cap, 4/12/76
WALSH, Benjamin - 12/9/74
WALWORTH, Elijah - 4/22/74
WALWORTH, William - 2/17/75
WARDROP, David - 11/8/76
WARNER, Daniel - 4/19/76
WARNER, Ely - 4/15/74
WARNER, Moses - 1/6/75
WARNER, Nathaniel - 1/27/75
WARNER, Mr.- 12/23/74
WARREN, Mrs. Abigail - 6/9/75
WARREN, Jacob - 6/9/75
WARREN, Moses - 9/9/74
WASHINGTON, George - notes 16, 38
WATERHOUSE, Abraham - 6/28/76
WATERHOUSE Jr., Abraham - .12/30/74
WATERMAN, Joseph, - 7/19/76
WATERMAN, Joseph - 12/16/74; 11/22/76; 12/6/76
WATERMAN, Nehemiah - 7/29/74; 10/21/74
WATERMAN, Rev. Silvanus - 11/4/74
WATERS, Josiah - 12/8/75

WATROUS, Daniel - 5/16/76
WATROUS, John -8/12/74; 1/27/75; 3/22/76
WATROUS, Capt. - 7/26/76
WATSON, John - 5/20/74; 5/5/75; 5/16/76
WATTLES, Captain John - 3/10/75
WATTLES, Sluman - 3/10/75
WAY, Jr. Ebenezer - 10/28/74
WAY, John - 6/7/76
WEAVER, Samuel - 1/28/74
WEBB, Charles - 7/7/75
WEBB, Joseph - 12/2/74; 1/20/75
WEBB, Orange - 10/18/76
WEBB, Samuel - 12/23/74
WEBB, William - 12/6/76
WEBB, Col. - 3/29/76
WEBB, Captain - 10/21/74
WEEDEN, Richard - 1/26/76
WELCH, Rev. Daniel - 6/3/74; 12/29/75
WELCH Jr., Ebenezer 4/29/74
WELCH, Capt. John - 8/30/76
WELCH, Mrs. Martha - 12/29/75
WELCH, William - 6/7/76
WELLES, Jonathan - 4/15/74
WELLES, Levi - 1/27/75; 12/6/76
WELLES, William - 7/15/74
WELLS, John - 3/31/75
WEST,. Abial - 5/19/75
WEST, David - 8/16/76
WEST, Jabez - 3/10/75
WEST, Capt. Joshua - 12/30/74; 10/18/76
WEST, Nathaniel - 9/9/74
WEST; Zebulon - 10/6/75
WETMORE, Prosper - 12/1/75 ;10/11/76; 11/15/76; 12/6/76
WHALEY, Alexander - 4/5/76

WHEATS, Samuel - 2/4/74
WHEELER, Abeleny, - 4/1/74
WHEELER, Charles - 10/11/76; 11/15/76
WHEELER, Joshua - 4/1/74
WHEELER, Jr., Shepherd - 2/3/75
WHEELER, Truman - 2/4/74
WHEELER, William - 7/19/76; 11/15/76
WHEELER 3rd, William - 7/7/75
WHEELER, Capt. Zacchus - 3/1/76
WHEELER, Capt. - 9/20/76; 12/13/76
WHIPPLE, Daniel - 10/11/76
WHITAKER, Mary - 1/14/74
WHITE, Abigail - 6/17/74
WHITE, Capt. Jonathan - 4/19/76
WHITE, Phillip - 12/2/74
WHITE, William - 12/2/74
WHITE, Rev.- 4/1/74
WHITING, Amos - 1/20/75
WHITING, Col. John - 7/12/76
WHITING, Mrs. Philenach - 7/12/76
WHITING, Col. - 4/19/76
WHITLEY, Caleb - 7/19/76
WHITMAN, Rev. Mr.- 9/1/75
WHITMORE, Aaron - 9/30/74
WHITMORE, Ephraim - 11/15/76
WHITON, Elijah - 5/31/76
WHITTLESEY, Hezekiah - 4/15/74; 9/9/74
WIATT, Elijah - 7/22/74
WICKHAM, Thomas 7/ 22/ 74
WIGHT, Joseph - 11/22/76
WILCOX, Ephraim - 7/19/76
WILCOX, Stephen - 5/16/76
WILDMAN, John - 9/2/74
WILKES, John - note 10

WILKESON, James - 6/28/76
WILLES, Dyer - 1/14/74
WILLIAMS, Abigail - 3/11/74; 6/24/74;8/23/76
WILLIAMS, Col. Amariah - 5/16/76
WILLIAMS, Benjamin - 12/30/74; 9/22/75; 10/13/75; 10/18/76
WILLIAMS, David - 8/23/76
WILLIAMS, Mrs. Deborah - 1/6/75
WILLIAMS, Ebenezer - 7/15/74 1/6/75
WILLIAMS, Rev. Eleazer - 10/6/75
WILLIAMS, Elisha - 2/17/75
WILLIAMS, Elizabeth - 8/23/76
WILLIAMS, Mrs. Eunice - 10/6/75
WILLIAMS, Ez'l - 11/17/75
WILLIAMS, George - 8/18/75; 1/5/76; 5/16/76; 6/21/76; 12/13/76
WILLIAMSJr, George - 1/5/76
WILLIAMS, James - 4/8/74
WILLIAMS, John - 7/8/74; 10/14/74; 10/13/75
WILLIAMS, Nathaniel - 3/11/74; 6/24/74
WILLIAMS, Peleg - 7/26/76
WILLIAMS, Reverend Dr. Solomon
WILLIAMS, Thomas - 5/16/76; 10/18/76; 11/15/76
WILLIAMS, Capt. Veach - 12/30/74
WILLIAMS William - 4/15/74; 9/16/74; 12/23/74; 12/30/74; 4/14/75; 5/19/75; 11/3/75; 5/16/76
WILLIAMS, William Rev. - 3/15/76
WILLIAMS; Mr. - 8/2/76
WILLOUGHBY, Elijah - 5/12/75
WILLSON, James - 11/15/76
WILLWORTH, John - 6 /23/75
WILS, George - 11/15/76
WILLIAMS, John Still - 6/14/76
WINTHROP, John Jr., note 7
WINTHROP,' Mr. - 9/20/76
WITTER, Ebenezer 9/20/76
WITTER, Joseph - 7/12/76
WITTER, William - 4/15/74; 6/24/74
WOLCOTT, Erastus - 7/15/74
WOLCOTT, Oliver - 11/3/75; 5/16/76
WOLCOTT, Samuel - 10/18/76
WOLCOTT, Simon -1/28/74; 7/21/75
WOLCOTT Solomon - 10/6/75
WOLCOTT, Col. - 3/29/76
WOLLYS, Nathaniel - 2/24/75
WOLSEY, Ebenezer - 12/23/74
WOOD, John - 7/12/76
WOODBRIDGE, Dudley - 12/30/74; 4/21/75; 3/8/76; 3/22/76
WOODBRIDGE, Mrs. Mary - 6/16/75
WOODBRIDGE, Captain Paul - 1/28/74
WOODBRIDGE, Miss Sarah - 1/28/74
WOODBRIDGE, Rev. Mr. - 6/16/75
WOODWARD, Jonas - 9/29/75
WOODWARD, Joseph - 5/31/76
WOOLCOT, Simon - 6/17/74
WOOSTER, General - 8/18/75
WORDEN, Gideon' - 2/3/75
WORRELL, Thomas - 11/15/76
WORTHINGTON, Elias -

WORTHINGTON, Elias -
8/12/74; 1/27/75; 12/20/76
WORTHINGTON, Col. Wm -
4/15/74; 5/16/76; 12/20/76
WRIGHT, Capt. Dudley -
4/15/74; 8/12/74; 1/27/75
WRIGHT, Ezekiel - 4/14/75
WRIGHT, Jr., John - 12/2/74
WRIGHT, Jr. , Josiah - 4/14/75
WRIGHT, Capt. Seth- 11/10/75
WYLLYS, George - 2/7/76;
5/16/76; 11/29/76
WYLLYS, Col. Samuel - 4/14/75

Y
YEAMANS, David, - 1/21/74
12/9/74
YEAMANS, Moses - 1/27/75
YEDEL, Dr - 12/29/75
YORK, John - 10/11/76
YOUNG, Robert - 2/17/75
YOUNG, Simeon - 2/17/75

PLACE INDEX

Abington in Pomfret - 2/17/75
Albany - 7/8/74
Antigua - 3/11/74
Arkansas. - note 10
Ashford - 2/25/74; 3/4/74;
4/15/74; 9/30/74; 12/16/74;
5/16/76; 5/24/76; 5/31/76;
10/18/76; 12/13/76
Atchauge River - 2/18/74
Bahama Islands - 10/18/76;
11/15/76
Barbados - 9/13/76; Barbados -
10/11/76;
Barbary - 1/27/75
Barnegat Beach - 2/25/74
Bartletts Reef - 5/26/75
Beach street, New London-
3/4/74
Bedford into the Susquehanna
purchase - 7/15/74; note 2
Berkshire County - 2/4/74
Bermuda - 10/18/76; 11/15/76

Bethlem - 10/27/75
Black Point - 6/23/75; 12/6/76
Block Island. - 1/28/74; 9/1/75
5/24/76; 5/31/76; 6/21/76;
11/8/76
Boston Neck - 1/7/74
Boston Commons - 1/7/74
Boston Bay - 6/21/76
Boston - 2; 1/7/74; 2/11/74;
4/15/74; 6/3/74; 6/10/74;
6/24/74; 7/1/74; 7/15/74; 7/
22/ 74; 7/29/74; 9/9/74;
9/16/74; 11/11/74; 12/2/74;
12/30/74 1/27/75; 2/3/75;
2/17/75; 7/ 22/ 74; 3/10/75;
4/28/75; 5/5/75; 5/12/75;
5/26/75; 6/9/75; 6/16/75;
6/30/75; 7/21/75; 8/18/75;
12/22/75 12/22/75; 3/8/76;
3/15/76; 5/3/76; 5/10/76;
6/14/76; 6/21/76; 10/18/76;
note 4
Branford - 4/22/74; 11/25/74

Brattleborough - 10/11/76
Bridgehamton on Long Island - 12/1/75; 9/6/76
Bristol note 7
Brook haven - 4/5/76
Brookline, Pomfret - 7/7/75;11/17/75
Brooklyne of Canterbury - 5/10/76
Cambridge- 4/28/75; 5/12/75; 6/30/75; 9/1/75; 11/3/75; 6/30/75;1/19/76
Camp Roxbury - 8/11/75; 8/18/75
Canada - 7/1/74
Canterbury - 7/1/74; 7/15/74; 9/22/75; 5/16/76; 5/31/76; 7/12/76; 8/16/76; 9/6/76; 9/13/76; 10/18/76; 11/15/76; 12/13/76
Cape Ann, - 1/28/74
Cape Cod - 3/18/74
Capes of Virginia - 4/12/76
Caribbean - note 30
Casco Bay - 1/6/75
Castle William- 4/28/75
Charleston, South Carolina, - 1/7/74
Charlestown Hill - 6/30/75
Charlestown, Mass.- 4/28/75
Chatham - 2/18/74; 11/25/74; 12/2/74; 12/23/74; 2/17/75; 8/18/75; 1/5/76; 12/27/76
Chelsea [see also Norwich Landing] - 4/1/74; 6/10/74; 6/24/74; 8/19/74
Chelsea Society in Norwich - 3/1/76 ; 3/8/76; 4/5/76; 12/20/76
Chester in the Susquehanna Purchase - 3/10/75; 11/1/76; note 2

Chesterfield society - 3/3/75
Cohees - 3/31/75
Colchester - 1/21/74; 2/18/74; 3/4/74; 3/11/74; 4/1/74; 4/15/74; 5/20/74; 6/3/74; 7/1/74; - 8/12/74; 11/18/74; 12/2/74; 1/6/75; 1/20/75; 1/27/75; 4/28/75 ;6/2/75; - 6/9/75; 8/4/75; 8/11/75; 8/25/75; 9/22/75; 10/6/75; 12/8/75; 1/26/76; 3/22/76; 4/5/76; 5/31/76; 6/7/76; 8/2/76; 8/9/76; 9/20/76; 10/25/76; 11/1/76; 12/6/76; 12/20/76; 12/27/76; note 2
Connecticut river - 2/4/74; 2/25/74; 2/3/75; 7/14/75; 12/27/76
Cornhill - 12/2/74
Coventry - 2/4/74; 8/19/74; 9/9/74; 3/24/75; 3/31/75; 5/5/75; 2/23/76; 5/16/76; 10/18/76
Coventry, North parish - 2/11/74
Dedham in Norwich - 12/8/75
Delaware River notes 2, 16
Denison's Wharf - 9/1/75
Dominica - 8/9/76
Dorchester Point- 4/28/75
Duck Island - 2/4/74; 10/21/74; 3/10/75; - 6/9/75
Durham - 1/20/75; - 4/14/75
East Granby - notes 6, 7
East Haddam - 1/28/74; 2/25/74; 3/18/74; 4/15/74; 6/17/74; 7/1/74; 7/15/74; 9/23/74; 1/6/75; 1/20/75; 2/10/75; 3/3/75; 3/31/75; 10/27/75; 11/10/75; 11/17/75; 11/24/75; 12/29/75; 1/5/76; 1/26/76;2/9/76; 3/22/76;

4/19/76; 5/10/76; 5/16/76;
6/28/76; 7/12/76; 7/19/76;
8/2/76; 8/16/76; 9/13/76
East Haddam Landing -
4/15/74; 9/23/74; 10/14/74
;11/1/76; 11/22/76;12/13/76;
12/20/76
East Hampton - 7/ 22/ 74
9/2/74; 9/16/74; 12/2/74;
1/6/75; 3/15/76; 4/12/76
East Hartford - 2/18/74;
7/21/75
East Indies - 8/25/75
East Society of Norwich -
1/5/76; 2/23/76; 11/22/76
East Windsor - 5/20/74; 5/5/75;
5/16/76
Elderkin's Bridge - 12/13/76
Elizabeth town, NJ - 9/1/75
Enfield, New Hampshire -
5/24/76
Enfield,Ct.- 3/4/74; 7/1/74;
11/25/74; 4/28/75; 8/25/75;
9/15/75; 12/22/75; 2/23/76
Execution Rocks - 1/1375
Fairfield - 8/12/74; - 8/26/74;
12/23/74; 5/12/75; 10/27/75;
4/19/76; 12/6/76
Falmouth, Barnstable County -
12/9/74
Faneuil Hall 7/15/74
Farmington - 2/18/74; 7/7/75;
3/29/76
Faulkner Island, - 1/12/76
Fire Island inlet - 9/6/76
First Society of Hebron -
4/28/75; 4/19/76
First Society of Lyme - 4/21/75
First Society in Windham -
1/14/76
First Society in Woodstck -
5/5/75
Fishers Island Harbor - 12/9/74

Fishers Island - 12/9/74;
8/11/75; 8/18/75; 9/1/75;
9/8/75; 7/19/76; 11/8/76;
12/13/76
Fishing Creek - 6/3/74
Flatbush - 9/6/76
Fort George - 12/16/74
Gales Ferry - 7/7/75; 5/16/76
Gardiners Island - 8/11/75;
8/18/75; 12/20/76
Germany - 3/1/76
Glastonbury - 4/15/74;
7/15/74; 3/31/75; 12/1/75;
1/5/76
Goshen reef - 2/25/74; 9/9/74;
11/4/74; 10/4/76
Gravesend - 9/6/76
Great Rip - 10/14/74
Great Bridge in Norwich -
8/19/74
Great Burlington - 2/4/74
Green's Harbor, New London -
3/10/75
Groton Ferry - 11/3/75;
12/15/75
Groton - 1/14/74; 1/28/74;
4/15/74; 4/22/74; 5/13/74;
7/29/74; 7/29/74; 8/19/74;
9/2/74; 9/9/74; 12/2/74;
12/23/74; 1/6/75; 1/20/75 ;
2/17/75; 3/3/75; 3/17/75;
4/14/75; 5/5/75; 5/19/75;
5/26/75; 6/9/75; 6/16/75;
6/23/75; 7/21/75; 8/18/75;
8/25/75; 9/29/75; 11/3/75;
12/15/75; 1/26/76; 2/9/76;
2/16/76; 3/1/76; 4/5/76;
4/26/76; 5/3/76; 5/10/76;
5/16/76; 5/31/76; 6/7/76;
6/14/76; 6/28/76; 7/19/76;
7/26/76; 8/9/76; 8/23/76;
9/13/76; 9/20/76; 9/27/76;
10/4/76; 10/18/76; 10/25/76;

11/8/76; 11/15/76; 11/22/76; 12/6/76; 12/27/76
Guadalupe - 9/15/75
Guilford - 4/14/75
Gull Island - 6/7/76; 11/29/76
Haddam - 2/25/74; 4/15/74; 9/16/74; 3/17/75; 4/14/75; 10/6/75; 12/29/75; 2/7/76
Hadley - 7/19/76
Hadlyme - 7/1/74; 11/17/75; 12/13/76
Halifax - 5/24/76; 9/13/76; 10/11/76
Hancock in the Susquehanna Purchase - 7/15/74; note 2
Hartford, - 4/15/74; 4/29/74; 5/13/74; 5/20/74: 8/12/74; 9/16/74; 11/25/74;1/20/75; 3/3/75; 3/17/75; 4/14/75; 5/12/75; 7/7/75; 8/18/75; 9/1/75; 9/15/75; 3/8/76; 6/21/76; 9/6/76;- 12/20/76
Hartford County, - 4/15/74; 12/8/75
Hatfield - 4/14/75; 3/15/76
Hebron - 2/23/76; 3/15/76; 4/19/76; 5/3/76; 9/13/76
Hells Gate - 12/13/76; note 39
Hispanola - 4/22/74
Hopkinton, RI - 3/29/76; 7/12/76; 12/13/76
Hudson River note 21,
Huntington, Long Island - 9/6/76
Isle of Wright in Suffolk county -9/2/74; 9/16/74; 12/30/74
Jamaica - 5/13/74; 9/8/75; 5/3/76
Jordan - note 23
Jordan Brook - 3/29/76
Jordan Plain - 3/29/76
Kensington - 10/7/74

Killingly - 1/21/74; 5/16/76; 7/19/76; 10/18/76; 11/15/76
Killingworth - 2/10/75; 9/22/75;10/13/75; 5/16/76; 6/7/76; 10/18/76
Lebanon North Parish - 9/15/75; 9/22/75
Lebanon Village - 12/27/76
Lebanon First Society - 10/28/74
Lebanon - 1/14/74; 4/15/74; 6/3/74; 8/26/74; 9/9/74; 10/28/74 ;12/16/74; 12/30/74; 1/6/75; 2/24/75; 3/10/75; 3/24/75;4/14/75; 6/2/75; 9/22/75; 10/13/75; 1/19/76; 3/15/76; 5/10/76; 5/16/76; 6/7/76; 7/19/76; 10/18/76; 12/27/76
Lester's Rock. - 9/9/74
Lichfield County - 7/8/74; 5/3/76; note 2
Litchfield - 4/21/75; 5/19/75; 12/8/75
Little Rest - 6/21/76
London - 2; 2/25/74; 2/3/75; 10/20/75; 12/29/75; 3/15/76
Long Island - 7/15/74; 10/14/74; 10/21/74;11/18/74; 12/2/74; 1/1375; 10/6/75; 3/15/76; 4/12/76; 9/6/76; 9/13/76; 9/20/76; 10/18/76; 10/25/76; 11/8/76; 11/29/76; 12/6/76; 12/27/76; Note 37
Long Island Sound - 1/1375; 5/26/75; 6/23/75; 7/14/75; 1/12/76; - 6/7/76; 11/29/76; 12/6/76; notes 35 37, 39
Long Point in Stonington - 1/7/74; 4/22/74; 5/24/7; 10/11/76; 11/1/76
Long Wharf - 8/4/75; 4/5/76
Lyme - 1/14/74; 3/18/74;

4/15/74; 5/6/74; 5/20/74;
7/15/74; 8/19/74; 9/2/74;
9/9/74; 1/6/75; 2/3/75;
3/17/75; 4/7/75; 4/14/75;
4/21/75; 6/16/75;
8/11/75;8/18/75; 9/22/75;
10/13/75; 12/29/75; - 1/12/76;
1/26/76; 2/23/76;3/8/76;
3/22/76; 4/5/76; 4/19/76;
5/16/76; 6/7/76; 6/14/76;
6/28/76; 8/9/76; 9/27/76;
10/11/76; 10/18/76; 11/8/76;
12/6/76
Lyme East society - 3/11/74;
5/3/76
Lyme North Society - 10/20/75
Manhattan Note 37..
Mansfield - 2/18/74; 4/1/74;
4/8/74; 6/3/74; 9/30/74;
10/14/74; 11/11/74; 12/16/74;
12/30/74; 10/6/75; 12/29/75;
1/26/76; 3/8/76; 3/22/76;
5/16/76; 7/5/76; 10/18/76
Marlborough Society - 7/21/75
Martha Vineyard - 3/18/74;
12/6/76
Massachusetts Bay colony 2;
6/24/74;-7/1/74 ;7/15/74;
11/18/74; 11/25/74; 10/6/75;
10/11/76
Mattituck - 7/15/74
Meeting House Hill, New
London - 10/25/76
Middle Haddam - 12/29/75
Middleborough of
Massachuseettes Bay Colony -
5/16/76
Middlefield - 1/20/75
Middletown - 3/11/74; 7/1/74;
7/15/74; 8/5/74; 9/2/74;
11/11/74; - 11/18/74 ;12/2/74;
1/1375; 2/17/75; 3/17/75;
8/11/75; 10/6/75; 1/19/76;

3/15/76; 3/29/76; 4/12/76;
5/3/76; 5/10/76; 7/26/76;
9/13/76;10/18/76; 11/22/76;
12/27/76
Middletown; Upper Houses -
8/18/75; 12/1/75
Milford - 4/8/74; 7/29/74;
11/4/74; 10/27/75
Millington Society in East
Haddam - 12/20/76;- 6/7/76;
7/19/76; 12/27/76
Milton - 2/18/74
Mississippi - 1/14/74; 7/15/74
Mohawk River - 2/7/76
Mohegin - 4/5/76
Montauk - 5/10/76; 5/31/76;
10/11/76; note 37.
Montserrat - 7/26/76
Moule - 2/25/74
Mystic Meeting House -
10/28/74
Mystic River - 9/23/74; 3/17/75

Nantucket - 4/15/74; 10/14/74;
10/21/74; 12/9/74; 7/26/76;
2/6/76
Naraganset Bay - 10/4/76; note 2
Narrows - 9/6/76
New Britain - 2/18/74
New Hampshire- 3/4/74;
12/2/74
New Hartford - 5/3/76; 5/16/76
New Haven 3/18/74; 4/15/7;
7/8/74 ; 7/29/74; 8/5/74;
11/4/74; 1/20/75; 3/3/75;
3/31/75; 6/30/75; 7/7/75;
8/4/75; 5/31/76; 11/22/76;
11/29/76
New Haven County - 2/25/74;
4/5/76; 5/31/76
New Jersey, notes 10, 16
New London - 1/7/74; 1/14/74;

1/21/74; 2/4/74; 2/18/74;
2/25/74; 3/4/74; 3/11/74;
3/18/74; 4/8/74; 4/15/74;
4/22/74; 4/29/74; 5/20/74;
5/27/74; 6/3/74; 6/10/74;
6/17/74; 6/24/74; 7/1/74;
7/8/74; 7/15/74;
7/22/74;8/19/74; 8/26/74;
9/2/74; 9/9/74; 9/23/74;
10/7/74; 10/14/74; 11/4/74;
11/11/74; 11/18/74; 11/25/74;
12/2/74; 12/16/74; 12/23/74;
12/30/74; 1/6/75; 1/1375;
1/20/75; 1/27/75 2/3/75;
2/17/75; 2/24/75 3/3/75;
3/10/75; 3/17/75; 3/24/75;
3/31/75; 4/7/75; 4/14/75;
4/21/75; 5/5/75; 5/19/75;
6/9/75; 6/16/75; 6/23/75;
6/30/75; 7/7/75; 7/14/75;
7/21/75; 7/28/75; 8/4/75;
8/11/75;8/18/75; 8/25/75;
9/1/75; 9/8/75; 9/15/75;
10/6/75; 10/13/75;
10/20/75;10/27/75; 11/3/75;
11/17/75; 12/1/75; 12/8/75;
12/15/75; 12/22/75; 1/5/76;
1/12/76; 1/26/76; 2/7/76;
2/16/76; 2/23/76; 3/1/76;
3/8/76; 3/15/76; 3/22/76;
3/29/76; 4/5/76; 4/12/76;
4/19/76; 4/26/76; 5/3/76;
5/10/76; 5/16/76; 5/31/76;
6/7/76; 6/14/76; 6/21/76;
6/28/76; 7/5/76; 7/12/76;
7/19/76; 7/26/76; 8/2/76;
8/9/76; 8/16/76; 8/23/76;
8/30/76; - 9/6/76; 9/13/76;
9/20/76; 9/27/76; 10/4/76;
10/11/76; 10/18/76; 10/25/76;
11/1/76; 11/8/76; 11/15/76;
11/22/76; 12/6/76; 12/13/76;
12/20/76; 12/27/76; notes 10,
35; 37.
New London county - 3/11/74;
4/29/74; 9/16/74; 12/1/75;
3/1/76; 3/22/76; 4/5/76;
5/16/76
New London Ferry - 7/7/75
New London Great Neck -
9/9/74, 11/4/74; 1/1375;
5/26/75 ; 8/18/75; 9/22/75;
10/20/75; 11/17/75; 12/15/75;
3/1/76; 6/7/76; 11/1/76;
11/22/76; 12/6/76; 12/20/76
New London-on Jordan Plain -
5/5/75
New London North parish -
1/7/74; 1/21/74; 2/11/74;
6/3/74; 11/25/74; 12/2/74;
8/4/75; 10/13/75; 3/1/76;
5/24/76; 6/28/76; 7/5/76;
8/2/76; 11/15/76; 12/13/76
New York -1/7/74; 2/4/74;
2/25/74; 3/11/74; 6/3/74;
9/16/74; 11/18/74;
2/3/75;2/24/75;; 7/7/75;
8/18/75; 8/25/75; 3/15/76;
3/29/76 ;4/12/76; 4/19/76;
5/10/76; 9/20/76; 9/27/76;
10/25/76; 12/6/76; 12/27/76;
notes 2, 16
New York City 7/ 22/
74;9/27/76; notes 30, 37, 38, 39
New Providence - 4/12/76
New Utrecht - 9/6/76
Newbury Port - 4/19/76; 8/2/76
Newent in Norwich - 6/3/74
;10/13/75; 4/19/76; 12/13/76
Newport 4/12/76; 5/31/76
Newport in the Susquehanna
Purchase -3/18/74
Newport -1/7/74; 3/18/74;
4/22/74; 7/1/74; 12/16/74;
2/3/75; 4/28/75; 7/7/75;
7/21/75; 7/28/75; 8/18/75;

9/8/75; 10/6/75; 1/19/76; 2/23/76; 3/29/76; 5/31/76; 8/9/76 ; 12/13/76
Newton - 3/3/75
Niantic - 6/23/75; 2/23/76; note 23
Niantic river - 5/6/74; - 6/24/74; 7/8/74; 4/7/75
North Carolina, note 10
North Hampton - 3/15/76
North Quarter of Lyme - 7/12/76
North Society of Preston - 3/29/76; 6/14/76
North Society of Stonington - 5/10/76
Norwalk - 3/18/74; 7/22/74
Norwich, Norwich - 1/14/74; 1/28/74; 2/4/74 2/11/74; 2/18/74; 2/25/74; 3/4/74; 3/11/74; 3/18/74; 4/1/74; 4/8/74; 4/15/74; 4/29/74; 5/20/74; 5/27/74; 6/3/74; 6/10/74; 6/17/74; 6/24/74; 7/1/74; 7/15/74; 7/22/74; 7/29/74; 8/19/74; 9/2/74; 9/16/7; 10/7/74; 10/14/74; 11/25/74; 12/23/74; 12/30/74 1/20/75; 2/3/75; 2/10/75; 2/17/75; 2/24/75 ; 3/3/75; 3/24/75; 3/31/75; 4/7/75; 4/14/75; 4/21/75; 5/5/75; ; 5/12/75; 6/23/75; 7/7/75; 9/22/75; 10/13/75; 11/17/75; 12/1/75; 12/8/75; 1/5/76; 1/19/76; 1/26//76; 2/9/76; 3/1/76; 3/8/76; 3/15/76; 3/22/76; 3/29/76; 4/5/76; 4/19/76; 5/16/76; 5/24/76; 5/31/76; 6/7/76; 6/14/76; 6/28/76 7/19/76; 8/16/76 10/11/76; 10/18/76; 10/25/76; 11/1/76; 11/8/76; 11/15/76;

11/22/76; 12/6/76; 12/13/76; 12/20/76; 12/27/76; note 21.
Norwich Green - 2/9/76; 3/29/76; 6/14/76
Norwich Landing [see also Chelsea] - 1/21/74; 3/11/74; 4/1/74; 5/6/74; 5/13/74; 5/27/74; 9/23/74; 10/28/74;12/9/74 11/18/74; 3/31/75 ;1/26/76; 3/8/76; 3/15/76; 3/22/76; 3/29/76; 5/31/76; 6/28/76; 9/6/76; 10/11/76; 11/8/76; 11/15/76; 11/22/76; 11/29/76; 12/20/76
Norwich Meeting House - 2/4/74
Norwich West Farms - 2/4/74; 6/14/76/ 12/20/76; 12/20/76
Nova Scotia - 4/22/74; 5/27/74; 11/4/74; 3/24/75; 3/31/75; 5/5/75
Oyster Ponds - 3/11/74; 3/31/75 ; 8/18/75
Pacific Ocean.note 2
Patuxet - 9/1/75
Pechanga in Saybrook - 11/18/74 11/22/76
Pennsylvania - 2/11/74; note 2
Pequatanack - 9/20/76
Philadelphia - 7/1/74; 7/15/74; 8/12/74; 8/26/74; 9/16/74; 11/4/74; 11/11/74; 11/18/74; 12/2/74; 12/23/74; 12/30/74; 11/3/75; 4/12/76; 6/28/76; 8/30/76; note 21
Pine Island - 9/9/74
Plainfield - 4/15/74; 7/15/74 ;6/9/75; 7/7/75; 11/17/75; 5/16/76; 5/24/76; 10/18/76; 11/15/76; 12/6/76
Plum Island - 6/23/75; 8/18/75; 9/8/75; 9/15/75
Pomfret - 2/4/74; 5/27/74;

6/10/74; 7/15/74; 2/3/75;
2/17/75; 6/2/75; 9/15/75;
5/10/76; 5/16/76; 5/31/76;
7/5/76; 10/18/76
Poquonnock - 12/15/75
Post Road - 10/28/74; 5/5/75;
3/29/76; note 23
Preston - 1/14/74; 1/21/74;
3/11/74; 4/15/74; 6/24/74;
10/28/74; 12/2/74; 2/10/75;
3/17/75; 3/24/75; 8/18/75;
10/20/75; 11/24/75; 3/29/76;
5/16/76; 8/16/76; 9/13/76;
9/20/76; 11/22/76; 12/6/76;
12/27/76
Preston North Society- 3/25/74;
1/19/76
Providence - 12/16/74; 4/28/75;
9/1/75; 9/15/75; 10/6/75;
5/24/76; 10/11/76; 10/18/76
Race, the - 5/31/76; 10/11/76;
11/29/76
Rhode Island - 2/3/75; 7/21/75;
10/6/75; 1/19/76; 2/23/76;
10/11/76; 10/18/76; 11/8/76;
12/6/76; 2/13/76
Ridgefield - 2/3/75; 3/3/75
Riverhead, Long Island - 5/6/74
Rocky Hill - 7/14/75; 2/7/76
Rope Ferry - 1/14/74; 3/29/76
Roxbury - 5/12/75; 5/31/76
Sag Harbor - 3/10/75; 9/15/75;
12/8/75; 11/1/76; 11/15/76
Salem - 12/2/74;
Salem on the Susquehanna
River - 1/12/75; note 2
Saybrook - 2/4/74; 2/18/74;
3/11/74; 4/15/74; 9/9/74;
12/30/74; 4/14/75; 7/7/75;
7/14/75; 8/11/75; 9/22/75;
9/29/75; 10/13/75; 5/16/76;
5/31/76; 6/7/76; 8/9/76;
8/23/76 ;10/18/76; 11/1/76;

11/22/76; 12/6/76
Say Brook Bar - 5/31/76
Saybrook ferry - 2/3/75
Second Society in Lebanon -
11/10/75
Second Society, Windham -
1/20/75; 12/22/75; 5/10/76;
;3/17/7; 1/6/75; 1/20/75;
1/27/75; 2/3/75; 2/24/75;
3/17/75; 3/31/75; 4/14/75;
4/28/75; 6/23/75; 7/7/75;
8/4/75; 8/11/75; 9/1/75;
9/8/75; 9/22/75; 9/29/75;
12/8/75
Shagwogonneck reef - 9/8/75
Sharon - 2/11/74; 7/8/74
Sheffield - 9/20/76
Shelter Island - 1/20/75;
10/4/76; 11/22/76
Shetucket River - 2/4/74
Simsbury - 5/6/74; 6/24/74;
7/22/74; 10/7/74; 2/3/75; notes
6, 7
Somers - 3/4/74 9/9/74; 11/1/76
South Brimfield - 11/17/75
South Carolina - 1/28/74
South Hampton, New
Hampshire - 12/2/74
Southampton, Long Island -
1/21/74; 5/6/74; 7/15/74
;12/2/74; 12/23/74; 12/30/74;
2/24/75; 3/15/76; 8/9/76;
11/1/76
Southold, Long Island -
3/11/74; 1/1375; 10/6/75;
1/26/76; 11/8/76; 11/15/76
South Kingston - 8/2/76
St. Eustatia.- 3/4/74
St Vincent - 2/16/76

Stafford - 4/19/76
Stamford - 7/7/75
Staten Island - 9/6/76

279

Stewart's Wharf, New London - 11/1/76
Stockbridge - 12/2/74
Stoneham, Massachusetts - 3/15/76,
Stonington - 1/7/74; 1/14/74; 1/21/74; 3/4/74; 3/11/74; 3/18/74; 4/15/74; 4/22/74; 5/20/74; 6/24/74; 7/22/74; 7/29/74; 9/2/74; 10/14/74; 10/28/74; 11/11/74; 12/23/74,12/30/74; 1/6/75; 1/20/75; 1/27/75; 2/3/75; 2/24/75; 3/17/75; 3/31/75; 4/14/75; 4/28/75; 6/23/75; 7/7/75; 8/4/75; 8/11/75; 9/1/75; 9/8/75; 9/22/75; 9/29/75; 12/8/75; 1/26/76; 3/29/76; 4/5/76; 4/12/76; 4/19/76; 5/3/76; 5/10/76; 5/16/76; 5/24/76; 6/14/76; 6/21/76; 7/19/76; 8/2/76; 8/16/76; 9/13/76; 10/11/76; 10/18/76; 10/25/76; 11/1/76; 11/15/76; 11/22/76; 12/6/76; 12/20/76
Stonington Long Point - 2/17/75; 3/31/75 ;10/6/75; 10/20/75; 11/8/76
Stonington Second Society, Windham - 5/10/76
Stratford - 4/19/76
Suffield - 5/13/74
Suffolk county 7/ 22/ 74,
Suffolk County, Long Island - 12/2/74 ; 12/30/74
Susquehanna River - 1/27/75
Swansey in Glamororganshire, Wales - 4/19/76
Thurlow in the Lackawana - 7/15/74; 10/13/75; note 2
Tolland- 3/25/74; 7/1/74
Town Wharf - 8/4/75; 4/5/76
Trenton. note 16

Tryon county - 2/7/76
Uxbridge - 3/29/76
Village, in Lebanon - 2/24/75
Virginia note 3
Voluntown - 12/22/75; 4/26/76; 5/16/76
Wales Bridge, 8th Society of Norwich. 4/29/74
Wallingford - 5/6/74; 7/8/74; 11/4/74; 7/7/75
Warwick 9/22/74; note 2
Warwick township in Susquehanna Purchase - 2/10/75
Watch Hill - 8/2/76
Waterbury - 1/20/75
West Indies - 1/21/74; 2/4/74;7/29/74; 11/18/74; 1/6/75; 4/21/75; 9/1/75; 12/15/75; 6/14/76; 7/12/76; 8/2/76; 12/27/76
West Parish, Saybrook - 2/4/74
West Shepard Walk, Norwich - 2/4/74
Westbrook - 7/19/76
Westchester Parish in Colchester - 12/9/74
Westerly - 7/8/74 ;2/3/75; 11/3/75; 8/2/76; 9/13/76; 11/8/76
Westfield, Massachusetts Bay - 12/23/74 ;10/11/76
Westford parish, Ashford - 2/25/74
Westmoreland - 5/19/75; 9/22/75; note 2
Wethersfield - 7/8/74; 8/26/74;12/2/74; 1/20/75; 4/7/75; 4/14/75; 2/7/76
Winchester, Susquehanna Purchase - 6/3/74 ;7/1/74; 9/9/74; 10/14/74
Willimanic River - 8/18/75

Winchester - note 2
Windham County - 1; 9/16/74 5/16/76; 12/6/76
Windham - 1/14/74; 2/4/74; 2/11/74; 3/4/74; 3/18/74; 4/1/74; 4/15/74; 4/22/74; 6/10/74; 7/1/74; 7/8/74; 7/15/74; 10/14/74; 10/28/74; 11/4/74; 11/25/74; 12/2/74; 12/23/74; 1/26/76; 2/23/76; 3/8/76; 3/29/76; 4/26/76; 5/10/76; 5/16/76; 5/24/76; 5/31/76; 6/21/76; 7/26/76; 10/18/76; 11/8/76; 11/15/76; 11/29/76; 12/13/76; note 2
Windsor - 4/8/74; 5/6/74; 1/20/75; 1/27/75; 2/3/75; 2/17/75; 2/24/75; 3/3/75 ;3/10/75; 3/17/75; 3/24/75; 4/14/75; 5/5/75; 7/21/75; 8/18/75; 9/22/75; 10/6/75; 11/3/75; 12/8/75; 12/22/75
Woodbury - 12/8/75
Woodstock - 7/8/7; 5/5/75 4; 1/26/76; 5/10/76; 5/16/76; 5/24/76; 7/26/76; 8/23/76; 10/18/76
Worchester - 6/28/76
Worthington parish in Middletown - 12/27/76
Wyoming Valley note 2
Yentick - 2/4/74

GENERAL INDEX

Ames Almanac - 2/4/74
Anderson's Pills - 11/15/76
Andrea Doria -
Anglican Church - note 9
Articles of Confederation - note 2
Battle of Brooklyn - note 37
Battle of Bunker Hill - 6/30/75
Battle of Concord- 4/28/75; note 29
Battle of Lexington 4/28/75; note 29
Battle of Long Island - 9/6/76; note 37
Battle of Princeton - note 16
Battle of Trenton note 16
Battle of Long Island,
Boston Tea Party 2
Braddick's Passage Boat - 6/10/74; 4/5/76
Breed and Howland - 10/7/74
Brig *Andrea Doria - 6/28/76;* 8/2/76

Brig *Bolton* - 4/12/76; 6/14/76
Brig *Bomb*- 11/29/76; 11/15/76
Brig *Cabot* - 6/28/76
Brig *Defense - 6/21/76; 10/4/76 ;10/18/76;*
Brig *Middletown*- 5/3/76
Brig *Minerva* - 4/22/74
Brig *Pitt* - 7/29/74
Brig *Royal* - 5/31/76
Bristol Mine - note 7
Capt. Clark's tavern 12/13/76
Captain Wheeler's Tavern - 12/13/76
Christopher Leffingwell's Tavern - 9/6/76
Church and Hallam - 6/30/75
Coffee House, Norwich - 5/16/76
Colchester Lottery - 4/1/74
Colchester Meeting House - 4/15/74
Columbia University - note 3
Committee of Correspondence

[Correspondents] - 11/11/74; 11/18/74; 12/2/74; 12/30/74; 2/10/75
Committee of Inspection and Observation - 12/2/74; 12/23/74; 12/30/74; 1/6/75; 1/27/75; 2/10/75;2/24/75 ; 4/21/75; 6/23/75; 8/25/75; 9/22/75; 10/13/75; 10/27/75; 1/26/76; 2/16/76; 3/8/76; 3/22/76; 4/12/76; 4/26/76; 5/24/76; 6/14/76; 7/26/76; 8/9/76; 9/13/76; 9/20/76; 9/27/76; 10/11/76; 10/18/76
Committee of "Pay Table" - 11/17/75
Common Sense - 3/1/76; 5/31/76; note 16
Connecticut Gazette - 1;2;10/27/75; 4/12/76; 5/10/76; 5/16/76; 8/23/76
Connecticut Gazette and Universal Intelligencer 1,2
Continental Association - 6/3/74; 11/11/74; 11/18/74;12/2/74; 12/30/74; 1/6/75; 1/27/75; 2/3/75; 2/17/75; 3/3/75 , 4/21/75 ; 8/25/75; 10/13/75; 4/26/76
Continental [or General] Congress - 8/12/74; 8/26/74 ;11/4/74; 11/11/74;11/18/74; 12/2/74; 12/23/74; 12/30/74; 1/6/75; 2/3/75; 2/10/75; 2/24/75;; 3/3/75; 4/21/75; 7/28/75; 10/13/75; 10/27/75; 11/3/75; 4/12/76; 4/26/76; 5/24/76; 7/12/76; 8/9/76; 8/16/76; 9/20/76; 11/1/76; note 3
Copper Hill, note 6
Council of Safety - *7/5/76; 9/6/76*

Crisis - 5/5/75; ,note 16
cruiser *Greenwich* - *12/6/76*
Daughters of America - 5/10/76
Declaration of Independence - 7/12/76; note 37.
Delaware Purchasers - 2/18/74; 7/29/74; 10/21/74; /5/76
Distilhouse in New London - 12/6/76
Distillery - 7/1/74
East India Company - 1/7/74; 3/11/74
Edwards' Life and Sermons - 8/18/75
Eliot's tavern - 3/22/76
Fenning's Spelling Book - *1/21/74; 4/7/75*
Fire of 1776, the - note 38
First Church of Mansfield - 10/6/75
First Ecclesiastical Society in New London - 4/21/75
First and Second Delaware Purchases note 2
Fly - 6/28/76
Fort Trumbull - 8/2/76; 8/9/76
Free Masonry - 7/29/74
Freebetters New England Almanac - 10/27/75;
galley *Shark*- *11/15/76*
General Hospital in New York - 8/9/76; 9/13/76; 10/18/76; 11/22/76; 11/29/76
General Post Office - 9/20/76
General Assembly 1/14/74; 3/11/74; 3/18/74; 4/1/74; 4/15/74; 6/24/74; 7/1/74; 7/8/74; 9/2/74; 9/9/74; 11/4/74; 11/18/74;3/3/75; 4/14/75; 6/9/75; 7/7/75; 8/18/75; 11/3/75; 1/5/76; 3/22/76; 5/16/76
Great Commoner, the note 19

Green and Spooner - 6/17/74
Green Plumb - 10/4/76; 10/25/76
Harvard College - 3/15/76
Hessians note 16
HMS Adventurer - 10/18/76; 11/15/76
HMS Asia - 9/6/76
HMS Cerebrus - 5/10/76; 5/24/76; 5/31/76; 8/2/76; 11/8/76; note 35
HMS Clarendon - 12/6/76; 12/6/76
HMS Eagle - 9/6/76
HMS Experiment. note 22
HMS - Glasgow - 4/12/76; 6/14/76
HMS John - 10/18/76; 11/8/76; 11/15/76
HMS King Fisher - 7/14/75
HMS Lady Gage - 2/3/75
HMS Lark - 11/8/76
HMS Lively - 6/30/75
HMS Metlin - 11/8/76
HMS Nautilus - 7/7/75
HMS Oliver Cromwell - 10/11/76
HMS Phoenix - 9/6/76
HMS Roebuck - 9/6/76
HMS Rose - 7/7/75; 8/18/75; 10/6/75; 9/1/75; 9/8/75;note 22
HMS Sally - 10/18/76
HMS Swan - 7/7/75
HMS Tristam, - 12/30/74
House of Commons - note 11
Intolerable Acts. - 2
Iroquois note 2
Jachin and Boaz - 7/29/74
Judgments of Whole Kingdoms and Nations concerning the Rights, Powers and Prerogatives of Kings and the Rights, Privileges and

Properties of the People - 7/1/74
Lackaway [Lackawana] Purchase - 10/13/75; note 2
Lebanon Meeting House - 10/28/74
Lee & Jones - 4/19/76
London Coffee House - 6/10/74; 8/26/74; 9/2/74; 4/21/75; 7/21/75; 9/1/75; 11/17/75; 3/29/76
Loyal Nine, The - note 4
Mohawk Indians -2
Mohegan Indians -2/18/74; 3/18/74
Mr. Wait's Writing Room - 11/8/76
Nathaniel & Elizabeth - 8/2/76; 10/11/76
New Gate prison - notes 6, 7
New York Mercury - 9/1/75; 10/18/76
New South Meeting House, Boston - 9/1/75
New London Gazette 1, 2
New Gamut or Rules of Music, A - 9/9/74
Newgate prison [see also Simsbury mines] - 3/4/74; 4/8/74; 5/6/74 10/7/74
Niantic Tribe - 4/5/76
Norwich Lottery - 6/3/74
Norwich Wharf Bridge lottery- 3/4/74; 5/6/74
Parliament - 2; 6/3/74;6/10/74; 6/24/74; 7/1/74 7/15/74; 7/ 22/ 74 1/1375; 2/10/75; 10/27/75; 4/12/76; note 10
Princeton University note 3
Proclamation Act of 1763 2,
Prosperity - 9/15/75
Quartering Act of 1765.2
Reverend Mr. White's Meeting

283

House - 4/1/74
Rhode Island ferry - 8/18/75
Roman Church - note 9
Sabbatarian Church - 1/6/75
Sabbatian Baptist meeting house - 3/29/76
schooner
schooner *Bachelor* - 11/15/76
schooner *Belona*, 4/12/76
schooner *Dolphin* - 7/8/74
schooner *Hawk* - 6/14/76
schooner *Hannah and Elizabeth* - 10/11/76
schooner *Indian King* - 4/22/74
schooner *King of Prussia* - 4/1/74
schooner *Mary and Elizabeth* - 9/13/76; 12/6/76
schooner *Mississippi* - 1/14/74
schooner *Sally* - 11/8/76; 11/15/76; 12/6/76
schooner *Spy* - 5/31/76 ;9/13/76; 10/11/76

schooner *Two Sisters* - 11/18/74
Sign Post, the - 1/21/74
Sign of the Golden Ball - 3/17/75; 7/21/75; 4/5/76; 8/16/76
Simsbury mines [see also Newgate prison] - 4/8/74; 11/4/74; 11/25/74; 2/3/75; notes 6, 7
sloop *America* - 10/18/76
sloop *Betsy and Polly* - 10/7/74
sloop *Commerce* - 7/26/76
sloop *Cumberland* - 5/27/74; 3/31/75
sloop *Dove* - 4/8/74
sloop *Elizabeth* - 7/1/74
sloop *Fancy* - 12/9/74
sloop *Fanny* - 2/25/74
sloop *Lydia* - 12/15/75
sloop *Lyon* - 12/27/76
sloop *Macaroni* - 7/12/76
sloop *Polly* - 2/25/74

Other Heritage Books by Richard B. Marrin:

Abstracts from the New London Gazette*:
Covering Southeastern Connecticut, 1763-1769*

Abstracts from the New London Gazette*:
Covering Southeastern Connecticut, 1770-1773*

*A Glance Back in Time: Life in Colonial New Jersey (1704-1770)
As Depicted in News Accounts of the Day*

Going to Court in Texas: Riding the Circuit, 1842-1861

The Paradise of Texas, Volume 1: Clarksville and Red River County, 1846-1860

Passage Point: An Amateur's Dig into New Jersey's Colonial Past

*Runaways of Colonial New Jersey: Indentured Servants,
Slaves, Deserters, and Prisoners, 1720-1781*

Other Heritage Books by Richard B. Marrin and Lorna Geer Sheppard:

Abstracts from the Northern Standard *and the Red River District [Texas]:
August 20, 1842-August 19, 1848*

Abstracts from the Northern Standard *and the Red River District [Texas]
Volume 2: August 26, 1848-December 20, 1851*

Abstracts from the Clarksville Standard
(Formerly the Northern Standard*)
Volume 4: 1854-1855*

Other Fireside Fiction by Richard B. Marrin:

The Retaking of America